SO-CKH-164

ANIMAL PROGRAMS IN PRISON

ANIMAL PROGRAMS IN PRISON

A Comprehensive Assessment

Gennifer Furst

FIRST**FORUM**PRESS

A DIVISION OF LYNNE RIENNER PUBLISHERS, INC. • BOULDER & LONDON

Published in the United States of America in 2011 by
FirstForumPress
A division of Lynne Rienner Publishers, Inc.
1800 30th Street, Boulder, Colorado 80301
www.firstforumpress.com

and in the United Kingdom by
FirstForumPress
A division of Lynne Rienner Publishers, Inc.
3 Henrietta Street, Covent Garden, London WC2E 8LU

© 2011 by FirstForumPress. All rights reserved

Library of Congress Cataloging-in-Publication Data
Furst, Gennifer.
  Animal programs in prison : a comprehensive assessment / Gennifer Furst.
  Includes bibliographical references and index.
  ISBN 978-1-935049-34-0 (hbk. : alk. paper)
  1. Criminals—Rehabilitation—United States. 2. Human-animal relationships.
  3. Animals—Therapeutic use. 4. Corrections—United States. I. Title.
HV9304.F87 2011
365'.66—dc22   2010049928

British Cataloguing in Publication Data
A Cataloguing in Publication record for this book
is available from the British Library.

This book was produced from digital files prepared by the author
using the FirstForumComposer.

Printed and bound in the United States of America

∞ The paper used in this publication meets the requirements
   of the American National Standard for Permanence of
   Paper for Printed Library Materials Z39.48-1992.

5 4 3 2 1

Contents

Acknowledgments   *vii*

1   Introduction   1
2   The Logic of Animal-Assisted Activities   13
3   The Evolution of Prison Programming   33
4   Contemporary Programs   67
5   Who Benefits and Why: Theoretical Implications   99
6   Emerging Ideas in Punishment   135
7   The Future of Animals in Prison   155

Bibliography   *163*
Index   *177*

Acknowledgments

The ideas in this book are the result of more than ten years of studying our country's criminal justice policies and, concurrently, considering human-animal relations in this context.

There were many who believed in the project from the very beginning: these include Dr. Doug Girardi of the New Jersey Department of Corrections and my mentors from the City University of New York Graduate Center and the John Jay College of Criminal Justice, Dr. Barry Spunt, Dr. Larry Sullivan, and Dr. Michael Jacobson.

I thank Andrew Berzanskis of Lynne Rienner Publishers for sticking with me for three years and going above and beyond; Dr. Sheetal Ranjan for her superior indexing and her constant faith; Deanna Sidoti for editing and imparting to me the value of ohm; and, of course, Dr. Maria Soda.

For their unwavering support: Betsy and Sasha Scalzo and Linda and Emma Gurick, who pushed me to the finish line.

Two anonymous readers provided me with their very constructive comments.

To my boys: Angel and Tiger of Fulton Street in Brooklyn; Little Leaguer of Philly; and Baby Hudson from the depths of north Jersey. Tioga, you are this girl's best friend; that was a fateful Election Day 2004—a sad day for America but a great day for us. Lincoln: Baby Pie, I hope you find the peace I never will.

E.V. always and forever.

I take responsibility for any errors, typographical or otherwise. I would appreciate your feedback: furstg@wpunj.edu.

1
Introduction

*"The degree of civilization in a society can be
judged by entering its prisons."*
—Fyodor Dostoyevesky

*"The greatness of a nation and its moral progress
can be judged by the way its animals are treated."*
—Mahatma Gandhi

*"He who is cruel to animals becomes hard also in his dealings
with men. We can judge the heart of a man by his
treatment of animals."*
—Immanuel Kant

"Man is the cruelest animal."
—Friedrich Nietzsche

What happens when human and non-human animals interact? What
lessons can be drawn by criminal justice scholars and practitioners? In
this book I explore what social science has demonstrated about human-
animal relationships, specifically the value of establishing these relations
within the confines of the criminal justice system. I argue that criminal
justice scholars should consider what we have learned about a topic
seemingly unrelated to their own field: how people can benefit from
interacting with non-humans. While the so-called "touchy feely" topic
of cute, fuzzy animals may seem anathema to the traditional, male-
dominated field of criminology/criminal justice, it is no longer possible
to dismiss the potential in connecting people and animals.

Animals are increasingly being incorporated into programs inside
prisons across the United States and abroad. The programs are appealing
on an intuitive level and are consistently regarded as successful
according to ample amounts of anecdotal information. However,

criminal justice researchers have largely ignored the trend. The logic of prison animal programs is rooted in a developed therapeutic literature regarding human-animal interactions. Physicians and psychologists have recommended companion animals for a variety of illnesses including blindness, deafness, recuperation from surgery, high blood pressure, chemical addiction and a range of disorders associated with aging (Arkow, 1998; Beck & Katcher, 1996). Animal-assisted therapy has been used as an effective intervention with the elderly, those who have been physically or sexually abused, and people with chronic mental illness (ibid). The relaxing effect of animals has long been recognized by dentists and doctors who have fish tanks in their offices. Companion animals offer a unique bonding experience for humans. In fact, more people in the United States have pets than children (Shepherd, 2008).

Some people may wonder what animals can offer prison inmates and the criminal justice system. At the same time, more and more non-humans are spending time behind prison walls. The animals are being incorporated into programs that promise positive outcomes at a number of levels. In this book, I seek to understand the potential of these programs to benefit not only the program participants, and animals, but also both the prison and outside communities. In order to understand current prison-based animal programs (PAPs) it is necessary to consider them through the lens of the United States history of correctional programming. How do these programs fit within the country's current policies regarding punishment? Do inmates who participate in PAPs demonstrate changes that are different from or more significant than inmates who participate in other programs—or no programs which is the usual—administered inside prison facilities? I also explore why these programs are proliferating—why are they so appealing, not just nationally but around the world? Given this, why haven't they been more widely studied by academics and researchers?

In the rest of this introdutory chapter, I explain the traditional goal of having inmates participate in programs in order to reduce recidivism, or return to prison. I introduce the idea of personal transformation, or internal change within an individual, as another way of measuring program "success." I also describe the ever increasing consensus among academics, researchers, and now even politicians that our current policies that are punitive and revenge-oriented are just ineffective. We are currently witnessing an era of punishment that some regard as neither purely punitive nor purely rehabilitative. Therefore the place of PAPs within the current paradigm of U.S. punishment is discussed.

In chapter 2, I introduce the logic of human-animal interactions (HAI), specifically prison inmates and animals. Shelter animals and prison inmates share a number of qualities that make them well-suited to create a symbiotic relationship. I examine the findings that the impact of these relationships has social implications beyond those received by the participants. The work being done by incarcerated people provides restitution and much-needed work for the community. Once released, former convicts will be living in society among fellow human beings but they often go unprepared for reintegration. We have seen that contact with animals can positively impact this transition. Here I review the vast evidence we have about the social, psychological, and physical benefits of HAI.

In chapter 3, I examine the history of United States correctional programming. In doing so it is necessary to understand the rise of the prison as the country's favored form of punishment. The story is sordid and has roots in the practice of enslaving Africans—the effects of which we still see when we look at the vast racial disparity of who is incarcerated today. The end of slavery did not mean the end of indentured servitude; black people continued to be exploited for their work when went from plantations to prisons and their farms. Prison farms are the first examples of inmates working with animals but given the policies that made these farms de-facto slave plantations, coupled with the inevitable slaughter of the farm animals, they are not the therapeutic animal programs I define as PAPs. But given the work with animals and the idea of work as rehabilitative—present throughout the history of prison programming and continuing to this day—it is necessary to follow the development of the farm programs. Further, I examine how both the use of prisons and work programs have consistently been driven by the desire for economic profit.

Having established the definition of a true PAP, in chapter 4 I explore the evolution of the programs. I review how they began and the history of how they came to be so common inside prisons. After examining the past, I present data from my own national survey of programs currently being administered throughout the United States. I provide a snapshot of today's PAPs—including what models are most common and the animals participants are working with, as well as program characteristics such as their size and policies for choosing participants.

Largely missing from the limited research that has been conducted on PAPs are theoretical explanations for why the programs produce effects. In chapter 5, I present an in-depth analysis of two such programs—one with male participants and the other female. Using these programs as prototypes I suggest desistance from crime, first demonstrated inside prison by the program participants' efforts to remain free from infractions, as an alternative to measuring a program's worth solely on official rates of recidivism. A person's internal transformation, which can be inspired by participation in a PAP, lends itself to an alternative paradigm of viewing program effects. Building on prior theoretical work by researchers in the field I present preliminary ideas about why prison-based animal programs produce the outcomes we repeatedly see.

Current economic conditions have permitted a dialogue to begin regarding the usefulness of the country's reliance on prisons. Rather than being labeled soft on crime, politicians have started to listen to the decades old message from researchers that prisons do not work. It is unfortunate that it has taken such dire national economic conditions to listen to reason, but reformers have to be thankful for the opportunity. Evidence of this change can be found in the National Criminal Justice Commission Act of 2009, sponsored by Senator Jim Webb (D-Virginia), and passed in July 2010, that calls for a thorough evaluation and is assigned to develop recommendations for improvement at each stage of the criminal justice system. In chapter 6 I examine a number of emerging ideas in punishment, so-called alternative programs that build on this momentum for change. The programs discussed in this chapter demonstrate the duality of our current model of punishment that seeks to both punish and reform.

Finally, I conclude with a broad discussion of how animals can help prison inmates in their quest for personal change, while creating an opportunity for incarcerated people to give back to the community. I also examine the expanding future roles for animals in prison. I close by asserting that we should critically reconsider our ideas about non-human animals and their place in our society. Not only may we be on the brink of major criminal justice policy reform but also significant modification in our recognition of the sentience of beings other than humans.

The interview data referred to in chapter 5 were collected at two prison animal programs and chosen for a variety of reasons. The programs differ on a number of criteria which allowed for comparison. One program is in a male facility while the other is in a female facility. They both utilize dogs but have different designs: the male program socializes rescued adult greyhounds, while the female program socializes puppies to go on to specialized service training. The programs are administered by different non-profit organizations and have different staff. While the prisons are different security levels, the male prison is medium-security and the female facility is maximum-security, their location in the same state means they abide, in general, by the same overall security guidelines and are governed by the same commissioner.

In addition, the program in the female facility is part of a firmly established network administered by the affiliated non-profit organization while the program in the male facility is the only one administered by that other non-profit organization. Applying to one state department of correction for access to its facilities was also a practical consideration.

How I Became Aware of Animals Inside Prisons

It was fall 2000 when I first read a New York State Department of Correctional Services newsletter describing the puppy program that had been in place at one of the state's maximum-security women's facilities for over a year. Initially I thought it was a cute idea, certainly novel. The story was accompanied by a picture of a group of smiling women and young Labradors. The photo struck me —I could never recall ever seeing smiling inmates pictured in this newsletter. My next thought was that while women might be entrusted with dogs, there would never be a program like this in a men's facility.

The idea stuck with me. I began thinking about how animals had positively influenced my life and the lives of others I knew. Whether walking or driving by I would always look at dogs I passed and feel myself smile. I knew dogs could be therapeutic for people—older people and people who needed encouragement to get out and walk for exercise. Shortly after reading about New York's first program in the women's facility I learned the state had instituted a similar program at a medium-security men's facility. I was pleasantly surprised I had been wrong about dogs and male inmates, and impressed with the state for taking such a step.

I became more interested in visiting a dog program first-hand. In spring 2001 my job with a nonprofit prison watchdog agency brought me to a medium-security male facility with a dog program. I knew I had to make sure a stop at the program made it on to the day's agenda. It was cold, raining and dreary on the day of the visit. We were told we would not see the program until the end of the day and only if time permitted. When the time came my colleagues and I were driven in a prison van with metal mesh on the windows to the stand-alone building where the program was housed, near the perimeter of the facility compound. The one-story structure looked like a military barrack—long and narrow. There was a small fenced-in yard behind the drab one story beige building.

Walking into the "puppy unit" was like walking into another dimension—it was like no other prison unit I had ever experienced, especially in generally tense male facilities. It did not take my two degrees in psychology to recognize the men here were different from others I had met behind prison walls. Inside this building there was kindness and hope; inmates were smiling. These men had pride in their work and they were eager to show us what they and the dogs had accomplished. I will never forget the satisfaction one man had in introducing me to his bilingual dog—he had taught her commands in both English and Spanish. Something special was going on and I left that day knowing I had to explore this phenomenon further.

I must also make a note about the scope of this work. The book is not simply about animal programs in prison—it could not be. The topic is too complex and part of a much larger landscape. Non-human animals, prison inmates and incarceration are intertwined in ways I was not even aware of when I began. I see each topic as a string—each with its own forward trajectory that intersects the other strings. In telling the story of where we are I found I had to explore where we were and how we got here. Nothing is as simple as we think (and hope) it will be.

Penology

In the mid 1970's the sociologist Robert Martinson and his colleagues infamously reported that efforts at offender rehabilitation had failed and declared that when it comes to prison programming nothing works (Lipton, Martinson, & Wilks, 1975; Martinson, 1974). While criminal justice policy turned more punitive and largely based on politics of fear in the ensuing years (see Beckett, 1997) researchers of correctional treatment have devoted significant energy toward discovering what programs are more or less effective at reducing recidivism for different offenders (see, for example, Harland, 1996; Lipsey, 1992, 1995; McGuire, 1995, 2002; Ross, Antonowicz, & Dhaliwal, 1995). Today, there is agreement that "the view that 'nothing works' is simply wrong: some rehabilitation programs can have a positive effect in reducing recidivism. The effect is not always large, although sometimes it is; nor is it always present, although on average it is. However, it is there and that cannot be ignored" (McMurran & Hollin, 1995, p. ix). Our current paradigm of punishment has been described as "braided" (Hutchinson, 2006, p. 443) or "hybrid" (Hannah-Moffat, 2005, p. 29) as there is growing evidence of the blurring of lines between the punishment-rehabilitation duality. In fact some have gone even further and called for a revolution in penology that recognizes "the transformative possibilities of the human subject" (Arrigo & Milovanovic, 2009, p. 6).

Recidivism, defined simplistically as a return to prison, is actually a complex phenomenon based on a number of factors and can be the result of any of several actions on the part of the offender or parole officer. The limits of the treatment-punishment dichotomy are increasingly being recognized by researchers who acknowledge "there is non consensus" regarding what works in corrections (Visher, 2006). Therefore rather than recidivism researchers are increasingly framing the discussion of desistance from crime in terms of transformation or self-change within offenders and former offenders (e.g., Maruna, 2001; Veysey, 2008; Visher & Travis, 2003; Ward & Maruna, 2007). People who adopt "valued social roles" have been found to experience transformation (Veysey, 2008, p. 3). People who "learned new, or organized existing skills to support the new role, surrounded themselves with people who reinforced the new role, and rewrote their life narrative to tell a story of strength and resilience instead of hopeless victimization" are able to more successfully desist from crime (Veysey, 2008, p. 3).

Participating in prison programming is believed to have the potential to achieve a number of positive outcomes. At a most basic level programs can improve the safety and control of the prison environment. A number of researchers (e.g., Lawrence, Mears, Dubin, & Travis, 2002; Mears, Lawrence, Solomon, & Waul, 2002; Travis & Petersilia, 2001) recommend utilizing a broader definition of benefits that includes not only reduced recidivism, but more long-term goals including improved health and family relationships that can also lead to public safety. When programs are "held to the sole criterion of reduced recidivism, many programs, in fact, may not be effective. Other measures…may be more appropriate for assessing their effectiveness" (Mears et al., 2002, p. 68). Reliance on decreased levels of criminality may "substantially understate the range of outcomes and goals that prison [programs] may yield and that are frequently included to justify them…..Indeed, the ability of many programs to exert a strong and direct effect on recidivism may be relatively nominal, especially given the range of factors that can contribute to criminal behavior" (ibid). It is the nature and scope of the changes, or transformation in program participants, therefore, that needs to be documented (Lawrence et al., 2002).

One type of prison programming that appears to influence transformation is based on the principles of animal-assisted therapy (AAT) or animal-assisted activities (AAA) which have been incorporated into an increasing range of programs (Arluke, 2008). People with various physical and emotional needs interact with (e.g., train, groom, pet) an assortment of animals (e.g., dogs, horses, llamas) in many different settings (e.g., prisons, nursing homes, schools). While there is mounting evidence of the effectiveness of AAA and AAT (see Becker, 2002; Fine, 2000; Wilson & Turner, 1998), "studies so far have only provided solid statistical proof of the benefit, not an explanation for it" (Franklin, Emmison, Haraway, & Travers, 2007, p. 44). Within the field of criminal justice the trend has gone largely ignored. Could it be that criminologists are hesitant to consider the distinct contributions of a non-human animal in creating a relationship formed with a prison inmate? Perhaps it is due to the paradoxical nature of the programs which have been implemented not to treat inmates but to provide a service to the community. The benefits to the participants and the positive press the facility inevitably receives are considered collateral. Some may argue the intention of the programs is irrelevant—positive outcomes are positive outcomes—but others could argue that if not specifically designed to benefit inmates, they are just another example of ill-conceived prison programming. So while PAPs positively affect inmates, the benefits to participants may be viewed as almost accidental, dismissing the programs as evidence of the coming of a new era of enlightened prison practices—practices that recognize the possibility of "recovering, reclaiming, and transforming one's sense of self, of expanding the capabilities to affect others, to be affected, and to experience a continual metamorphosis" as a human being (Arrigo & Milovanovic, 2009, p. 6).

Terminology

It is worthwhile to note language and terminology here. In previously published work on this topic I have referred to prison-based animal programs as PAPs. I received feedback from a few female scholars who associated the acronym with a yearly gynecological procedure they do not look forward to. I thought a catchy acronym might be useful to gain wider acceptance and recognition of the programs but was unable to come up with anything that would spell out something more likeable such as "dog" or "pet." Going along with the idea of catchy acronyms, many times these programs have cute names such as Program Pooch or Pound Puppies; the sweet names, ironically, make it easier dismiss the important work being done (Gromstein, 2008). Charming names are not congruent with the paramilitary nature of prisons and jail—they imply fun and games and some people believe punishment should not involve the pleasure of having a dog.

Continuing with names and labels, some make distinct distinctions between animal-assisted activities (AAA) and animal-assisted therapies (AAT); activities may be therapeutic but they need not be. Animals, usually dogs, have been utilized in activities ranging from being present to help ease anxiety in children learning to read aloud to accompanying nervous victims testifying in court to visiting nursing home residents. At a broader level, the program participants are taking part in what has been termed human-animal interaction (HAI). In this work the terms will be used interchangeably.

Another classification of animals are those animals regarded as working, such as those involved with law enforcement agencies trained to detect explosives, illicit substances, and counterfeit DVDs, as well as those trained to assist in the daily activities of people with differing abilities. Officially, distinctions are also made between assistance or comfort animals and service animals which are specifically trained to do work or perform tasks for the benefit of an individual with a disability according to the American with Disabilities Act of 1990 (see www.ada.gov/pubs/ada.htm). Comfort animals can be found in hospitals and nursing homes. "Psychiatric service animals" are increasingly being recognized; these animals retrieve pills, work with autistic children, and warn of oncoming panic attacks. Moving beyond service dogs for the blind, "monkeys for quadriplegia and agoraphobia, guide miniature horses, a goat for muscular dystrophy, a parrot for psychosis and any number of animals for anxiety, including cats, ferrets, pigs, at least one iguana and a duck" have been documented (Skloot, 2009). The distinction between assistance and work animals is significant as service animals cannot be denied access to a business or other place animals are not commonly permitted. A lack of clear guidelines leads to difficulties for those needing the animals, such as having to fight or sue a co-op or condo board in order to be able to keep the animal in a building with a rule prohibiting dogs (Raftery, 2010). The controversy surrounding these issues is beyond the scope of this work.

There are also differing names given to the larger philosophical or academic area of study. Sociobiology, once used to refer to the study of gender differences between male and female humans, was then applied to the study of interactions between humans and other animals. The term human-animal relations is more frequently being replaced by human-animal studies, while there has also developed an interdisciplinary study of non-human animals as cognizant and having emotional lives similar to humans. Some argue about the very label applied to animals; the term "companion animal" is preferred to "pet." Companion animals are not owned and are more equitable to their human counterparts—their individual sentience is acknowledged. Since we are all animals, some insist on distinguishing between human and non-human animals rather than between humans and animals or non-humans. The division is meant to point out the tendency toward anthropocentrism, or using humans as the measuring rod to which all other beings are compared and therefore regarded as inferior. Some prefer to refer to all of us as creatures.

Some researchers and academics debate whether the term rehabilitation should be used as "there is something vaguely preachy and evangelical" about the term (Ward & Maruna, 2007, p. 2). Then there is re-entry, a hot topic in the United States (Petersilia, 2003; Travis, 2000; Travis, 2005), or resettlement in the United Kingdom (Ward & Maruna, 2007) which can be substituted with reintegration, coined by Australian John Braithwaite over 20 years ago (1989). Desistance from crime has become widely used for its lack of the prefix "re-" but has been described as an awkward way of "describing the process of 'going straight' or self-reform" (Ward & Maruna, 2007, p. 4). So, rather than "rebranding" (p. 6) terms and the distraction it brings with it, it has been suggested rehabilitation's "long, well-known and well-documented history....[while] not always pretty" (Ward & Maruna, 2007, p. 7) offers a more stable basis for moving forward with the topic. If rehabilitation, transformation, and desistance are troublesome terms, so too is the debate about "what works." Given the lack of consensus regarding much of this area of study, maybe "what helps" should be considered (Ward & Maruna, 2007).

In this work, the terms rehabilitation and transformation will both be used. Despite the limits of the word rehabilitation the programs are rehabilitative in the sense that participants do experience a change, or are affected by, their interactions with animals; the programs are therapeutic. While the term transformation is preferable to rehabilitation when one considers the semantics of the words, both are used in this work. While I often question tradition, the term rehabilitate is more well-known and accessible to readers. The debate over the most appropriate term is beyond the scope of this work and will continue to be argued by academics for years to come. A typology of PAPs based on that proposed by Hines (n.d.) appears in Table 1.1.

Whatever terminology is used, there is an undeniable trend of a growing number of PAPs; the programs are alluring on a number of levels. The flexibility of the program models, their relatively low cost to implement, and the continually growing, even if largely anecdotal, evidence of their success make them a good bet. Given all that is wrong with prisons, the possibility of finding and implementing reliable and effective treatment programs is appealing. Not only can some of the more than two million incarcerated people benefit, but programs that pair inmates with homeless animals make it possible to help an inordinate number of animals as well. Participants of PAPs make a contribution to a larger social issue when the program is designed to rescue unwanted animals that would otherwise be destroyed (Lai, 1998). Most recently, the great demand for work and service dogs has created a market where the large blocks of time had by prison inmates makes them ideal candidates to conduct the intensive and time-consuming training required for animals to go on to specialized service work. Inmates can be viewed as engaging in noble work that also serves the community and fills a need. Having inmates and animals help each other

Table 1.1: Prison Animal Program Typology

PROGRAM TYPE	DESCRIPTION
Visitation Programs	Companion animals brought to facility by humane society or nonprofit organization at specified times
Wildlife Rehabilitation Programs	Participants care for injured wildlife which are then released
Livestock Care Programs	Farm animal care including milking and calf raising; fish breeding
Pet Adoption Programs	Animals are adopted and cared for by individual inmates
Service Animal Socialization Programs	Assistance/work puppies or dogs are raised and taught basic commands; dog goes on to specialized training
Vocational Programs	Participants are trained/certified in animal grooming/handling/care
Community Service Programs	Participants train and care for animals (including dogs and wild horses) which are then adopted out to the community
Multi-Modal Programs	Usually vocational program component and community service program component

in a symbiotic relationship, regardless of the motivation for establishing such a program, makes it possible to achieve a win-win-win situation.

Some could argue there is a certain irony that is created when a program pairs those who society has judged as "bad" with others viewed as vulnerable or even helpless. So then are PAP participants valiant or do they remain villainous? Prison inmates who work with animals represent a group with a uniquely contradictory status. Adding to the social duality of PAP participants is how the work tends to violate traditional gender norms. Engaging in what is frequently nurturing work stands in stark contrast to the big, mean outlaws sitting in cages—how the general public often characterizes prison inmates. In fact, most PAP participants, like most prison inmates, are male.

Apart from unwanted animals there are few groups less revered than prison inmates. In the eyes of the law, both inmates and animals are property, albeit of little value. Both have been caged, experimented on, and their work poorly rewarded. Significantly, since help generally comes from above (i.e., we give to those less fortunate than ourselves), there are not many opportunities for inmates to help those worse off than themselves. But when given the opportunity, the results have been shown to be powerful—as will be explored in the rest of this book.

2
The Logic of Animal-Assisted Activities

Science has been rethinking the interactions between human and non-human animals for over two decades. The National Institutes of Health (NIH) Technology Assessment Workshop on the Health Benefits of Pets (1988) brought particular legitimacy to the area. Moving beyond anecdotes and popular media, several NIH-funded studies were published in medical journals at the time, and human-animal interaction became an acceptable avenue of research (Beck and Katcher, 2003). In fact, in 1987 the NIH proposed that "all future studies of human health should consider the presence or absence of a pet in the home, and, perhaps, the nature of this relationship with the pet, as a significant variable" (Beck & Katcher, 2003, p. 80).

Why Animals

The vast majority of the existing research regarding animal assisted therapy (AAT) has been conducted with populations other than prison inmates (Lai, 1998; Moneymaker & Strimple, 1991). Perhaps most developed is the literature on the benefits of animals in working with the elderly (e.g., Baun & McCabe, 2000; Perelle & Granville, 1993; Siegel, 1990); the treatment has also been applied to a variety of chronic and terminal illnesses (e.g., Batson, McCabe, Baun, & Wilson, 1998; Becker, 2002), including AIDS patients (e.g., Gorcyca, Fine, & Spain, 2000) and autism-spectrum symptoms (Nimer & Lundahl, 2007). In addition to using animals to encourage recovery from physical illness, pets have successfully been introduced to psychiatric populations for whom "there is so much loneliness and rejection in an institution that pets can have a real impact" (Lee, 1987, p. 232). It should be no surprise then that AAT have become widely implemented in prisons.

The first documented use of AAT is recognized as occurring at the York Retreat in England, regarded as one of the first modern mental institutions, established in 1792 by a Quaker group (Beck & Katcher, 1996; Graham, 2000; Lai, 1998). Farm animals were used to teach the patients self-control through positive reinforcement with the weaker and needy animals. The approach was vastly different from the general manner in which people with mental illness were treated at the time. By 1860, during the course of her work with wounded men in the Crimean War, the English nurse Florence Nightingale noted that "a small pet is often an excellent companion for the sick, for long chronic cases especially" (Nightingale, 1860/1969, p. 103). In 1867 epileptics institutionalized at Bethel, in Germany, were treated with animal therapy. The center still utilizes pet therapy treatments for the patients with physical and psychological disorders housed there today (Beck & Katcher, 1996). The first recorded use of animals in therapy in the United States was in the early 1940s at the Army Air Corps Convalescent Hospital in Pawling, New York (Arkow, 1998; Beck & Katcher, 1996). Men recovering from service-related injuries worked with farm animals as part of a regimen of non-stressful activities.

Physiological Underpinnings

Despite being utilized in programs, little formal research that specifically examined how people and animals interact was conducted before the 1960s. Clinical research that scientifically studied the effects of animals on people began, by accident, during a series of studies from 1977 to 1979 of patients with severe coronary heart disease (Beck & Katcher, 1996). At the University of Maryland, Alan Beck and Aaron Katcher found that divorced, single, and widowed men and women died from heart disease at higher rates than those who were married. The scientists designed an exhaustive study to examine what other social factors could have produced such results. They examined variables such as type of neighborhood, number of social encounters, birth place of parents, life changes, and measures of mood. After the first year, 14 of 92 patients died. As predicted, some of the social variables examined differed between the living and the dead, but it was pet ownership that best predicted who lived or died (see Table 2.1). Incredulous of their data, the researchers rechecked their work and found they had not erred. They verified that better health did not make owning a pet more likely, but was, in fact, an effect of the having a pet.

Table 2.1: Mortality of Pet Owners Versus Non-Pet Owners with Severe Coronary Heart Disease

Mortality	Pet	No Pet	Total
Living	50	28	78
Dead	3	11	14
Total	53	39	92

After documenting the effects on heart disease, Beck and Katcher conducted an experiment designed to compare pet owners talking to a stranger with those talking to (and touching) animals, which is how most people interact with their pets. They found that participants' blood pressure was highest when talking to the researcher and lower when at rest, but lowest when the participants were talking to and petting their animals. And "since that first conclusion, that unlike talking to people, talking to animals reduces stress and blood pressure, the validity of the observation has been confirmed by many others investigators" (1996 , p. 81).

The calming effect of animals is also mediated by how people talk to their companion animals. By recording the interactions, the researchers were able to watch people's facial expressions while talking with their animals. Pet owners generally talk to their animals "with softer, higher-pitched voices than normal, their conversation punctuated with simple questions…and with their attention fully on the animal to the exclusion of all else" (1996, p. 82). They found the effect present for not only dog and cat owners, but bird owners as well.

While in most social interactions, American men are viewed as engaging in touch less often than women, the same cannot be said in how the genders relate to their pets. The researchers found "men and women touched their dogs as frequently and for just as long….There were no significant differences between the sexes" (1996, p. 89). The intimacy that is established between people and their companion animals stems from the lack of language exchanged between them. "They ask no questions; they say no words that hurt; they offer no advice" (1996, p. 93). Companion animals never reject their masters.

Even the mere sight of an animal can reduce tension. In a series of experiments, Katcher and a research partner had children come into a room with either a lone researcher or the researcher accompanied by a friendly dog. The children's blood pressure was lowest when the dog was present. Some children saw the dog when they first entered the room, while for others, the dog entered later. The children who saw the dog upon first coming into the room had the lowest blood pressure, "suggesting that the initial sighting of the dog labeled the whole situation as safe" (1996, p. 105). Various permutations of this experiment demonstrated that the presence of one's own dog lowered blood pressure more than when paired with a strange dog. Fish were also found to have similar calming effects. The researchers explain their results with a seemingly simple fact: "We relax whenever any neutral visual event draws our attention outward and interrupts our ongoing train of thought" (1996, p. 110).

The fact that animals have relaxing and reassuring effects on people is reflected in the ways in which animals are increasingly being used in everyday work. As airports have become increasingly tension-filled places, the presence of explosives-detecting dogs can actually produce a calming effect, in addition to being more accurate than machines. At Los Angeles International Airport, the dogs have been described as cheering people up and providing passengers with a sense of security (Sterngold, 2002). According to one security officer, "Strolling through a terminal here with Jackson was like being with Julia Roberts on a crowded street. Nearly everyone who noticed her responded with a smile or an outstretched hand, followed by kissing sounds" (p. A24). The officers partnered with the dogs also report feeling more relaxed when on the job.

Courthouse Dogs is another example of the healing power of dogs being used in the criminal justice system (www.courthousedogs.com). The goal of the organization is to promote "justice through the use of well-trained dogs to provide emotional support for everyone in our criminal justice system" (ibid). Since 2003, courthouse dogs have been used in courtrooms to comfort sexually abused children while testifying and during interviews, and are present to provide support for specialty court defendants such as participants in drug courts and mental health courts. Anyone who has ever been called for jury duty knows the setting can be stressful and tension-filled as (often agitated) potential jurors learn their fate; dogs can bring calm to the courthouse and help employees maintain their composure in a largely repetitive and adversarial environment. Courthouse dogs need not be placed in a courthouse but can be found in child advocacy centers and domestic violence shelters. As with PAPs, courthouse dogs can bring a sense of normalcy and grounding to all members of the staff, from judges and lawyers, to administrators and court officers.

While the relationship between pet-ownership and health has been documented, the understanding is not considered comprehensive. Perhaps a web model comes closest as it "considers the many complicated and convoluted relationships among the pet, its owner, and the multiple social systems in which they exist" (Brasic, 1998, p. 1012). The components of the relationship do not neatly add up to what ultimately results. There appears to be synergy, or, according to the principles of Gestault psychology, the effects of animals are greater than the sum of their parts.

Psychosocial Effects

While Beck and Katcher were conducting their first experiments, other researchers were investigating the effects of companion animals in psychiatric treatment (Beck & Katcher, 1996). The AAT program at Lima State Hospital for the Criminally Insane (today Oakwood Forensic Center) in Ohio, established in 1975, remains one of the most oft-cited animal-assisted programs, and was the first formal program to use a maximum-security population (Graham, 2000; Lai, 1998; Lee, 1987; Moneymaker & Strimple, 1991). The program at Oakwood had a number of psychosocial goals including to: improve self-esteem; provide non-threatening, non-judgmental affection; and induce a responsible attitude within the participants (Lee, 1987). Socially, the staff at Oakwood hoped the animals would: stimulate communication; improve the atmosphere of the unit; provide the participants with a pro-social focus of attention; offer a diversion; and finally, serve as companionship. After a number of years, the program was evaluated by comparing patients on a unit with animals to those on a unit without animals. Both wards had comparable patients and were of equal levels of security. The patients with pets required "half as much medication, had drastically reduced incidents of violence and had no suicide attempts during the year-long comparison. The ward without pets had eight documented suicide attempts during the same year" (ibid, p. 232).

The research regarding the psychosocial benefits of AAT can be categorized into four types: loneliness and depression; attention and calming; socializing effect; and motivating effect (Hart, 2000). A review of the literature regarding the effects of animals on human health found that "the benefits derived from companion animal contact are consistent with the research reported during the past two decades in the literature on human social support" (Garrity & Stallones, 1998, p. 3). Of 25 empirical studies examined, 16 reported some advantage to having contact with animals, while 11 studies reported no advantage to animal contact (ibid). The researchers report that "pet association probably benefits a person both directly and as a protective or buffering factor when the person is threatened by life circumstances" (p. 19). Due to the great variability in the types of studies included in the researcher's review, they conclude that positive effects are not present for all people in all circumstances; they call for additional research to determine the factors that mediate therapeutic treatment effects. In a meta-analysis of the effectiveness of working with animals in treating depression, researchers found a medium effect size that was statistically significant, meaning AAA/AAT were associated fewer depressive symptoms (Souther & Miller, 2007). In a meta-analysis of 49 AAT studies, Nimer and Lundahl's (2007) also found that "AAT was as effective as or more effective than other interventions….these findings suggest AAT is a robust intervention worthy of further use and investigation" (p. 234).

More recently it appears that there is general acknowledgement that pets can be beneficial in a variety of ways. In a survey of parents with an epileptic child who also owned a dog, 20 percent said their dog was able to predict when seizures were coming (O'Neil, 2004, p. F6). While the phenomenon is not understood, it does appear to be learned as it develops only after the dog has witnessed at least one seizure and appeared in dogs untrained for the purpose. According to the study's lead author, even if a family dog cannot identify seizures, owning a dog is still probably beneficial. "Families in the survey who had dogs reported higher quality-of-life scores over all. 'At some point, they should consider a dog for the same reasons we all do,' Dr. Kirton said" (ibid). Doctors have seemingly come to prescribe pets as good medicine. According to a survey of nurses who worked on units where AAT was utilized, "the unspoken healing bond between the patient and the animal radiated back and absolutely affected other members of the health care community" (Halm, 2008, p. 375).

Behavioral Effects.

Changes in psychology often accompany changes in behavior. In studies of children with attention deficit/hyperactive disorder, "calming the children was an initial first step. With their attention mobilized and directed outward, agitation and aggression diminish, creating a better teaching environment" (Hart, 2000, p. 70). Improvements in both conduct and attendance were noticed after a dog made regular visits to a school for severely behaviorally handicapped children (Woods, 1991). Arkow (1998) discusses several behavioral studies that further demonstrate the range of potential treatment effects in psychiatric populations. In one experiment, mentally ill offenders were videotaped answering questions both with and without a dog present. Patients spoke more words and answered more quickly when a dog was in the room (Corson, Corson, & Gwynne, 1975). In another study, physically-ill depressed outpatients laughed more readily and maintained a sense of humor after becoming pet owners (McCulloch, 1983).

Pro-social experiences with animals can also lead to pro-social relations with other people. Margaret Mead is credited with uncovering the relationship between how people treat animals and how they treat other people (Moneymaker & Strimple, 1991). Research has since demonstrated a relationship between a triad of maladaptive behaviors that occur during adolescence—enuresis, fire-starting, and animal cruelty—with antisocial tendencies in adulthood (ibid). Thus prison inmates, who are overwhelmingly diagnosed with antisocial personality disorder, can greatly benefit from the opportunity to interact with animals in order to learn how to better interact with people.

Having a companion animal can instill responsibility and "inspire and motivate people to engage in constructive activities that they would not have otherwise" (Hart, 2000, p. 69). To that end, researchers recently found older adults living in an assisted living facility who walk with dogs are more consistent about walking than those people who walk with another person (Parker-Pope, 2009). They report that among the humans, partners were increasingly likely to make up an excuse to skip a walk (ibid). The dog walkers were more consistent in their activity as it was necessary for the well-being of the dog. The human participants who were driven to the animal shelter to walk the dogs demonstrated enthusiasm about their activities and while back at the facility spoke about looking forward to their walks.

The responsibilities and care-giving activities associated with a pet are ties to a reality that can otherwise be absent for an institutionalized person (Lee, 1987). Companion animals also provide the person with an outlet to demonstrate his ability to commit, not only to the tasks required in animal care, but also to the living creature that relies on him. The needy animal "stimulates innate nurturing responses, and offers a sense of mastery" (Arkow, 1998, p. 8). Being responsible for another living creature not only teaches respect and appreciation for other forms of life, but also provides an educational opportunity. Animal-assisted therapy programs often include lessons in how to care for specific types of animals. For any institutionalized population, the ability to learn new skills can be especially rewarding; for prison inmates, the skills can lead to viable job opportunities when released.

Animals in Prison

The unconditional positive regard received from an animal can be of particular significance to prison inmates who have been identified as a population vulnerable to "social isolation that leaves people without the social or family support they need during a...crisis" (Hart, 2000, p. 60). The companionship that develops is also a source of security in an adversarial environment (Arkow, 1998; Lee, 1987). With animals, prison inmates are given the opportunity to interact with a living being with no interest in their past actions or mistakes. Animals can provide a feeling of acceptance, while also fulfilling a basic human drive to nurture (Walsh & Mertin, 1994). Especially for males, who, it has been noted, "have few socially-acceptable outlets for touching and caressing," the mutual affection that a relationship with an animal provides can be therapeutic (Arkow, 1998, p. 2). For inmates who live lives absent of touch and acceptance, animals are able to "stimulate a kind of love and caring that is not poisoned or inhibited by the prisoners' experiences with people" (Beck & Katcher, 1996, p. 153). Clearly, then there are multiple therapeutic psychosocial and behavioral implications for pairing prison inmates with animals.

The prison programs examined here differ in several aspects from animal-assisted therapy or activities with other populations. Most importantly, the animal is not present specifically for the benefit of the program participant (inmate). The animals are not used in conjunction with clinical methods, such as psychoanalysis, in order to more effectively communicate with the patient or client. In prison, the programs do not have a clinical or psychological counseling component. Participants undergo screening procedures that consider personal characteristics such as the nature of the individual's crime and prior institution behavioral record, but there is no regular program contact with a clinician. The programs implemented in prisons utilize AAT techniques differently; participants not only interact with animals, but they work with or train them as well. Due to the unique nature of these prison-based programs in which offenders work with and train animals, these programs will be referred to as prison-based animal programs (PAPs).

Prison-based animal programs differ from one prison to another in a number of aspects. Most basically, the type of animal used differs; dogs – whether puppies or rescued strays – are most commonly utilized. The nature of the animal-inmate interaction differs as well; in some programs participants take their animal with them everywhere, while in others, the time spent with the animal is more limited and training-oriented. The animal training being undertaken differs; in some programs participants socialize dogs for a domestic life as a pet, while in others the animals are challenged to learn the obedience necessary to go on to training for elite service work as a guide or working dog. Another common model of PAP is one that includes inmates working with horses. Again, the specifics differ from program to program but inmates may learn how to train and groom horses, whether retired racehorses or wild horses who they are taught to domesticate. The presumed treatment effects on the participants also differ among programs; some inmates may give and receive unconditional positive regard for the first time, others learn patience, while still others may acquire vocational licensure to groom animals or assist veterinarians. Regardless of the details of the program, however, there is ample anecdotal evidence that indicates these programs are popular with inmates, staff and administrators alike, effectively modify prison behavior, and retain their participants.

What We Still Need to Study

There are two competing perspectives by which to explain the findings about the potential benefits of animals on people. In exploring loneliness and the importance of social support for people, Lynch (1977) was one of the first to discuss animals as a type of social support. The social support theory has driven much of the reasoning regarding the human-animal bond and directed the research conducted on the topic. The biophilia hypothesis from E. O. Wilson (1984) argues that from an evolutionary sense humans are predisposed to pay attention to animals, as well as the natural environment, for survival (Kellert & Wilson, 1993). While contemporary research on HAI generally focuses on the benefits to people when involved with positive, prosocial interactions with animals, humans have relied on killing, eating and wearing animals for their own survival. Therefore, the evolutionary predisposition has not necessarily been to the benefit of nonhuman animals (Katcher & Wilkins, 1993).

And it has been pointed out, the theories, along with cultural factors that determine which animals we let sleep in our beds and which animals we eat and wear, are not easily isolated; therefore it is difficult to specify one definitive reason for benefits from interactions with nonhuman animals (Beck & Katcher, 2003; Lawrence, 1993). In addition, there is not sufficient research regarding whether activities such as hunting and fishing "done in a family or social context [are] as protective of health as keeping a pet" (Beck & Katcher, 2003, p. 81). It is possible a brutalization effect is created by choosing an instrument, stalking, killing, skinning, eating, and decorating with animals gotten through a process some think of as sport and others regard as barbarian. And since there are many prison farms across the country, the potential violent environment produced by raising animals and engaging in their slaughter is discussed further later in the book. And while much has been learned about HAI, there is still considerable need for additions to be made to the research literature.

While many call for the need for additional quantitative data collected through controlled experiments, others note that "although quantitative data are invaluable, qualitative data should always supplement them" (Conniff, Scarlett, Goodman, & Appel, 2005, p. 393). The need for mixed methodological approaches of study is due to the "deep, enduring and complicated relationships between humans and animals [that] do not lend themselves to study merely by objective means and measurement...[but] require intuitive methods of study" as well (Mallon, 1994, p. 98). At the same time, we have reached the saturation point of anecdotal reports and case studies. In order to demonstrate the value of AAA and AAT "to more skeptical audiences such as administrators of budgets who might fund AAT interventions or research" rigorous studies are needed (Nimer & Lundhal, 2007, p. 235). What can be agreed upon is the need for research that answers the questions of "how" and "why" working with animals is beneficial under various conditions; there is a "dearth of theories aimed at explaining the mechanisms through which animals influence medical interventions" (Nimer & Lundhal, 2007, p. 235). The authors conclude "more research and theory development is needed" (ibid.).

Maximizing the benefits from human animal pairings can only be understood with additional research on how the various ailments, disorders, or challenges the human brings to the relationship are best matched with a specific animal or specific type of animal (Nimer & Lundhal, 2007). For example, battered women or abused children may benefit more from working with feral cats, with their lack of trust for humans and need for slow integration with people, than with exposure to a friendly dog. But if it is known that a shelter dog is homeless and has a history of being abused, might that increase the benefits for some people? Will an older person paired with a dog for companionship and exercise who knows the animal has a complicated and sordid history experience a non-therapeutic pressure to cure the dog or make up for the sad past? Can petting a soft, fuzzy rabbit bring about the same calming effects as watching fish glide through the water of a tank?

There is also little known about those who do not benefit from interacting with animals. There is evidence that some people who are drawn to relationships with animals display evidence of having difficulty developing close relations with people (Brown & Katcher, 2001). Might these people benefit from tending a garden or being in a lush, green, white snow scape, or otherwise enjoyable outdoor environment? In addition, there are countless people who have fears, phobias, and allergies to certain animals. Some people are simply just not animal people, whether due to smell, cleanliness, assumptions about intelligence and sentience or other characteristic of the animal.

It is also necessary to consider the possible problems associated with human animal bonding. The inevitable death of an animal may cause enough grief to outweigh the benefits of the interactions (Beck & Katcher, 2003). We do not know the effects of extending a sick animal's life on the person; "we do not know which owners would benefit and which would suffer" (Beck & Katcher, 2003, p. 86). The increasingly recognized disorder of animal hoarding is another possible risk that is taken when promoting human-animal interactions (ibid). The outright physical abuse of animals may also occur when some people are provided with access to animals. There is an established link between how people treat animals and how they treat humans (see Hensley & Tallichet, 2009; Petersen & Farrington, 2007; Schlesinger, 2001). In addition, there is evidence of the presence of animal abuse in homes where domestic violence takes place (see Currie, 2006; Piper & Myers, 2006; Volant, Johnson, & Gullone, 2008). In the call for additional research into animal assisted therapy and activities, there are specific suggestions. Beck and Katcher (2003) argue that the U.S. Census should ask questions about animals in households, as well as the use of gardens and other green spaces. Information of this type could not only illuminate patterns of public health problems, but also aid in decisions about how to direct resources. The authors also call for additional interdisciplinary studies on this broader area of human animal bonds.

To that end, the first Human Animal Interaction Conference was sponsored by the Research Center for Human-Animal Interaction (ReCHAI), housed at the University of Missouri's College of Veterinary Medicine (www.rechai.missouri.edu), in October 2009. The conference was also sponsored by the International Society for Anthrozoology (ISAZ), a non-profit academic organization established in 1991 with the goal of promoting the scientific and scholarly study of human–animal interactions (www.isaz.net). The ISAZ publishes the academic journal *Anthrozoos* which is meant to serve as an outlet for multidisciplinary research regarding the interactions of people and animals (www.bergpublishers.com/?tabid=519). The ISAZ also held their 18th annual conference during this meeting. One of the places speakers came from is The People-Pet Partnership (PPP) located at Washington State University's College of Veterinary Medicine. The PPP conducts research on the human-animal bond and how it can be utilized in a variety of areas. In addition to research that benefits veterinary medicine and veterinary education, the PPP "aims to conduct innovative research that will result in identifying, promoting, and facilitating the HAB" (www.vetmed.wsu.edu/depts-pppp). Another group is the Center for the Interaction of Animals and Society (CIAS) located at the University of Pennsylvania's School of Veterinary Medicine (research.vet.upenn.edu /cias/Home/tabid/1889/Default.aspx). The (CIAS) is a multi-disciplinary research center established in 1997 to provide a forum for addressing both the practical and moral issues surrounding the interactions of animals and society. Among the research being conducted at the Center are projects that examine the behavioral development of assistance canines and pet dogs and the monitoring of the health of search and rescue dogs used at the World Trade Center and Pentagon after the September 11th terrorist attacks (research.vet.upenn.edu/Research/tabid /1907/Default.aspx).

Perhaps the oldest and largest group promoting the positive effects of human-animal interactions is the Delta Society. Based in Washington State, the Delta Society emphasizes the healing connection of animals, people, and medical professionals. The group is largely educational: healthcare professionals are taught how to incorporate animals into their treatment of patients; people with disabilities are provided with service animal resources; and people are encouraged to volunteer their animals as therapy animals in their local communities (Delta Society, 2008). Another national group, Canine Companions for Independence (CCI), provides trained dogs for people with disabilities. Based in Santa Rosa, California, CCI breeds its own dogs that have been chosen for their heritage as highly trainable. Until 1996, when CCI started its Prison Puppy Raising Program, volunteer caretakers were recruited from the local community. Today, dogs can receive their initial socialization for 15 to 18 months either inside or outside prison walls.

Having discussed animals and the research regarding the positive effects of HAI, it is now crucial to understand the context in which PAPs operate. Right now, prisons and the criminal justice system at large are facing a changing climate initially brought on by difficult economic conditions. Although "the enactment of draconian legislation in the face of public anxiety is a time-honored political strategy," with the economic downturn we have seen that is safer for politicians to call for change (Grabosky & Shover, 2010, p. 643). And socially, the population is growing tired of their tax dollars being spent on prisons and not, for example, schools, particularly as cost-saving yet more effective programs are being considered.

Incarceration in America Today: The Decline of Prison Programming

Once the failure of treatment and nothing works had been declared, criminal justice policy in the United States became characterized by the need to get tough on crime and criminals (Mauer, 2001; McGuire, 2002). In most state's adult systems, determinate sentencing replaced indeterminate sentencing and rehabilitation as a goal (Mauer, 2001). The 1980s saw the war on drugs, and the 1990s truth in sentencing and three strikes policies that emphasized punishment and retribution (ibid). After nearly three decades of get tough policies, the result has been an incarceration rate that is highest in the world. In 2008, the United States incarcerated 1 of every 100 adults in prison or jail; one of every nine black men between the ages of 20 to 34 is behind bars (The Pew Center on States, 2008). On any given day, 7.3 million adults, or 1 in 37, are under some type of criminal justice authority, including probation, parole, and federal, state, or local corrections (The Pew Center on States, 2009). Put another way, the U.S. has less than 5 percent of the world's population but nearly 25 percent of the planet's prisoners (Liptak, 2008). If the number of people affected by the criminal justice system does not shock you, the dollar amounts spent might. In 2008, states spent approximately $52 billion on corrections, an increase of over 303 percent since 1988 (Scott-Hayward, 2009). Only funds spent on Medicaid have increased at a greater pace (ibid).

In 2008, over 600,000 people, more than 1,600 each day were expected to be released from state and federal prisons (Visher & Travis, 2003). As a result, the issues surrounding inmates returning to the community have received significant attention in recent years (Travis & Pertersilia, 2001; Veysey, 2008). Given not only that prisoner re-entry is an increasingly pressing issue for communities, but also the constant need for effective inmate control in prison and thereby safety for all living and working inside, an environment seemingly prime for programming has been created. However, "programming has not kept pace with the number of offenders entering prison. In fact, the proportion of inmates receiving programming has steadily declined in the past decade" (Mears, Lawrence, Solomon, & Waul, 2002, p. 66).

The need for programming is also driven by the nature of the people we choose to incarcerate. The majority of inmates suffer from multiple problems, including lower rates of educational achievement and employment, increased rates of substance abuse and prior physical and sexual abuse, and physical and mental health disorders (Andrews & Bonta, 2003; Lawrence et al., 2002; Mears et al., 2002; Veysey, 2008). When these characteristics are co-occurring, "the risks of recidivism, relapse into drug use, unemployment, etc., are compounded" (Mears et al., 2002, p. 67).

An Ideal Time for Change.

Thus, we have created grand warehouses full of over 2 million people, most of who will be released. Their prison experience will determine their experience upon release; therefore their experience inside is crucial and where PAPs can make a great contribution. Some authors suggest creating "the virtuous prison" where moral goodness or moral excellence is fostered (Cullen, Sundt, & Wozniak, 2001). While critics may argue that virtuous is a concept too value laden, it is important to remember that "rehabilitation is, at its core, a moral enterprise. It depends on the existence of social consensus about shared values— about what is right and what is wrong....it accepts a standard for moral and legal behavior" (p. 269). A prison of this type has a positive agenda rather than one of simply inflicting pain. Inmates in these facilities can be shown that they "are not a form of refuse but have the human dignity to be renewed; that offenders are worth investing in because they can change and contribute to society" (p. 276). Inmates in a virtuous prison do good—that is they engage in activities that go beyond benefiting themselves, but society as well. Sometimes these activities are referred to as part of restorative justice efforts, which will be discussed later.

Currently, we face national economic conditions that, coupled with a budding realization that we have relied on a "remarkably simplistic and inflammatory public and political discourse on the value of prisons" (Jacobson, 2005, p. 9), have created an environment that appears ideal for change. According to Attorney General Eric Holder, "we've reached an important point for updating our goals, for modernizing and refocusing our strategies, and for compiling the latest and best thinking we have on the most effective, and most economically viable, ways to reduce violent crime" (Holder, 2010 available at www.justice.gov/ag /speeches/2010/ag-speech-100713.html). Prison-based animal programs are relatively inexpensive to operate, with the animals, their medical care, and food and other supplies donated by the administering non-profit organization. The participant (inmate) labor is free as their work is generally considered voluntary. The cost to the facility is the space the program requires and the security staff needed for that space. The economics of the programs are significant given the argument that due to "tight budgets, shifts in public opinion and priorities and new research that confirms the efficacy of ...programs....the United States is in a historical moment of limited duration, when a radical shift away" from the policies of mass incarceration of the last three decades can occur (Jacobson, 2005, p. 6).

States spent more on corrections in 2008 than on education and transportation infrastructure (Pew Center on the States, 2009). But as state officials across the nation continue to struggle with budget shortfalls, they are making and considering policy changes that would reduce prison populations and reduce the number of people under parole supervision (American Press, 2009, retrieved from www.msnbc.msn .com/id/28592088; Scott-Hayward, 2009). A number of states are establishing sentencing reform committees and task forces (Scott-Hayward, 2009). The changes represent the most significant modifications in corrections policy since the tough on crime climate began in the 1970s. Under the pretext of being fiscally responsible, politicians can now support programs and policies that would both save money and improve corrections without appearing soft on crime. For example, in California Governor Arnold Schwarzenegger wants to eliminate parole for all but violent or sex offenders. In August 2009, a federal panel of judges ordered the size of the California prison system to be cut by approximately one-quarter within two years (Moore, 2009b). Mass over-crowding has led to chaotic conditions. Days after the judges' orders, a riot broke out at the California Institution for Men in Chino, injuring more than 250 inmates (Moore, 2009a). While no staff members were hurt during the 11-hour riot, and inmates made demands, 10 of the state's 33 prisons were put on indefinite lockdown to prevent further disturbances (ibid). In New York, Governor Paterson has changed sentencing policy including the Rockefeller Drug laws that inflicted long mandatory sentences for first-time nonviolent drug offenders.

For the fiscal year 2010, the corrections budgets of at least 22 states have been cut (Scott-Hayward, 2009). According to *The Fiscal Crisis in Corrections: Rethinking Policies and Practices,* published by the Vera Institute of Justice in July 2009, states are looking at three areas in which to make cost-saving changes: operating costs, re-entry and community corrections, and population reduction (ibid). In increasing the efficiency with which their departments are managed, state departments of corrections are closing facilities, allowing staff attrition and reducing benefits, and placing an increased burden on inmates by making them pay for medical care.

Of course, reductions are also being made in prison programming. According to the Vera report, at least 19 states are seeking to cut costs through programming reductions. Returning inmates who violate probation or parole is a significant cost to correctional systems, with little to no demonstrated positive outcomes—policies that generate very little bang for the buck. Departments are also improving programs that allow offenders to remain outside of prison facilities, a less expensive, and in many cases more effective approach known as community corrections. Community corrections is tied into recidivism, or return to prison; the transition back to the community is obviously less abrupt when a person has not left the community and has been able to maintain ties to family and employment. One of the reasons we spend so much on prisons is because we have a staggering number of people behind bars, therefore fewer people behind bars would mean less money expended. There are groups of inmates, such as the elderly, who can safely be let out of prison; the cost of their care in the community (i.e., Medicaid, etc.) would then be shared by both the state and federal governments. Clearly, officials are re-evaluating the long-standing practices that have failed to reduce crime or drug use but instead drove up prison budgets with few or no positive results for the public.

The federal government is not ignoring the issue of overcrowded and costly prison systems. In March 2009, Senator Jim Webb, a Democrat from Virginia, introduced a bill that "would establish a national commission to review the system from top to bottom" (New York Times, 2009, Nov. 29). The National Criminal Justice Commission Act of 2009 would bring together criminal justice experts who would evaluate "a range of policies that have emerged haphazardly across the country" and recommend reforms (ibid). In July 2010, the House of Representatives passed the National Criminal Justice Commission Act, H.R. 5143 (The Sentencing Project, July 2010). The commission will have 18 months to review the country's entire criminal justice system and make recommendations for reform. Speaking at the 2010 Project Safe Neighborhoods Annual Conference in New Orleans in July 2010, Attorney General Eric Holder demonstrated this increasing recognition for the need to "commit to being clear about what works, to being responsive to research and analysis, and to being pragmatic in determining how and where our resources can be used most effectively" (Holder, 2010 available at http://www.justice.gov/ag/speeches/2010/ag-speech-100713.html). While civil libertarians and Democrats might be expected to call for reform, Republicans and "some religious groups object to prison policies that appear to ignore the possibility of rehabilitation and redemption, and fiscal conservatives are concerned about the cost of maintaining the world's largest prison population" (Liptak, 2009, Nov. 24). As it has become more difficult to deny ours is a flawed system, driven in large part by over-criminalization (e.g., drugs), a wider audience is recognizing the dire need for both legislation and action that create improvement. Despite spending $60 billion on prisons and jails at the state level each year "People who have been incarcerated are often barred from housing, shunned by potential employers and surrounded by others in similar circumstances. This is a recipe for high recidivism. And it's the reason that two-thirds of those released are rearrested within three years. It's time for a new approach...and any real effort ...must include a strong focus on preparing for reentry. Effective reentry programs provide our best chance" (Holder, 2010 available at www.justice.gov/ag/speeches/2010/ag-speech-100713.html). Enter prison-based animal programs as one ingredient in this new recipe.

We are also facing other social conditions that make animal programs inside prison a logical development. While there has always been a demand for service dogs for people with disabilities, post-9/11, the use of working dogs for security purposes has greatly increased (Baker, 2008; Sterngold, 2002). The domestic demand for explosive-detecting canines is unprecedented, with canines being added to law enforcement teams posted in locations from train stations to court houses (see, for example, Jones, 2003). Agencies including the Transportation Security Administration, established after 9/11 to oversee airport security, are using canines which are seen as being "quicker and hav[ing] fewer false alarms" than technological devices; the dogs are viewed as having "no downside" (Sterngold, 2002, p. 24). And with the Christmas Day 2009 attempted terror attack on a plane flying from Amsterdam to Detroit, Michigan, there is an even greater reliance on explosive-detecting canines. While there is a renewed focus on small incendiary devices that are not detectable with traditional metal detector machines, the existing methods of detecting these devices are limited. The so-called puff machines, designed to detect explosives by testing the air around a person, are expensive and difficult to maintain while waiting for the results after swabbing a passenger for evidence of explosive material is time consuming. Pat-downs would have to become significantly more frequent (every passenger not only those randomly chosen), and more thorough (with closer contact over a greater area of the body). The perpetrator of the Christmas Day incident packed the explosive powder inside his underwear, in the crotch. Even a pat-down fitting today's stricter standards would not have found those explosives; only a (naked) cavity search would have been effective.

Airport safety check points could start to look a lot more like prison gates after time spent in the yard: systematically and closely patting down each person that passes through. Most people have not experienced this type of search outside of law enforcement environments: airports could become more institutional and punitive places. As airports come to mirror prisons, law enforcement and safety agencies will justify a high level of control and the enforcement of strict rules as increasing peoples' safety. Like prisons, we want to keep weapons out of airports and off airplanes but we are experiencing the criminalization of air travel. However, canines (with handlers who are not holding large automatic weapons across their chests) can effectively prevent having a trip to an airport seem more like entering a police state. Quite simply, canines, can give travelers "a visceral sense of security that machinery" cannot. Rather than heavily armed security officers, dogs can bring reassurance to travelers, as well as the officers who handle them (ibid). In fact, the day after the failed attack, the front page of The New York Times featured a picture of a large, gold-colored dog sniffing suitcases that were laid out over the floor in an airport. Standing around the dog and his handler, a corporal from a Michigan county police department, were a number of people who had stopped and were smiling as they watched the team work (Pugliano, 2009).

There is also the need for assistance animals for the ever-increasing number of returning disabled war veterans. While estimates vary, the military does acknowledge a significant number of returning veterans suffer from Post-Traumatic Stress. These social circumstances have lead to unique partnerships between prison facilities and law enforcement agencies, as well as the federal Department of Veterans Affairs (Strom, 2006). One program assisting returning veterans with Traumatic Brain Injury (TBI), Post Traumatic Stress Disorder (PTSD), or other physical injury is Dog Tags: Service Dogs for Those Who've Served Us, a program under the auspices of Puppies Behind Bars (www.puppiesbehindbars.com/about_service.asp). The dogs learn 82 commands in order to become service canines. As one participant said, "we give people who receive these dogs their freedom, and that is something that was taken away from us" (Berger, 2008a, p. 1). Participants in these prison programs are providing a valuable service in raising these dogs which are generally provided for free and include a training period where the canine and the recipient learn to work together. An example of one veteran who received an assistance canine for help with PTSD demonstrates the power of this program model. The first veteran paired with a dog through Dog Tags returned to the prison facility where the dog was trained to share his thanks with the dog handlers as well as report on how successful the dog was at reminding him to take his medication and serving as a barrier from approaching strangers (www.puppiesbehindbars.com/about_service.asp). This former soldier was able to communicate the sense of freedom the incarcerated women gave him, while the participants could experience first-hand the positive impact they made for this valued member of our society. The work inmates are doing inside prison is important. Prior to be paired with his dog, the 47- year-old veteran fought in "the worst days of the Iraq War. He sustained such severe concussions and post-combat stress, from car bombs while patrolling with his Army National Guard Unit, that for a time he was too frightened to leave his home" (Berger, 2008, p.1). When flashbacks of dead bodies and brutal fighting hit, his dog is beside him to remind him that he is in the supermarket, not on the battlefield; his dog is also nearby when he wakes up from nightmares in the middle of the night. The psychological pain that imprisons this veteran is being lessened by people locked inside a prison of mortar and stone.

This chapter began by pointing out that animal-assisted therapy and activities are increasingly being incorporated into programs in a wide variety of places. Human animal interactions have been recognized as therapeutic for many people and research about the phenomenon continues to be conducted by a number of organizations. Animals can positively influence people physically, psychologically, socially, and behaviorally. Prison-based animal programs can be therapeutic for a number of reasons. The unique nature of animals—including their unconditional regard and nonverbal communication—make them ideally suited to work with prison inmates. And when the animals have experienced violence or are homeless or otherwise unwanted, there is the obvious parallel between them and the experiences of (too) many inmates. A symbiosis can be formed that benefits not just the specific creatures participating, but the larger community beyond prison walls as well. Add to this the current economic climate and its ensuing influence on criminal justice policy, and an inexpensive program that can help so many is just a plain no-brainer.

3
The Evolution of Prison Programming

Prison-based animal programs are a massive improvement in the evolution of prison programming, but to understand why we need to examine the history of prison programming in the United States. A sizeable amount of that history actually involves inmates working with animals but not in PAPs. For those in the know, animals in prison are nothing new. There is a long history, which continues today, of prisons having agricultural animals with inmates performing related duties. I argue, however, that these programs do not reflect the positive rehabilitative elements of a true PAP. Among the reasons for the PAP-prison farm distinction is the farm's origins from slave plantations, connecting them to issues of race and the exploitation of labor. In addition, agricultural work with animals is inherently different from building rehabilitative relationships: the animals are being raised only to best prepare them for slaughter. Fattening up a pig or cow is not the same as trying to train a service dog or socialize an abandoned or abused animal. The interactions with farm animals do not generate the pro-social, redemptive, or therapeutic relationships—described in the previous chapter—that are necessary for a program to receive the label of a PAP. Thus PAPs offer an alternative model to how animals have historically been incorporated into prison programming.

So how did we get where we are with prisons and programming? The answer is not simple or linear. The first jails were holding places for people prior to trial and for those unable to pay fines (Christianson; 1998; Friedman, 1993; Weiss, 2005). They were putrid, dungeon-like places where males and females, young and old, were kept in one room. Until the start of the 1800s, punishments were generally corporal, public, and took on various forms of torture. From the start, prisons incorporated some type of labor. Justifications for prison labor changed over time, from having rehabilitative uses to generating profit for private business and/or government agencies; "prisons became quasi-economic institutions, and their impact, directly and indirectly, on the wage and price market generated political controversy and conflict that would severely limit its reformative potential" (Weiss, 2005, p. 529). Inmate labor, Jim Crow era laws that continued slavery through convict leasing and the prison plantation have left their mark on the history of today's prison farms. As a result, this sordid history differentiates modern-day farm programs from other PAPs, "evidencing the slavish origin of penal systems" (Sellin, 1976, p. 178). The emancipation of slaves is what shaped the development of prisons, their programs, and the development of prison farms. Therefore examining the role of slavery is crucial to understanding the history of prison programming.

Early U.S. Prisons

It is misleading to consider the activities demanded of inmates in early American prisons programmatic. At Eastern State Penitentiary in Philadelphia and Auburn State Prison in New York in the 1820s, generally considered the institutions from which prisons as we know them evolved, incarcerated people were put to work. The competing Pennsylvania and Auburn models, as the approaches came to be known, both included inmate labor if in different forms. Under the Pennsylvania model conceived by Quakers, inmates remained isolated from each other and the world, providing them with time to reflect, or ask for penance, for their wrongs. In solitary cells they were limited to reading the bible and engaging in small handicraft activities (Christianson, 1998). The earliest programs arose out of these penitentiaries and a need to teach inmates to read the Bible (Linden & Perry, 1983). Because of high rates of illiteracy, literacy programs were developed in order to facilitate inmates' understanding of the religious materials that would lead to their reform. In contrast, in the Auburn or congregate system, inmates worked together in silence in prison shops during the day and returned to single cells to sleep at night.

The Auburn system ultimately became the model of choice for a number of reasons. Complete isolation, as at Eastern State, required more space and more staff to oversee inmates spread out over a large facility. Increased space equated increased costs to build and maintain the facilities. And with inmates only able to engage in small handicraft activities, the Auburn model was associated with a greater output of products for the state's profit. The north's contract system had inmates remain in prison while working for private contractors who then sold the products of the inmate labor, including items such as shoes, on the free market. However, northern trade unions fought the practice which was viewed as taking away jobs from law-abiding workers who would lose out to the cheap products of prison labor (Weiss, 2005).

Under the guise of reformation, the north experimented with what came to be known as the Reformatory Movement in the late 1800s. Beginning with Elmira in New York in 1876, states attempted to send young first-time offenders to facilities that were supposed to be more like schools than prisons. Educational and vocational classes, coupled with indeterminate sentencing which allowed for early release with good behavior, would encourage rehabilitation (Rotman, 1995). Massachusetts, Michigan, Pennsylvania, and Indiana followed with similar facilities. However, a lack of vocationally trained instructors and overcrowding led to the end of the movement by the early 1920s (Roberts, 2005).

Southern Postbellum Justice or Presenting Farm Work as Therapeutic

When the 13th Amendment was passed in December 1865 at the end of the Civil War, many believed it indicated the end of slavery. A closer examination of the 13th Amendment indicates something more subtle: "Neither slavery nor involuntary servitude, except as punishment for crime whereof the party shall have been duly convicted, shall exist within the United States." Although Lincoln's policy was supposed to bring emancipation from slavery, the effect was not as clear and immediate as most history textbooks would have us believe. Slavery did not just disappear in the south: "It remain[ed] embedded as a function of law and other social institutions and, therefore, a feature of U.S. culture" (Adams, 2007, p. 9). It is legal and permissible to make a person who has been convicted of a crime work against his or her will.

What some may call a caveat to the ban on slavery became the foundation for the South's approach to punishment and prison programming. According to penal historian Blake McKelvey (1935, p. 143), "the war and its aftermath were the dominant factors in separating the South from the Union in penological matters for at least half a century" (cited in Weiss, 2001, p. 272). Freedom meant plantation owners lost their source of free labor, and poor white farmers lost what made them distinct from slaves, but still emancipation did make not make blacks equal to whites. Meanwhile, "the ex-slave had become a scapegoat for the South's humiliating defeat.... and...a living symbol, a daily reminder, of all that had changed" (Oshinsky, 1996, p. 14). The political economy created a situation where profit became the core of punishment in the South.

Poor whites suddenly became similar to freed blacks—an intolerable situation. Neither group owned land to farm and so had to rely on wealthy land owners to rent them equipment, including animals, for a meager economic survival. In response, Mississippi passed a series of acts known as the Black Codes: "their aim was to control the labor supply, to protect the freedman from his own 'vices,' and to ensure the superior position of whites in southern life" (p. 20). Other southern states, including Alabama, Florida, Georgia, Louisiana, South Carolina, and Texas also adopted the Black Codes which created categories of crime that were specific to blacks: mischief, rude gestures, cruelty to animals, selling alcohol, and living with a white person. Intermarriage was punishable with a life sentence in the state penitentiary (ibid). Central to the Black Codes was the Vagrancy Act which required all ex-slaves to have documentation verifying their employment, and the Enticement Act which made it illegal for anyone, black or white, to entice a worker away from an employer; this both controlled the price of black labor as well as prevented plantation owners from "stealing each other's Negroes" (Oshinsky, p. 21, 1996). The laws criminalized blackness (Blackmon, 2008).

The Codes created a great influx of criminal cases that overwhelmed the local courts leaving the town sheriff to determine the punishment, generally a fine the freedman could not pay. The solution was to have the offender work off his debt for a white man to whom he was then leased. Many times, black men were arrested and simply auctioned off to local farmers to repay their debt. It seemed nothing had changed from prior to the Civil War. With the Reconstruction Act of 1867, states were forced to rewrite their constitutions and adopt the Constitution's 14th Amendment which guaranteed the Bill of Rights at the state level. It is important to note that while the North spearheaded the movement to invoke the act, it was not without self-interest. By providing blacks in the South with rights, it was believed they would not travel to the North's cold climate (Oshinsky, 1996). Dissatisfied with the forced policies, the South returned to its unwritten code of settling personal wrongs outside the law—the result was an explosion of violence; "the ex-slaves could no longer count on the 'protection' that went along with being the master's valuable property" (p. 25). Writing in the *Souls of Black Folk* (1903/1990, p. 129), W. E. B. Du Bois noted that whites were "'tacitly assumed' to be actual or de facto members of the police system" (quoted in Adams, 2007, p. 136). Quick, simple judgment marked by a schedule of fines that charged for each additional step in the judicial process created a system where blacks avoided accruing debt by acquiescing to the charges so as to minimize their sentence of indentured service. Indeed, "the span of time from arrest to conviction and judgment to delivery at a slave mine or mill was often no more than 72 hours" (Blackmon, 2008, p. 66). And the best way to make a guilty black person give up crime was through work, which it so happened was plentiful.

What had once been the realm of the plantation master now became the purview of the criminal justice system; the courts became a way to re-enslave the blacks (Du Bois, 1902/1990). Low-level disobedience, most commonly stealing, overwhelmed southern courts and southern prison populations turned black. For example, under the Pig Law, grand larceny was defined as stealing any farm animal or property worth over ten dollars, and could result in a five-year prison sentence (Oshinsky, 1996). But having been largely destroyed during the Civil War, states would need to construct new facilities to house offenders. Just when it seemed like the burned out and gutted pre-War prisons would burst, along came Edmund Richardson, a rich white businessman in need of cheap labor to work the land he purchased in the Yazoo Delta of Mississippi. He would feed, clothe, and guard the state's felons in exchange for their labor. "At the time, it seemed a stop-gap measure to deal with rising crime rates until a new prison could be built. It did not turn out that way" (Oshinsky, 1996, p. 35). The result was Parchman Farm (now Mississippi State Penitentiary), the country's largest prison plantation at the time, covering 20,000 acres (Oshinsky, 1996; Taylor, 1999). Another infamous prison plantation established at nearly the same time with the same profit-driven motivations was Angola, or the Louisiana State Penitentiary, today's largest maximum-security prison in the country. And as with Parchman, Angola is still a fully operational farm today, with 18,000 acres of land. Angola is often compared to the island of Manhattan—it is approximately the same size and both are surrounded by water on three sides. At Angola, the nearest town—at the side attached to land—is 20 miles away and virtually unpopulated (Shere, 2005). These plantations were hardly transformed from places where slaves were once kept—they simply became prison farms where the same people, now called convicts, were kept and put to work which some argued was actually good for them.

Inmates, nearly all of whom were former slaves, carried out the duties they had performed prior to emancipation. They used horses to plough fields of crops and maintained herds of animals including cattle and pigs. Black men, and some women, could still be found in the fields harvesting crops by hand under the scorching hot sun. Their living conditions were as deplorable, if not more so, than when they were enslaved. Prison barracks, when they did exist, were dilapidated buildings that barely provided shelter in what could be cold winters. Food was also scarce, more so than when these black men and women lived as slaves. The incentive to maintain the people who were once an investment for private land owners disappeared as prisons were operated according to a traditional business model seeking to maximize profit with no regard for the highly replaceable people, really no more than machines or tools that performed the work.

Angola is actually named for the home country of most of the original slaves who worked the plantation (*Angola: The Farm*, 1997). Angola was a "slave-breeding plantation—where the 'crop' was human beings, ...the owner believed the 'best' slaves came from that African country" (Shere, 2005, p. 41). After the Civil War, the state was able to incarcerate men on the site without fee; the men were there to farm the land. They were also instrumental in building the levee system on the Mississippi that leads to New Orleans (Shere, 2005). In following with the barbaric treatment of the time, when a man died while working on the levee—whether due to exhaustion, heat stroke, or other malady, his body was dumped into the levee, thus requiring less dirt for fill (ibid).

Codified first by Mississippi in 1876, the Leasing Act made convict leasing law. The state did not completely end imprisonment, but reserved it for convicts serving sentences of ten years or more, and these were largely whites who went unpunished but for the worst acts (Oshinsky, 1996; Sellin, 1976). All other offenders were eligible for leasing, whether those serving state sentences of several years or those sentenced to less than a year in county jail but unable to pay court fees and fines. The work ranged from mining, laying railroad tracks, building roads, clearing swamp land and forests for farming, the turpentine industry, and any work free laborers would refuse (Blackmon, 2008; Oshinsky, 1996; Sellin, 1976; Webb, 2005; Weiss, 2001). "Convict leasing was not about justice, equal treatment, or making the punishment fit the crime. Convict leasing was about profits, brutality, and racist ideas" (Oshinsky, 1996, p. 78). The obligation of southern states to punish the quickly growing population of black people labeled criminal lead to "cash-strapped governments [sending] felons directly from the courts to the labor market, making criminal justice a major conduit to labor-hungry capitalist developers" (Weiss, 2001, p. 272). Historian Alex Lichtenstein (1996) notes that convicts had a "reputation for providing reliable results in work that whites would not usually deign to or be asked to do...convict leasing was not simply a 'continuation of or replacement for slavery.' It was part of the machinery of 'progress'" (p. 113). The justification for the leasing system was that the work socialized blacks to their full potential. As a lesser, genetically inferior race more animal-like than human, blacks were believed to be designed for arduous labor (Blackmon, 2008; Oshinsky, 1996; Sellin, 1976; Taylor, 1999). It was believed that unless hungry or compelled, blacks would not work. As different from whites, they required different punishments—mere confinement would not be viewed as punishment to blacks (Blackmon, 2008; Litwack, 2009; Oshinsky, 1996). The best punishment was work, which might even be rehabilitative for some.

All of the work was dangerous, and included employment in brick yards, the turpentine industry, lumber camps, coal and iron mining, and rail road construction (Adams, 2007; Oshhinsky, 1996). A benefit of convict leasing was the flexibility afforded to meet the needs of the customer (Adams, 2007). After toiling 10 and 12 hours or more each day, the conditions of confinement were deplorable at best. Some convicts slept on the ground yards from where they worked, most went bare foot, under-nourished, and generally neglected in terms of their health or general well-being. Death, disease, accidents, and maimed men were common (Blackmon, 2008). Beatings— generally lashings, or torture were the norm for failure to work to one's full potential or for any number of minor infractions. "They were hung from makeshift crucifixes, stretched on wooden racks, and placed in coffin-sized sweatboxes for hours at a time" (Oshinsky, 1996, p. 79). Inspectors entering the prison and mine camps found desperate conditions for convicts; according to a report of one member of Alabama's Board of Inspectors of Convicts "many of them are unfit for such labor, consequently it is not long before they pass from this earth….If the State wishes to kill its convicts it should do it directly and not indirectly" (Blackmon, 2008, p. 288). The inspector went on to suggest "it would be more humane and far better to stake the prisoner out with a ring around his neck like a wild animal than to confine him in places…that are reeking with filth and disease and alive with vermin of all kinds— nurseries of death" (p. 289). In 1885, George Washington Cable, a Louisiana prison inspector described Angola as "the system at its worst. So complete … is the abandonment, by the State, of all the duties it owes to its criminal system that … it does not so much as print a report" of conditions (1885, p. 168-169, quoted in Adams, 2007, p. 138). In 1888, Frederick Howard Wines, a social reformist who was collecting data for the 1880 U.S. Census described convict leasing as

> the greatest blot upon our American prison system. It is…a virtual abdication of the direct responsibility of the government for the treatment to be accorded to convicts. The best that can be said of it is that the states which have adopted it do not know what better to do.

> The leased prisoners are all in southern states....Their condition is for the most part deplorable in extreme, especially in the county chaingangs. Of this class of convicts...nine-tenths are negroes....The system is, however, so inherently vicious, involving as it does, an enormous death-rate and an extraordinary number of successful attempts at escape, that it does not meet the approval of the better class of citizens in the southern states, and it is undoubtedly doomed to speedy extinction (Wines, 1888 quoted in Rafter, 2009, p. 293).

By the 1890s there was widespread public objection to the conditions of leased inmates that had been revealed in newspaper reports. Convict leasing was outlawed in Louisiana in 1901 and the state bought the Angola farm. Inmates went from working for private industry to working for the state on the plantation.

As the generation of freemen begat a new generation who never knew slavery, the "'New Negro,' born in freedom, undisciplined by slavery and unschooled in racial etiquette" had to have their impulsive nature controlled—the only answer was to return blacks to the plantation environment, whether through prison farms or sharecropping (Litwack, 2009, p 13). Whites "disseminated racial caricatures and pseudo-scientific theories that reinforced and comforted ... their racial beliefs and practices" (p. 14). Whiteness "long escaped a specific identification with 'race,' it being 'normal' and therefore invisible in the mainstream" (Adams, 2007, p. 8). Irrespective of any theory driving the thinking, emancipation was a policy in name only. For southerners at the time, "slavery does not, nor can it, just go away. It remains embedded as a function of law and other social institutions and, therefore, as a feature of U.S. culture" (Adams, 2007, p. 8-9). Just as those blacks who could not afford to pay fines were forced to work in prison camps, freedmen not caught up in the criminal justice system could not pay for the land or equipment necessary to establish their own independent farms. As a result, a system of sharecropping and remaining as a tenant on their former masters' land rose and blacks were kept in the same socioeconomic position as when they were enslaved (Blackmon, 2008; Litwack, 2009; Oshinsky, 1996).

Prison farms were not limited to the South, but were presented as a progressive way to reform inmates and improve the conditions of incarceration in the North as well (Howe, 1913; The New York Times, 1916; The New York Times 1911). In the early 1900s, penologists in the North believed having the opportunity to farm was not only healthy, being out in the fields with exposure to the open air, but was a luxury compared to toiling away in the closed shops typical for northern inmates. In 1911, New York State had plans to replace Sing Sing Prison with the New York State Prison at Wingate, New York. The new prison would be an improvement in a number of ways, including its use of the scientific segregation of inmates. Wingate was promoted as a "great model farm" that would be "self-supporting" (The New York Times, 1916). A 1913 letter to the editor of The New York Times, written by the director of People's Institute, argued the prison farm built on the site of the Columbus, Ohio Penitentiary was developed to save men, not money (Howe, 1913). The People's Institute was a community educational center for working class adults and immigrants that sponsored lectures and adult education classes on topics such as social science and nutrition and health (Wingfield, 2003). However, in addition to the agricultural work, there would be "furniture, soap, hosiery, and woolen factories…[and] operated along the lines of scientific penology" (ibid). In keeping with the Progressive Movement, the new Ohio prison would allow for the investigation into the causes of criminality. According to a 1916 report by the State Commission of Prisons, New York's Wingdale would be a great improvement since at Sing-Sing,

> there is no broad acreage or farming land where the criminal guests of the State can work in the open air in the tilling of the soil, no herds of cows to be milked nor orchards to be kept in order and plucked of their fruit in due season, no fields of hay to be mown, nor fields of potatoes and cabbage and turnips to be cared for, and there are hundreds of Sing Sing's inmates who would welcome release from the shops to be assigned to these agricultural labors (The New York Times, 1916).

Despite the claims of farms being enlightened programming, the writers of the State Commission of Prisons report perhaps believed New York State Government might be enticed to adopt the farm model due in part to its cost saving aspects. The writers of the report noted the importance that planners "take into consideration that the State of New York purchases hundreds of thousands of dollars worth of industrial and farm products yearly, which might be produced in State institutions" (ibid). Clearly claims of science and progress as well as financial gain were difficult to untangle even in the North.

As the lease system was finally abolished in the early 1920s, southern states increasingly turned to the chain gang as a means of improving their roads for the new automobile age (Sellin, 1976). The conditions in the chain gangs were as deplorable as those of the prison camps, and like the camps, the chain gangs were designed to exploit inmate labor to maximize profit with minimal cost. Shackles and chains were worn at all times, and lashings and torture continued to be relied upon as punishment for the most minor infraction, whether attempting to escape or not working at what the guards considered maximum output. Chains remained in use in the south until after World War II (Sellin, 1976). Slowly, the use of penitentiaries returned but profiting from inmate labor remains common practice to this day. Prohibition in 1919 and the Great Depression both changed the make-up of prison populations—there was an increase in the population of white inmates (Oshinsky, 1996).

The Political Economy of Inmate Labor

As has been outlined thus far, the nature of both the type of prison programs and punishment being administered at any point in time has been inexorably tied to the state of political, social, and economic conditions outside prison walls. The beginnings of inmates working with animals were clearly not PAPs being administered for the rehabilitation of either the inmates or the animals. Instead, the work was exploitative of both the inmates and the animals. While farms continue to operate on prison grounds and with inmate labor today, it is necessary to examine prison labor broadly, irrespective of working with animals. The events that produced the current era of programming and work is no less driven by the forces of politics and profits than it was 200 years ago. Today, however, the picture is complicated with little differentiation between work, education, vocational training, and other types of programs. And the prison industrial complex, whereby companies and organizations profit from the existence of prisons, still figures into decisions about work and programs inside carceral facilities. In comparison, PAPs that truly hold the potential to benefit and transform those who participate continue to demonstrate their worth for all involved.

The capitalist system of production creates and requires a surplus population for competition within the labor pool—the best should be hired for the job for the betterment of the owner. A seminal Marxist work by economist Georg Rusche and legal scholar Otto Kirchheimer theorized that "every system of production tends to discover punishments which correspond to its productive relationships" (1968, p. 3). At any given time, our society's punishments have reflected the most effective way in which to exploit labor. Rusche and Kirchherimer's *Punishment and Social Structure* (1939/1968) was revisited in the 1970s and 1980s "when millions of 'permanent' industrial jobs—high paying unionized manufacturing jobs—were lost to technological change, corporate deregulation, the globalization of labor markets, increases in capital mobility, and free trade" (Weiss, 2001, p. 255). With a labor market no longer flush with jobs, soaring unemployment occurred alongside exponentially growing prison population, causing some to argue prisons had become a place to store an oversupply of labor (D'Alessio & Stolzenberg, 2002; Weiss, 2001; Zimring & Hawkins, 1993). Not surprisingly, this exponential growth in the incarceration of people of color coincided with their portrayal as the dangerous classes (Sheldon, 2000; Wacquant, 2001). Today, prison labor has become an "economic resource for employers in labor intensive sectors of global competition" (Weiss, 2001, p. 255). As corporations struggle for survival in a global economy where outsourcing to other nations is common, bringing industry inside prisons keeps jobs in America while still maintaining the low wage benefits of transnational labor markets.

Going back to the sixteenth century, a timeline of industrial advancements parallels penal programming practices. When economic prosperity resulted in a surplus of jobs, prison conditions reflected the idea of less eligibility, where the lowest paid free workers had a higher standard of living than those incarcerated. In this way, the number in society's poorest classes were adjusted for with the use of penal sanctions; "cycles of unemployment and levels of imprisonment were medicated by 'moral panics' and 'judicial anxiety'" (Weiss, 2001, p. 258, n. 6). Research has shown "a consistent and significant relationship between labor surpluses, prison admissions, and incarceration rates, unmediated by crime rates" (ibid).

Technological change coupled with population rates came to intervene in prison conditions. With the industrial revolution and advances in medicine that allowed for population growth, eighteenth century Europe saw great numbers of its population leave the hinterlands and migrate to cities. The technological advances that created machines that could do the work of several people lead to competition for employment. History shows "European prisons soon deteriorated into deterrent-based regimes of solitary confinement and unproductive labor, such as rock busting, [and] work on the crank" (Weiss, 2001, p. 259).

The United States offers an opposing picture. As a result of the influx of people into the cities, where industry was unable to meet the demand for workers, we see the primary form of punishment being shaped by the need for labor. As described above, the Auburn model of the penitentiary beat out the Pennsylvania model in part due to the increased output of congregated inmates, compared to the limited piece work at Eastern State Penitentiary. The cheap and abundant production at Auburn lead to its use as a means of strike-breaking as owners could simply turn to convict labor to meet their demands (Weiss, 2001). At Auburn, production replaced punishment and was justified as being able to train inmates with discipline which would create a good citizen upon release. Between 1835 and 1885, most northern states implemented the private contract system modeled at Auburn (Weiss, 2001). Prison was presented as a way to enter society—in marked contrast to today where transition back to society is not a priority, as demonstrated by the draconian practice of long-term solitary confinement that is the hallmark of the modern-day super-max movement.

As the economic markets changed, the use of convict labor was scaled back. Prisons could not maintain the technological advances being made in machinery and labor unions grew in strength. The start of the twentieth century saw prison labor limited to state use. The Great Depression brought with it the Hawes-Cooper Act of 1929 and the Ashurst-Sumner Act that prohibited the interstate commerce of products made using convict labor. License plates became the default item produced by convict labor. With the decrease of productive work inside prisons came a decrease in the morale inside prisons. While profit and the commodification of convict labor are easily criticized as the exploitation of inmates, prison administrators then "had even less occasion to take notice of prisoners as individuals, furthering their objectification" (Weiss, 2001, p. 262). In contrast, participants in PAPs are individuals who are making contributions to society—another beneficial aspect of PAPs. Between the 1920s and the end of World War II the tactic of prison administrators changed from hard labor to hard time, characterized by the routinized treatment of inmates in the Big House model of prison in the 1930s and 1940s (Weiss, 2001). Rapidly, a growing number of men were warehoused in enormous, intimidating structures of brick and stone built in a square-shape to form a recreation yard in the center. The medical model of inmate transformation, popular in the 1950s and 1960s was abandoned in the 1970s as the result of a number of politico-economic conditions. As described above, the War on Drugs and increasing conservatism of Republicans who took on a tough on crime stance further reduced inmates' rights and worsened conditions inside prisons. A series of laws, including the Justice System Improvement Act and the Federal Prison Industries Enhancement Act, both passed by Congress in 1979 relaxed laws to allow inmates to work; private labor quickly entered prisons as a way to maximize profits (Jacobsen, 2009; Albright, n.d.). State-use production, at slave-like pay, became the model inside prisons. It is worth noting that prison inmates are not included in the unemployment rate, often used as an indicator of the health of the country's economy. Reporting unemployment rates that actually reflected the true number of people not employed would create a much bleaker picture.

Chief Justice Warren Burger, the longest serving on the Supreme Court in the 20th century, played an important role in the development of modern-day prison labor. Nominated by President Richard Nixon in 1969, he replaced Chief Justice Earl Warren. He restricted or outright reversed many of the civil liberties granted by the Warren Court during the 1950s and 1960s, such as permitting the "good faith exception" to the exclusionary rule. If law enforcement, in good faith, believe their warrant is legal and valid, proceed with a search that produces incriminating evidence, that evidence is no longer subject to the exclusionary rule and is admissible in court to be used against the defendant.

Judges who are strict constructionists believe the U.S. Constitution should be read as it was originally intended or written, not as a document that evolves with society. When deciding cases, they are certainly not concerned with the norms of other countries—our forefathers were creating a new and unique republic different from all other countries. While Burger was regarded as a strict constructionist, he did look to other countries for more efficient methods of prison management that made them less of a burden on society. In his public comments about the American judicial system, he often compared it to those of Scandinavian countries such as Norway and Sweden (Raspberry, 1983; Sitomer, 1984a). His ideas about prison labor came from what he saw overseas during his visits to prisons in (at the time) the Soviet Union, China, and Scandinavia over the course of 25 years (Raspberry, 1983).

Off the bench, Warren was more outspoken than most justices today. He made known his opinion of what he regarded as the U.S. criminal justice system's slow and cumbersome nature. His favorite cause, though, was prisons. In a 1983 commencement address at Pace University in New York, he called for changes that would "transform prisons from 'human warehouses' into places of education and training and into factories and shops for the production of goods" (Sitomer, 1984b, p. 3). Burger's crusade led him to publicly argue for the benefits of "training inmates in gainful occupations and taking off the backs of American taxpayers the enormous load of maintaining the prison systems of this country" (Shutt, 1982, p. 2). He promoted the Scandinavian system with its shorter sentences, less crowding, better food, more privileges, and most importantly inmates that were "virtually always work[ing], often producing—for market-adjusted pay—products for public consumption" (Raspberry, 1983, p. A23). Even better, he said, are the Chinese who "instead of installing factories in prisons, they build prisons by putting fences around factories" (ibid). In June 1984, he spearheaded "Factories with Fences," a forum at George Washington University co-sponsored by the Brookings Institution, a nonpartisan public policy think tank organization based in Washington, D.C. The conference was a "proselytizing effort that brought together several hundred legislators, penologists, and prison officials" (Raspberry, 1984, p. A21). Again, as with early prison farms that used former slaves as free labor, we see capitalistic motivations driving prison programming that is in stark contrast to PAPs.

Shortly after that forum Burger toured Minnesota State Prison at Stillwater, where inmates assembled computer equipment for Control Data, with the company's founder Bill Norris. For little more than minimum wage, other inmates worked at computer programming, software development, and data processing (Raspberry, 1984, A21). Norris acknowledged his company was not a charity; he saw "unmet societal needs as profitable business opportunities" (ibid). He believed the training inmates received as a result of working for his company inside prison led them to be employable once released. In fact, he built several new factories in inner-city neighborhoods where many of the employees lived in the community. Providing someone with an opportunity for employment, he argued would prevent a person from going to prison in the first place and from returning once released. His approach can be summed up by his belief that "when you think about it, there really isn't much difference between an inner-city-poverty-stricken neighborhood and a prison" (quoted in Raspberry, 1984, p. A21).

However, with the advanced economies of the 1980s and 1990s requiring skill at high levels of digital technology, the outsourcing of factory jobs to other nations lead to the creation of "a large, relatively permanent group of young male offenders and ex-offenders who for the most part are unlikely to be productive members of the workforce in the foreseeable future" (Freeman, 2000, p. 191). Many were unable to "adapt to the economic metamorphosis of the 1970s and 1980s. The structural adjustments caused by globalization were rendered even more disruptive by the historical shift in the U.S. mode of governance away from rehabilitative social services provision toward punitive containment" (Bourgois & Schonberg, 2009, p. 150). Adding to the problem in the 1970s were the veterans returning from Vietnam who faced a labor market of largely unskilled non-union jobs in service industries (Weiss, 2001). In a perverse relationship, this shift helped drive the explosion of the prison population that has gotten us to the point where some would need to be incarcerated in order to find employment. Prison has become the norm in many communities comprised of "young 'underclass' males" who have "little prospect of returning to an unsupervised freedom" (Garland, 2001, p. 178).

Structurally, prisons have always been rooted in a country's political economy. And currently in the U.S. it would seem that convict labor "fits well with the continuing transformation of America into a nation of small government, big corporations, and big prisons" (Wright, 2003, p. 118). Supporters of this political landscape are neoliberalists who support deregulation, free market enterprise, and privatization (http://www.globalexchange.org/campaigns/econ101/neoliberalism.html). There are three potential perspectives used by neoliberals in discussing convict labor today: pure marketers, social benefit advocates, and the human services capital tactic (Weiss, 2001). Current conditions have created noncompetitive control of government markets whereby state and federal governments must purchase goods from prisons, regardless of the price or quality of the products. Those coming from the pure market perspective ignore criminal justice issues and propose privatizing "prison industry under voluntary inmate participation, with contracts awarded to the highest bidder, eliminating all government market preferences and restrictions, extending union membership, and applying all labor laws and minimum wage requirements" (Weiss, 2001, p. 267). Social benefit advocates bring an important caveat to the pure marketer's perspective. Prison labor will most likely take jobs from the least skilled, lowest classes who may then turn to crime, thus increasing prison populations. The classes most likely to commit crime are also those most likely to be victimized, thus confounding the ability to calculate the costs and benefits of prison labor. They argue that inmates who are most likely to be employed upon release be involved in prison labor, and that the products be importable and competitive, but it is difficult, if not impossible, to ensure these conditions of convict labor are used in the private sector. The human capital services perspective, while taking into consideration crime, prison, and criminal justice, still calls for privatization much like the pure marketers. The industries' convicts participate in what should be those most likely to be outsourced from the United States so as to minimize competition with the labor of free workers.

While the arguments about using convict labor in private labor markets is being disputed by academics, researchers, advocates, and politicians, you may be asking yourself why an incarcerated person would work at a low-skill job s/he would likely not take outside prison. In some states inmates are paid pennies an hour, while others are paid minimum wage which is subject to deductions for various expenses accrued by the inmates. Most income is subject to deductions for child support, victim compensation funds, medical co-payments, and in some cases, the inmate's own room and board (Wright, 2003). According to a prisoner in Washington state, "'Due to the deductions, the more you make, the more they take. You pay taxes and can't vote and have no say in how the money is used. You pay for room and board yet you're still subject to the same shit food and conditions. Even with the money you earn, there isn't much you can buy with it due to property limits'" (Wright, 2003, p. 115). People on both sides of the prison walls work at jobs they dislike because they need the money. However for inmates it is not technically slavery because of the salary earned. According to one member of industry, "'It's more like serfdom, or like being a domesticated animal'" (Wright, 2003, p. 115). Again we see an inmate-animal connection.

Prison-based animal programs come from this long history of programming for offenders. The question of what activities inmates should engage in is still being answered. Prison-based animal programs clearly improve on past attempts at programming in a number of ways, as will be demonstrated. Rather than exploiting either inmates or the products of their labor (i.e., trained animals), PAPs nurture restitution on the part of inmates who are giving back to society and helping the animal as well. That they themselves benefit is often collateral to what else occurs in the process of participating in a PAP. So little of the account of past attempts at prison programming actually consists of improvements for inmates; PAPs are one of a few bright spots in a long history of misguided programs too often established on a foundation of disingenuous motivations and a desire for profit.

Working versus Volunteering

As mentioned above, it can be difficult to separate a prison's work programs from vocational programs. It is also necessary to recognize the subtleties of work versus volunteer programs. Some argue work is voluntary, but as discussed above it is increasingly less so. Therefore, it is necessary to question how voluntary any program participation is inside prison—do prison inmates really have freedom of choice? And what of the men and women who do not have the luxury of volunteering their time. Many if not most inmates need a paying job—whether for the fees they are charged for their own incarceration or basic necessities from the commissary. It is very difficult to survive solely on items issued by the state or, in the case of private prisons, the facility. Only the bare minimum is distributed. Things as basic as a pen and paper have to be bought at the commissary. And how about the stamp to mail a letter? We know maintaining ties with family members contribute to criminal desistance but what if a prisoner does not have the money to purchase the items needed in order to stay in touch? And since the vast majority of our country's prison population comes from the lower socio-economic status, family members (who are more likely to have dropped out of an inmate's life versus remain in it) probably cannot afford to give money for commissary items. For many incarcerated people volunteering may not be a luxury they can afford—literally. People inside prison need to earn money to survive—just like those of us on the other side of prison walls.

Even the distinction between working and volunteering can be difficult to surmise. What in some places is considered community service, such as participation in dog programs inside New York and New Jersey prisons, can be a paid job in other states. In contrast is Colorado where PAP participants working with shelter dogs make $1.50 per day, amongst the highest pay inmates can earn in the system (Peters, 2006). Similarly, in Massachusetts, where inmates work training service canines, the compensation can reach $30 each week (Mulvany, 2008). Ohio presents an interesting example for examining work versus volunteerism. In Ohio, inmates are required to engage in community service. In 1998, Ohio "farmed out more than 1.9 million hours of these prisoners' volunteer labor to various public and nonprofit entities" (Burton-Rose, 1998). Each of Ohio's prisons adopts a school and fulfills the needs of that school including re-sanding and re-staining desks, making flash cards, coloring books and book shelves, as well as maintaining school grounds and landscaping. Inmates have also gutted out old buildings for use in government projects such as museums (ibid).

Much like PAPs, this sort of community service goes towards maintaining a prison's positive relations with the community. But if your community service is possibly less rewarding or meaningful, such as folding pamphlets for a non-profit agency, are we not back to forced labor? Positive relations must also be maintained inside a prison between inmates and staff and administrators. Participating in a community service job that is the pet project of a CO can drastically change an inmate's treatment. Dropping out of a community service job in order to take on another may insult a staff member or administrator which again, can bring about countless negative repercussions.

Another interesting example comes from California's Prison Fire Camps where minimum- and medium-security level prison inmates are kept in open rural locations where they are trained to respond to woodland fires and other natural disasters including mudslides. The camps, which date back to 1915, were California's answer to the South's prison farms and chain gangs. They began as road camps where inmates were housed outside the confines of prison walls in order to build what would become one of the most vast highway systems in the nation (Goodman, 2009). While involved in difficult, hazardous work the camps afforded prison inmates more freedoms compared to inmates housed behind prison walls. Is it really a choice when deciding between engaging in life-endangering work and living in a less restrictive and more comfortable environment or avoiding dangerous work by being locked inside?

From the 1920s to 1980s the road and fire camp residents were viewed as engaging in public works that saved both the taxpayers and the state precious money; any rehabilitative value was collateral (Goodman, 2009). During the hold of the rehabilitation model from the 1960s until the 1970s the state presented the camps as also providing rehabilitation through labor (ibid). Here again, we see the so-called braided, or what Goodman (2009) presents as "variegated penology" that is characterized by the presence of both punishment and rehabilitation-focused programs and policies. The lack of uniform logic or justification for administering a given program has often been a presence in the field of punishment (Goodman, 2009; Hutchinson, 2006). As programs come and go there has often been ambivalence about why that program should be in place. As with PAPs today, the goals of the programs are interchangeable. With road and fire camps we see the goals change over the course of decades. With PAPs the labor and rehabilitative outcomes are often cited as goals simultaneously.

A Schema of Genuine PAPs

In considering the definition of work it is also worth considering the definition of a PAP; it is not appropriate for all programs in which prison inmates work with animals to be labeled PAPs. There are a number of characteristics a program should possess in order to make it worthy of classification as a PAP. A true PAP should involve rehabilitative work or training being conducted with animals in an effort to improve the life circumstances of the animals. Similarly, the goal of the program should not be to produce non-human beings that benefit others by being consumed or otherwise exploited, but provide benefits through their companionship or work skills. While some may say service work is still exploitative of animals, we must navigate within the admittedly speciesest paradigm that non-human animals are only as worthy as what they can provide others; thus PAPs should involve humanitarian work with animals. Work, service, and companion animals in a PAP should receive a level of care and concern that is commonly extended to humans. The animals involved in a genuine prison-based program should not be present for entertainment purposes, such as in the case of a rodeo. A PAP may even be indicated by seeming out of place or in stark contrast for the compassionate work being conducted in what are often dangerous, violent places of punishment.

The work being conducted in a true PAP should be marked by its humanitarian social value. Programs that allow participants to engage in restitution to society, but not by performing distasteful jobs, can be PAPs. Programs where inmates have jobs connected to animals that non-incarcerated people can, and frequently do, choose to not accept are not PAPs. Slaughterhouse and agricultural programs fall into this category. The care for the welfare of animals should not be so as to result in increased profits or value (as when fattening up an animal for slaughter), but rather to nurture life regardless of its form. For some, a genuine PAP may even violate the standard of less eligibility whereby the life of an incarcerated person should not be better than the least fortunate non-incarcerated person. Many people cannot afford a companion animal or even acquire a needed assistance animal. In the case of the former, while an inmate may be provided with companionship by the animal, it is for an unambiguously limited period of time. In the case of the latter a PAP participant does not receive an assistance dog for help with a disability but is training the animal to help another, non-incarcerated person. Overall, real PAPs benefit all the beings participating.

While there are minimum requirements for a program to be labeled as a PAP, there is also a paradigm of an ideal PAP. The model PAP combines vocational and educational components in addition to the therapeutic outcomes that come from participation. Some programs offer participants the opportunity to train, for example, for certification as a veterinarian technician or animal groomer. A deeper level of understanding the animals they work with would also be included in an ideal program. Some programs go beyond learning about how to train dogs, but also include classes in the biology and health of the animals. Others even teach participants how to administer medicine and other healing techniques to the animals. A PAP that includes educational and vocational features offers participants the opportunity to gain tangible skills in addition to psycho-social therapeutic benefits.

In summary, below are checklists of characteristics a PAP should and should not possess. The mere presence of non-human animals in a prison does not make a PAP. There are a number of characteristics a program should possess in order to make it worthy of classification as a PAP. A true PAP should:

1) Have participants working to rehabilitate non-human animals in an effort to improve the life circumstances of the animals such as being able to find a caring forever home and being trained to perform helping tasks including companionship or work skills.
2) Involve humanitarian and compassionate work with animals where life is nurtured regardless of its form. The animals are provided with a level of care and concern that is commonly extended to humans.
3) The work with animals should have a positive social value that allows the participants to engage in a form of restitution to society.
4) Have potential for psycho-social therapeutic benefits for participants.
5) Attempt to successfully meet multiple goals.
6) Because of the compassionate work taking place, the program is seemingly out of place or in stark contrast to where it takes place—an often dangerous, violent place of punishment.

An ideal PAP would also include:

1) A vocational component: the opportunity to train, for example, for certification as a veterinarian technician or animal groomer.
2) An educational component whereby participants gain a deeper understanding of the animals with which they work. Participants would go beyond learning about how to train animals to include education in the biology and health of the animals.
3) Teach participants how to administer medicine and other healing techniques to the animals.

A PAP should not:

1) Produce non-human beings that benefit others by being consumed or otherwise exploited; the care for the welfare of the animals should not be so as to result in increased agricultural profits or value (as when fattening up animals for slaughter).
2) Have animals that are present for entertainment purposes, such as a rodeo.

3) Have inmates performing jobs connected to animals that non-incarcerated people can and frequently do choose not to accept; slaughterhouse and agricultural programs fall into this category.

Overall, real PAPs should humanely benefit and provide the opportunity to enhance the lives of all the beings participating.

Genuine PAPs are being administered across the globe and it is not beyond their scope to successfully meet multiple goals. But are multiple programmatic goals necessary? A question may arise for some—why do inmates need programming anyway?

Why Prison Inmates Need Programming[1]

Once the failure of treatment and nothing works had been declared, criminal justice policy became characterized by zero tolerance and the need to get tough on crime and criminals (Mauer, 2001; McGuire, 2002). Determinate or fixed sentencing replaced indeterminate sentencing and rehabilitation as a goal (Mauer, 2001). Many states have resorted back to practices that were once considered draconian. Still driven by economics today, programs' effectiveness is often measured by their ability to prevent recidivism—a complex process which results not only because a program fails or is not effective. A number of researchers (e.g., Lawrence et al., 2002; Mears et al., 2002; Travis & Petersilia, 2001) recommend utilizing a broader definition of programming benefits that encompasses more long-term goals including improved health and family relationships that can also lead to public safety. When programs are "held to the sole criterion of reduced recidivism, many programs, in fact, may not be effective. Other measures…may be more appropriate for assessing their effectiveness" (Mears et al., 2002, p. 68).

Academic and vocational programs are especially important for offenders as they commonly face greater deficits than people in the general population. Inmates suffer from a lack of general academic skills, and rates of illiteracy are high among this population. Studies have shown that approximately one-half of prisoners have below a sixth grade reading level and others have estimated it to be below the fifth grade (Tewksbury, 1994). According to this standard, nearly 75% of inmates are virtually illiterate (Tewksbury, 1994; Trites & Fiedorowicz, 1991), compared to a 20% illiteracy rate among the general population (Trites & Fiedorowicz, 1991). Only one-half of inmates possess a high school diploma (Lawrence et al., 2002; Smith & Silverman, 1994;

Tewksbury & Vito, 1994), compared to three-fourths of the general population (Lawrence et al., 2002).

In addition to their inadequate academic skills, prisoners also possess weak employment skills. Their work history and work skills are far below the national average (Lawrence et al., 2002). If these deficits are combined with the stigma of having a criminal record, future prospects for stable employment become bleak (Lawrence et al., 2002). "These deficiencies can obviously be linked with economic hardship, lowered self-esteem, and social alienation. It is no surprise that education deficits are strongly related to criminal activity" (Tewksbury, 1994, p.398).

Given the above, however, "programming has not kept pace with the number of offenders entering prison. In fact, the proportion of inmates receiving programming has steadily declined in the past decade" (Mears, Lawrence, Solomon, & Waul, 2002, p. 66). According to a report by the Urban Justice Institute, between 1991 and 1997 participation in vocational programs declined from 31% to 27% while participation in educational programs declined from 42% to 35% (Lawrence et al., 2002).

Participation in programming has a number of collateral consequences that go beyond acquiring knowledge of a topic or a specific skill. Programs not only affect the inmate's behavior after release, but positive effects are also seen during incarceration. Educational programs have been correlated with a decrease in disciplinary infractions (Taylor, 1993). Programs monopolize inmates' time and serve to restrict the negative influences of prison life (Harer, 1995). Programs provide an incentive to stay out of trouble (Taylor, 1992), particularly if disciplinary action can lead to the removal from a desired program. Educational and vocational programs can also facilitate positive communication with civilian staff members and help to reinforce law-abiding norms and values (Gaes et al., 1999; Harer, 1995; Taylor, 1992). Inmates who participate in programs are also serving as positive role models for other inmates (Taylor, 1992; Taylor, 1993). Prison-based animals programs also have the above positive characteristics, as well as numerous other benefits.

It is necessary to note the constant effort to balance the needs of inmates with those of the rest of society. All issues of programming, labor, and profit are moderated by the principle of *less eligibility*. Developed by the philosopher Jeremy Bentham in the late 1800s, the concept states that offenders should not receive any benefit or privilege that society's most disadvantaged do not have; conditions inside prisons should not be better than those outside (Quigley, 1996). If conditions inside prison surpassed those faced by people living in the lowest socioeconomic conditions, there would not be any incentive to remain law-abiding or maintain employment.

The philosophy persists to this day and can be seen when people complain about inmates having gyms and weights and cable TV. The uninformed criticisms ignore the behavior modification philosophy behind these privileges: working-out keep levels of frustration down and TV (as any person who has ever babysat for a child knows) has a numbing or calming effect. In addition, in the limited capacity in which these opportunities still exist they are considered privileges which create incentives to remain out of trouble so as to retain access to them. In the case of PAPs the uninformed criticism is why should inmates get to "play" with dogs all day? Prison-based animal programs are not about "playing" with animals as free members of society interact with their pets. Having a companion animal while in prison is not equal to having a pet outside prison walls. Participants in PAPs are still locked inside and continue to experience the other pains of imprisonment including the loss goods and services, heterosexual relations, autonomy, freedom of movement, and security (Sykes, 1958).

Modern-Era Programming

While work programs abound, educational and vocational programs continue to decline. Basic education classes have been administered in most prisons since the 1930s (Gaes et. al., 1999; Gerber & Fritsch, 1995). In 1965, higher education was brought inside prisons through Tile IV of the Higher Education Act, which included the Basic Education Opportunity Grants that came to be known as Pell Grants that funded college-level education for those who could otherwise not afford college, including inmates (Mentor, 2005; Taylor, 1993). By 1973, there were 182 college programs, in 1976 there were 273, and by 1982 there were 350 prison-based college programs being administered (Taylor, 1993). By the mid-1980s, approximately 90% of states were offering some type of prison-based college programming (Taylor, 1993). Through the 1970s vocational training opportunities were also numerous. Training in trades included construction trades, printing, welding, and various types of woodworking; cosmetology could often been found inside female institutions. California offered more than 50 different trades including car repair, hair styling, and radio and TV repair (Roberts, 2005).

Although inmates received less than 1/10 of 1% of all Pell Grants distributed (Mentor, 2005), the public did not like the idea of inmates getting a "free" education while many of their sons and daughters struggled to pay for college. With the passage of the Violent Crime Control Act (VCCA) of 1994 Pell grants for inmates were eliminated. Today, despite evidence that education is the best tool to give inmates to prevent their recidivism (Greenwood, Model, Rydell, & Chiesa, 1996; McCollum, 1994; Shrum, 2004), there are only a scattering of self-funded college programs around the country. However, even before President Bill Clinton signed the VCCA many states had already started to restrict funding for post-secondary education. In the five years prior to the elimination of Pell Grants approximately half of all states cut educational, vocational, and technological programming budgets (Currie, 1998; Lillis, 1994). For correctional facilities that have managed to maintain some of their programs, budget cuts have resulted in longer waiting lists for all programs, larger classes, and fewer program offerings (Lillis, 1994). The focus today is on general education such as reading and math, and increasingly, English as a second language. Other classes offered include parenting skills, anger management, communication, and dispute resolution (Mentor, 2005).

Examples of states offering vocational training can be found. In New York inmates can learn floor covering (i.e., how to refinish and polish various types of flooring); air conditioning, refrigeration and heating repair; and small engine repair (www.docs.state.ny.us /ProgramServices/vocational.html). Similarly, in Texas and California training is available in trades such as plumbing and electrical work; print and graphic occupations; welding; dry cleaning; landscaping; and vehicle repair (www.cdcr.ca.gov/Divisions_Boards/Adults_Programs /DEVOP.html). Of course, these types of vocational offerings are largely reliant on the presence of an instructor; vacant positions are not uncommon in prison programming.

It can be difficult to separate a state's prison work programs from those programs offered as vocational training. New Jersey Department of Corrections operates AgriIndustries which "trains inmates in food production technology" (www.state.nj.us/corrections/AgriInd.html). The Pennsylvania Correctional Industries manufactures inmate and CO uniforms, as well as state-issued shoes in large factory-like shops located inside the prisons. Learning about textiles could be considered a vocation, but factories that produce cloth and material are not common in the United States anymore with most clothing sold in the United States manufactured in foreign countries (Lafer, 2003). In this way though, goods once produced in foreign countries may be brought home, or "repatriated" (Weiss, 2001).

In our contemporary global economy prison labor privatization would "be bringing the Third World home, as a Trojan Horse, in the guise of more American jobs" (Weiss, 2001, p. 281). With capitalism, nothing is done without economically benefiting the producer. Prison inmates are often more motivated to work than free people, whether to interrupt the monotony of prison life or to earn the little they can for basic needs as described above (Weiss, 2001). In addition, inmates can be fired without concern of unemployment benefits (ibid). For a product whose market waxes and wanes, disposable employees are a benefit. As former slaves were on early prison farms we see inmates are still easily replaced and are treated as commodities, and like farm and so many other types of animals, not individual beings.

Challenges come with doing business inside prisons. Owners generally relinquish control over the production of their products; inmates stop all activity several times each day in order to be counted. A riot or other disturbance can halt production for days (Nash, 1998). Inmates are also transferred and paroled which costs the employer a trained (i.e., invested in) worker, thus employee turnover can be a problem (ibid). However, freed employees may be promised, if not delivered, employment in the community. Prisoner-workers are offered a status less than free workers, but are "raised above the level of non-being that attends the late modern penal status" (Weiss, 2001, p. 282).

Another indicator of the questionable motives of prison labor is industry's preference for hiring people serving life terms to avoid the costs of retraining (Wright, 2003). If the state or industry was concerned with providing inmates with marketable skills on the outside they would be assigning work based on individual inmates' needs. In fact, "employers look for prisoners who already have the skills needed for their jobs" (Lafer, 125). An additional contradiction of prison labor is its social cost of reducing wages for workers outside prison walls. While industry in prison continues to grow, traditional rehabilitative programs continue to be cut. Inmates working six to eight hour days do not have time for substance abuse treatment or educational programming. In some places where inmates are required to meet a work requirement, they are not able to substitute education or treatment in its place.

Prison labor also plays a role in prison management. Inmates consumed with work for up to eight hours each day are easier to control than those sitting in dormitories or cells. While boredom can breed deviance and trouble, forced labor remains an exception or a loophole in the 13th Amendment that both the state and capitalism have exploited. Some that support prison labor point to the discipline it instills, but prison life itself demands obedience of the incarcerated. Some argue that work teaches inmates how to learn to take direction, but again, each day is an exercise in training and accepting the hierarchical organization of prison life. Another so-called benefit of prison labor is that it teaches inmates how to work with others. But in a country where countless prisons operate above capacity, cells designed for one person hold two, and what was once a classroom or a mess hall has been turned into dormitories with men stacked two and three high on bunk beds, survival requires the ability to navigate social interactions. It may be "telling that training is also the justification offered for the Chinese prison industries" and work camps that hold their inmates (Lafer, 2003, p. 125). But does the United States really want social policy similar to a largely closed, secretive nation like China?

The above demonstrates the varying and often conflicting goals of correctional industry. The inmate is supposed to benefit through exposure to real world work skills that will improve employability upon release. The prison's institutional goals center on the management of the inmates. Work reduces idleness and maintains order—important to facility staff and administrators. And finally, society is supposed to benefit from the lower costs associated with operating the prison. By making rather than purchasing necessary goods, tax payers can view prisons as self-sustaining. Inmates are seen as earning their keep rather than taking from earnest, hard-working, law-abiding people. Community members' hard earned tax dollars can then be spent on what are viewed as more important things such as public education. Offenders have already cost communities criminal justice system resources in terms of tangible damages such as the time and effort spent by law enforcement officers put in danger, as well as overloading our court system which depends on the average person to fill jury responsibilities (yet another burden cast on the earnest working community member by offenders). Each of these tangible resources has monetary value. Intangible damages include the emotional scar to the victim and the psychological damage done to the larger community that now must live in fear of crime. Prison labor provides inmates with an opportunity to provide society with restitution in various ways, as well as pay for their dependent children and contribute to victim funds. But inmate labor also comes at a cost—most significantly it prevents inmates from participating in basic education classes as well as therapeutic programming such as drug or alcohol treatment, and anger management or parenting classes. Clearly, then, while inmate labor can have a number of capitalistic benefits, it also has costs. The myriad goals create great expectations to come from work, but as has been described there are mixed and even contradictory collateral consequences of putting inmates to work. And once again PAPs emerge as a uniquely beneficial alternative to capitalistic-centered programs. Prison-based animal programs stand out as a distinct opportunity to combine truly educational, vocational, and therapeutic goals.

Where Are We Today?

Although much of inmate labor is limited to state-use today, there is criticism of how it fits into the larger idea of the prison industrial complex (Christie, 2000; Schlosser, 1998). While the manifest function of prisons is to deter, incapacitate, deliver just desserts, and rehabilitate, the last decade has seen a rise in the critical view of prisons having a latent purpose of providing jobs, making profit, and warehousing classes of people who society has otherwise abandoned (Sheldon, 2005). Employment is created for civilians (e.g., administrative workers, plumbers, and teachers) and correctional staff employed inside prisons, as well as the workers who build the facilities. A cursory look at the trade magazine published by the American Correctional Association, "*Corrections Today*" shows page after page of advertising for private, for-profit companies that have developed to serve the field of corrections: healthcare services, locks, unbreakable meal trays, non-flammable mattresses, scanning devices, Kevlar gloves, body armor, stainless steel toilets, bed frames, desks, as well as products that are designed to service large groups of people such as industrial dishwashers and cookware that can hold hundreds of servings of soup or stew. Private, for-profit prisons, such as those run by the GEO Group exist to make their shareholders money based on the number of beds in their facilities that are filled—the same business model of a hotel.

Another part of the prison industrial complex comes from the cheap labor inmates provide, whether to the state or to a private corporation. Even if it is claimed convict labor is compensated at a rate similar to that in the outside world, inmates are paying fees for what was once basic care provided by the state. For example, in Washington state, inmates are charged a $10 shipping fee for their belongings when they are transferred between prisons (Albright, n.d.). Also in Washington, prisoners pay a $3 charge for each visit to the infirmary. In Pennsylvania, the pay scale ranges from 19 to 42 cents per hour with the opportunity to earn bonuses up to 70 cents per hour based on levels of production. Up to 30 percent of inmate pay goes to restitution, court fees, and child support (www.cor.state.pa.us/stats/lib/stats/ci.pdf). Net pay for inmates working in agricultural jobs in Florida and South Carolina ranges from 30 to 50 cents per hour (Weiss, 2001). There is much profit to be made when the cost of workers from the outside can be replaced by workers making wages equal to those in developing nations.

Today's work programs are administered with great variation from state to state; state use programs where the products are sold only to state agencies and not on the open market to the general public are most common. For example, the elevated lifeguard chairs along New Jersey's beaches are constructed inside prisons. In New York, a variety of school and office furniture and cleaning products are produced in prison-based factories under the name CorCraft (www.corcraft.org/webapp). The Pennsylvania Correctional Industries produces products similar to New York. Inmates also manufacture the uniforms they and the correction officers wear as well as state-issued shoes in large factory-like shops (www.cor.state.pa.us/stats/lib/stats/ci.pdf). Texas also has a comparable system with its Texas Correctional Industries (www.tci.tdcj.state.tx.us). It is not folklore that most states' license plates are also manufactured inside prison facilities. And of course, a number of states across the country teach agricultural skills, including equipment use and maintenance and animal husbandry, in conjunction with the prison farms that produce goods for inmate consumption throughout the system.

Unicor, the Federal Prison Industries, is the production arm of the Federal Bureau of Prisons. At the federal level, some type of work is mandatory of all inmates (Bosworth, 2002). According to the website, "it is the mission of Federal Prison Industries, Inc. (FPI) to employ and provide job skills training to the greatest practicable number of inmates confined within the Federal Bureau of Prisons; contribute to the safety and security of our Nation's correctional facilities by keeping inmates constructively occupied; produce market-priced quality goods and services; operate in a self-sustaining manner; and minimize FPI's impact on private business and labor" (www.unicor.gov/about/overview/). Providing inmates with employable skills for use upon their release and to aid in reducing recidivism are not part of Unicor's mission; not interfering with capitalism outside prison walls is a goal. For newcomers to the federal system, there is food services, grounds maintenance, or work cleaning as a porter or orderly. With time comes employment with Unicor, which can include assignments such as making office furniture and other items sold to federal agencies including the FBI or IRS. Unicor produces more than 30 products including law enforcement and military uniforms (Albright, n.d.). Among the divisions listed on their website (www.unicor.gov) are "Electronics," "Fleet Management," and "Recycling". The pay rate is approximately 12 cents per hour (Bosworth, 2002).

At various periods in time, numerous private corporations have utilized convict labor, often through a sub-contracting firm, making it easier for the corporation to claim ignorance of where the work was occurring. A Washington state firm hired inmates to wrap software for Microsoft; inmates in Oregon manufactured menu boards for McDonalds; and in South Carolina, inmates made lingerie for Victoria's Secret (until the public learned about it) (Gilmore, n.d.). Private companies including Nintendo, Dell, Boeing, IBM, and Colgate-Palmolive have all used convict labor (American Press, 2005). According to Starbucks their use of convict labor is limited to during the winter holiday season when demand for products sharply rises (ibid). Public relations problems lead most companies to move production once their labor production methods are discovered (Nash, 1998). One of the largest packaging sub-contracting firms, Signature Packaging Solutions of Washington state, ended its use of convict labor in May 2004 (A.P., 2005).

In addition to factory manufacturing work, and despite the tainted history of prison farms, inmates can still be found working on farms. As states make hiring undocumented migrant workers more difficult, farmers are turning to inmate labor. Again, one of the justifications is to help solve state-wide labor shortages in states where agriculture is the major industry. Under Arizona law that fines employers for knowingly hiring undocumented workers, farmers are increasingly relying on inmates (Hill, 2007). The head of the Arizona Department of Corrections Industries (ACI) arm reports being contacted daily by companies needing labor (ibid). One of the largest watermelon farms in the west, the family-owned LBJ Corporation, employs approximately 20 non-violent female offenders. Even with the women's help, the farm has been unable to harvest its entire crop in past years, needing additional labor (ibid). Arizona DOC is considering satellite facilities to house inmates near sites needing inmate labor. The ACI provides inmates to several agricultural companies, including a greenhouse and a chili cannery (ibid). The pay is a minimum of two dollars per hour with 30% going to room and board and the rest to restitution for victims, child-support, or a mandatory savings account program (ibid). The company is responsible for transporting inmates to and from the job and security costs on site. Colorado has similar agricultural inmate-labor programs (Mitchell, 2007). Inmates at Angola State Penitentiary de-bone chickens for a private company for four cents an hour (Gilmore, n.d.). Also similar to the farms of prisons past, there is still opposition to using inmate labor. Today the United Farm Workers of America fights for paying workers based on experience and skills.

Nonviolent inmates with little time left on their sentences in Kentucky stay in a minimum-security facility in a "nice neighborhood" with no fences. Inmates work clearing garbage on the side of the road and in the local forests, but they also work at the state's tree nursery harvesting trees. The mayor of the town where the facility is located appreciates the inmate labor in these tough economic times: "It's like having six employees who don't cost us anything" he said (Moss, 2008).

Given that they are ubiquitous and have their roots in slavery, it is necessary to examine whether prison agriculture operations, which bring with them the overtly cruel slaughtering of farm animals, are even profitable. Previous research has found "correctional industries historically have difficulty in accurately accounting for operating costs such that products could be accurately priced" (Connelley, Conklin, & Gordon, 1993, p. 261). Additionally, "indirect costs, overhead, capital, and maintenance costs were often hidden in budgets" even while potential social and institutional benefits were unmeasured or immeasurable (p. 262). A 1986 audit by the state found inaccurate record-keeping, operating losses, and cost overruns; it was recommended that ACI halt operations of the dairy farm, hog operations, crop and garden production, and slaughterhouse (Connelley et al., 1993). In a 1993 case study of Arizona Correctional Industries' hog operations, researchers examined the costs and profits from a traditional economic method and from a social impact perspective. The authors point out that "profitability has become an increasingly important criterion for evaluating their performance in an era of increasingly tight budgets" (Connelley et al., 1993, p. 257). However, the researchers found discrepancies in the amount of calculated profits based on the accounting method used. They suggest the debate regarding prison agricultural operations focus on the "social and correctional value of overhead and institutional charges associated with prison farms" because the current system obscures an accurate evaluation of the social costs versus the potential benefits (p. 275).

Another area of profit within the prison industrial complex can be clearly seen in telephone companies that have been exposed for benefiting from inmates and their families by charging them higher rates than the general public for collect, long-distance phone calls. Any inmate who wants to speak to an outside person must do so by making a collect call. Surcharges and inflated rates not only make the company more money, but it has been found that states have awarded phone contracts based on the extent of profit sharing (Schlosser, 1998). Profits are shared by the company and the prison; both the state and the company benefit from those in society least able to afford exorbitant prices. But with no choice in long-distance carrier, family members wishing to stay in contact with loved ones behind bars have no choice but to accrue large bills.

An Update on Southern Justice

Southern-style justice is often still unique by northern standards. It is impossible to ignore "the conjoined histories of slavery and black criminality" (Adams, 2007, p. 135). There is an improbable endurance of the plantation as an institution that has proved "itself ideally suited to the maintenance of order in general, an order that is disproportionately applied to black people" (p. 136). As discussed above, the Louisiana State Penitentiary, or Angola, has an infamous reputation—not only for its racist brutality, but also for its level of violence. If the men incarcerated there did not die a natural death of old age as a result of their life sentence, there was a good chance they succumbed to the conditions of America's bloodiest prison. In 1973, Wilbert Rideau, a reporter and one-time editor for the *"Angolite,"* the country's longest running prison newspaper, wrote that

> violence was a brutal, daily, reality. Double-bladed hatchets, swords, long steel knives, and Roman-style shields were commonplace. Men slept with steel plates and J.C. Penny catalogs [which served as improvised body armor—something done by inmates who feel threatened to this day] tied to their chests; even in maximum-security cellblocks, men slept with their doors tied and with blankets tied around their bunks as a means of protection and security (quoted in Adams, 1997, p. 138).

Sadly, most animals found inside southern prisons are still not involved in a PAP; the ideas of animals in prison for therapeutic and other positive purposes continue to be corrupted and change has been limited. What was Angola the slave plantation is today still a large farm on the banks of the Mississippi River where corn, soybeans, and other vegetables are grown and thousands of cattle roam; still, this is all tended to by inmates who are watched over by COs armed with shotguns and mounted on horses. "There are cattle and horses, and there are men working the fields, driving farm machinery, repairing equipment, maintaining bushes and flowers and trees in full bloom. From a distance, the workers look to be farmers, not prison inmates" (Shere, 2005, p. 37). All inmates enter the prison at the lowest level of freedom, privilege, and job type which earns them four cents per hour. Others become trustees who make 20 cents per hour and are under minimal watch while engaged in less back-breaking work in the fields under the hot Louisiana sun.

In a 1997 documentary *"The Farm,"* the viewer is introduced to Warden Burl Cain. While driving the film makers around the prison's thousands of acres, he notes that "it's like a big plantation in days gone by. We hate to call it that in a way, but it kinda is, because we have the, you know, the, it's the inmates in prison." He goes on to describe the conditions:

> Everybody here works; in the field lines with hoes and big sling blades; that's gonna be about 12 to 14 hundred a day with hoes. There's gonna be a vast number driving the tractors, operating all the equipment, unloading and loading trucks and trailers, running the warehouses. Everybody has a job. Everybody at Angola works, everyday....This is really good for morale at Angola because you start out with a ditch sling blade in the field or a hoe and you can have illusions of grandure that you might at some point get to drive the tractor....What is it to be warehoused and locked in a cell never to come out? You come outside, ya in the sunshine, ya out here working. It's good for ya and ya feel like you're healthier and you gonna live longer, and um, and um, it makes em busy so they're less violent too an'....You have to be a good businessman too, to run this place (*"The Farm,"* 1997).

The prison operates various enterprises worth multi-millions of dollars.

Cracks in the reputation of Angola began to emerge under the management of Burl Cain who was appointed warden in 1995, even though the facility was not removed from federal judge decree until 1997. The prison is still a place where 90% will die behind its walls, anyone with a sentence less than 40 years is not sent to Angola where the average sentence is 88 years; parole is unusual—life is life in Louisiana (Shere, 2005). Cain brought with him a new philosophy—one based on his deep religious beliefs. He urged inmates to think of their surroundings as "a 'community' where they could begin to experience what Cain would come to call 'moral rehabilitation'" (Shere, 2005, p. 27). According to Cain, "positive change…has to start behind the walls, because it won't happen on the streets" (p. 46). Cain believes inmates "remain human beings no different in their needs, and often no different in their continuing desire to make something of themselves" (p. 51). Cain is recognized for the philosophy rooted in the progressive idea of personal transformation that he brought to a place once marked with blood and deep hopelessness. However, while his approach may be contemporary and unique for a prison with such an infamous and dark history, it stands in contrast to the place Angola remains.

While there are no PAPs at Angola, men are still challenged to demonstrate "that something about their lives is worth noting and applauding....They want the public to see them as having worth and value despite what they have done that got them sent to prison" (p. 41). Opportunities for restitution include rebuilding wheelchairs for the Wheels for the World program for distribution in developing nations and other organizations that distribute bicycles to Louisiana's children in need. Men also serve as hospice volunteers, keeping vigil over sick and dying men that have lived and worked sometimes for decades. After September 11, 2001 the men donated $15,000 to the American Red Cross, and in 2005, $2,500 to Asian tsunami relief (Shere, 2005). More recently inmates were used as labor to clean BP's huge oil spill in the spring and summer of 2010.

Beside the farm animals at Angola, animals also appear in another well-known example of what is not a PAP: the infamous and controversial rodeo that takes place weekly in October and over one weekend in April (Shere, 2005). What began as a small, local event for prison employees has become the "Wildest Show in the South" according to Cain (Shere, 2005, p. 69)[2]. Like the farm, "the rodeo is a big moneymaker for Angola, providing funds for inmate programs and building projects such as chapels" (Shere, 2005, p. 68). There is a mock prison cell where members of the public can pay to have their picture taken by an inmate, and a plywood cutout of two inmates' bodies wearing black and white stripe prison uniforms and shackled with leg irons. The spectators can stand behind it and provide the faces for the bodies and pose for a picture (Adams, 2007).

Ironically, "the world from which prisoners have been ostensibly banished is one in which they continue to labor. Prisoners make items used constantly in daily life outside" (Adams, 2007, p. 145). Inmates sell the crafts they make in the hobby shops during the year, such as furniture, artwork, clocks, key chains, and leather and metal goods while inmate cooks serve southern delicacies such as crawdad stew to the thousands of people who enter Angola during this much anticipated event (Adams, 2007; Shere, 2005). Cain sees the rodeo as a chance for men "to bask in the glow of praise from outsiders.... [and] as an opportunity for the taxpaying public to see a clean, well-maintained prison...'where moral rehabilitation takes place and their tax dollars are well spent'" (p. 69).

While some see this "wildest show" as a display of skill and hospitality, others see it as creating an environment of violence and mistreatment of animals. Sure, the inmates are armed with body padding for protection when they are thrown or fall as the result of "an angry animal's kick," but bulls and wild cows are pitted against them in what has been compared to a Roman gladiator type of affair (Shere, 2005). Cain points out that all participation is voluntary and likens it to the running of the bulls in Spain, but safer since "at least here we have a fence they can climb over to get away" (Shere, p. 68). In 1998, the "Angola State Pen" gift shop was opened inside the State Penitentiary Museum, built on prison property outside the walls. There is also a golf course built by prison inmates on the grounds; prisoners may not play, but members of the general public can after a background check (Adams, 2007).

Conclusion

In this chapter, I have reviewed hundreds of years of prison programming history. A large part of the history of programming centers on inmate labor. The often contradictory and exploitative nature of inmate work required a review of the evolution of work as programming. Justifications for having inmates work, while often presented as therapeutic, have been largely driven by outside forces concerned with capitalism, not rehabilitation. Politics, combined with economics, have played a larger role in the development of programs than research about how to best help incarcerated people. As a result, the goals of prison programs have often been corrupted, thus complicating the history. Even the very nature of volunteering is not simple when engaged in by prison inmates. And while there is a long history of animals inside prisons, most of that history does not include PAPs. The development of genuine PAPs is therefore a welcome change from the past. The truly altruistic motives of PAPs mark them as vastly different from other programs that have dominated the evolution of prison programming. What follows is the history of the development of PAPs as they emerge from this murky environment that is punishment and programming in America.

Chapter 3 Endnotes
1. Credit must be attributed to Dr. Kimberly Collica for her assistance in writing this section.
2. The Oklahoma State Penitentiary in McAlster also has a rodeo that can be attended by members of the general public. The first rodeo, at the Texas State Penitentiary at Huntsville was held in 1931, but ended in 1968 as a result of safety concerns (Adams, 2007, p. 192, n. 12).

4

Contemporary Programs

While PAPs incorporate animals in an official program capacity, as demonstrated in the previous chapter, animals are not new to prisons. What is recent and innovative is having inmates working with animals with the explicit goals of rehabilitation and restitution, making the history of PAPs rather brief. In this chapter I first point attention to published reports that have provided bits about the importance of animals to incarcerated people and move on to describe the programs that are the direct descendants of today's PAPs and the events that led to their development and formal establishment as programs. I then present the recent research that has been conducted on these PAPs. To demonstrate the extent of the current national landscape of PAPs I conclude the chapter with data collected from my own national survey of the programs.

Several authors have described the presence and touched upon the role of animals inside prisons and what they can mean to inmates. Johnson and Chernoff's (2002) analysis of poetry written by inmates suggests that "perhaps the scarcity of opportunities to develop relationships with non-inmates and the difficulties inherent in connecting with fellow prisoners are responsible for the striking number of poems about the importance of animals" (p. 161). In *New Jack: Guarding Sing Sing*, journalist Ted Conover went undercover working as a correction officer in a New York State prison. Over the course of the year he worked inside, he found "even more than people on the outside, inmates appreciate pets" (2000, p. 270). Early in his ethnography of life inside prison, Pennsylvania inmate James Paluch (2004) makes reference to the birds that wait for him, greeting him (p. 23). He defends breaking the facility rule against taking food from the dining hall because "I take it for my babies...my bird friends" (p. 27). He mentions these birds again in a section of the text devoted to family; he describes how "normally, they just swipe up the bread and fly away, but today they stay on the ground and look up at me as if to say

'Thanks'" (p. 200). More recently, James Fisher who spent 27 years on death row in Oklahoma for a crime he did not commit told one of his lawyers about his pet mouse Jasper on their car ride out of Oklahoma— Mr. Fisher had been banished as a condition of his release (Barry, 2010). Johnson and Chernoff (2002) observe that "animals as diverse as pigeons and lizards may respond to the prisoners' ministrations and seem to reward their care" (p. 161).

Perhaps the most famous, misrepresented, case of animal-assisted activity inside prison is that of Robert Stroud, the "Birdman of Alcatraz." Rather than having cared for and learned about the birds that flew onto the prison island as reported, these events occurred while he was in solitary confinement at the U.S. Penitentiary in Leavenworth, Kansas (Earley, 1992). In 1916, he killed a correction officer in the dining hall and days later he was outside in an exercise yard where he came across a dying sparrow. After caring for and nursing the bird back to health, Stroud became a self-trained authority on birds and wrote a book about bird diseases (ibid). He remained in solitary confinement at Leavenworth until 1942 when he was moved to Alcatraz where he was prohibited from keeping any birds. The 1962 movie placed Stroud at the "Rock" of Alcatraz which was more infamous than the "Hot House" of Leavenworth.

California was again the source of national news regarding animals in prison nearly a decade later when, in 1975, elderly inmates at what was then the minimum-security California Institution for Men at Chino were charged with caring for that facility's stray cat population (Arkow, 1998). In 1976, administrators put a stop to inmates feeding feral cats at San Quentin (ibid). After years on facility grounds, the number of cats had grown unmanageable while other inmates were decidedly not cat people. Inmate fights, lack of animal medical care, and improper food and sanitation were among the problems that led up to the removal of animals. It would take several more years for animals to be officially sanctioned by prison administrators and incorporated into formal programs.

It seems almost obvious that there would be a general amount of concern about entrusting convicted offenders, often people with high levels of psychological and emotional needs, with vulnerable animals. It was auspicious, then, that a maximum-security psychiatric patient came across an injured wild bird on the grounds of Lima State Hospital, now Oakwood Forensic (Lee, 1987). The unit director was impressed by how the usually solitary and unresponsive patients risked punishment and were able to coordinate their efforts to hide the bird in a custodial closet and bring it scraps of food. Although the bird died, the staff noted the camaraderie created by the experience, and a 90-day trial period was implemented with three parakeets and an aquarium serving as unit mascots. Soon, convicted murderers, rapists, and other violent offenders voluntarily participated in a behavior modification program where success was rewarded with the opportunity to be able to eventually care for their own small companion animal.

The First PAPs

Credit for the first formal PAP is generally attributed to Sister Pauline Quinn and her work in bringing dogs to the Washington Correctional Center for Women (WCCW), a maximum-security prison in Tacoma, Washington (see Quinn, 2004). The People-Pet Partnership (PPP) Program was established in 1979 and co-founded by Dr. Leo Bustard, the Dean of Veterinary Medicine of Washington State College, and Linda Hines of the Delta Society, a human service organization with the mission of increasing the application of scientific knowledge about the benefits of animals on people. In the summer of 1982 Sister Quinn was able to begin a pilot program at the facility. After being well-received by both the inmates and the administration, a permanent program was established in the fall. Through the PPP, inmates enrolled in an 11-week course administered by Tacoma Community College; the dogs were rescued from the Tacoma-Pierce County Humane Society (Strimple, 2003). The class's purpose was to provide "community college classroom instruction for the women prisoners in canine husbandry and behavior, obedience training, and customized training designed to meet the special needs" of people with physical disabilities (Moneymaker & Strimple, 1991, p. 140).

While classified as a vocational program, prison administrators were also attracted to the program by the potential therapeutic benefits for the participants who received classroom and hands-on lessons with local shelter dogs, in training, grooming and job-seeking skills (Hines, 1983). As a result of the inmates' training, many homeless dogs were made more adoptable while others were sent to schools for more advanced training to work with people with disabilities. Administrators noted that some inmates were more cooperative while others said the women learned self-control. Rather than any incidences of animal abuse being reported, as was initially feared, the inmates quickly became concerned for the animals' welfare (ibid).

At the same time, in Virginia, a veterinarian helped establish a program built around a prison chapter of the national People-Animals-Love group (Arkow, 1998; Beck & Katcher, 1996; Graham, 2000;

Hines, 1983). Shelter animals were paired with inmates at Lorton Prison who were allowed to keep the animal if transferred or released, in what would be considered a pet adoption program. Another component of the program was training in an Assistant Laboratory Animal Technician course that paralleled a class offered by the American Association of Laboratory Animal Science (AALAS). While the course did not meet all AALAS qualifications for their full accreditation, inmates who completed the course would receive assistance in finding work in a laboratory or in a veterinarian's office upon their release (Moneymaker & Strimple, 1991).

Equine PAPs

Prison-based animal programs that involve horses developed uniquely from other PAPs and so deserve specific examination. Reminiscent of the evolution of agricultural programs, the story of equine programs is linked to politics, with justifications ranging from the need to protect farm land to the necessity of controlling the population of the animals. The story of equine programs is one with a sordid history and to this day these horses experience precarious treatment and conditions. The U.S. history with its native wild horses dates back to the 1770s, in the land that would become the southwestern United States. By the 1800s the number of horses grew so quickly that settlements up and down the California coast engaged in mass execution of the horses. Similar to today, the horses were viewed as an annoyance that risked the survival of farm animals in a competition for grazing land and water.

Catching wild horses, whether for sale back east or to put to death was difficult and required several trained men, themselves on domesticated horseback. First, a mustanger would frighten a herd into fleeing. Then, multiple men would keep the herd headed in the specified direction as well as keep them in a manageable group. Lastly, the horses were lead into a funnel-shaped trap that led them into a pen, or corral (Flores, 2008). Upon finding themselves trapped, the first animals to enter would seek escape, trampling and killing others. It was possible that out of one thousand horses trapped, 200 would live (ibid). The frightened angry animals would screech and scream as they fought to get out. After several hours of suffering, the defeated horses that survived would be easily secured with rope around their necks. One witness described with awe how a talented mustanger had "the ability to render them half-tame a short while after depriving them of their liberty" (quoted in Flores, 2008, p. 16). The wild horse trade allowed mustangers to enjoy the very freedom they were stealing from the horses they captured and sold.

Sadly, we have not advanced far from the history described above. Not until federal code passed in 1971 was the protection, management, and control of wild free-roaming horses and burros placed under the administration of the Bureau of Land Management (BLM), an agency of the Department of the Interior and the Department of Agriculture's U.S. Forest Service (www.blm.gov/wo/st/en/prog/wild_horse_and_burro /what_we_do.html).

To maintain what the BLM refers to as the balance between the land's natural resources, including water and grazing area and the needs of the livestock belonging to local ranchers, the agency catches thousands of the animals each year for sale and adoption through their Adopt a Wild Horse or Burro Program, established in 1971. The animals are supposed to go to people and groups that are able to provide-long term care for the animals but this ideal does not always occur as the BLM is constantly faced with an over-abundance of animals needing placement. The BLM reports that since 1971 over 250,000 wild horses and burros have been placed in private care through the program (ibid). However, according to the American Wild Horse Preservation Campaign (AWHPC), nearly "36,000 wild horses and burros adopted through the BLM's Adopt-A-Horse program are unaccounted for" (www.wildhorsepreservation.com/resources/study.html). So where are these lost horses? Although horse slaughter was outlawed in the U.S. in 2007, there are no prohibitions on horses being sold for slaughter as meat for human consumption in countries outside the United States. The BLM maintains they do not sell horses to so-called killer buyers who purchase and quickly resell the animals to someone who will ultimately sell them to slaughter plants in Canada and Mexico where the horse meat is shipped overseas to Asia and parts of Europe. However, during a study conducted by the AWHPC, the BLM's Wild Horse and Burro Program Director conceded that "about ninety percent of rounded up horses ended up at slaughter" (ibid).

With both the BLM and horse-specific animal welfare agencies overwhelmed, the first equine PAP was established in the late 1970s at the state penitentiary in Canon City, Colorado by veterinarian Dr. Ron Zaidlicz and his National Organization for Wild American Horses (NOWAH) with three wild mustangs obtained from the BLM. Together with the National Humane Association in Canon City, Colorado, NOWAH created the Wild Horse Prison Project. Inmates were provided with "both classroom and field instruction in all aspects of horsemanship from husbandry and training, to handling and appropriate veterinary and farrier skills" (Moneymaker & Strimple, 1991, p. 141).

Wild horses are not the only horses needing rescue and socialization however. Abandoned horses (just like cats and dogs) deemed too old, sick or simply unwanted, such as retired racehorses that no longer generate money for their owners but have become an expense, are sold at auctions across the country. The Humane Society of the U.S. partners with a number of groups to rescue these animals to prevent them from destruction. Here again, equine PAPs can play a role in taking in and caring for otherwise unwanted animals.

Evaluation Research

Unfortunately, there is only limited evaluation research on PAPs. In an evaluation conducted several years after its inception, Moneymaker and Strimple (1991) sought to quantify the treatment effects of the program at Lorton by examining disciplinary records. First, they found that 12% of participants were discharged from the program due to rule violations. They also found that approximately 11% of the participants (after an unspecified length of time) recidivated, while the remaining members of the sample did not return to prison (p. 146). Finally, they found that inmates who participated in the program showed "considerable change in their outlook toward others and their sense of self-worth, as well as their sense of achieving a better goal in life. This seems particularly true by the fewer altercations and problem behavior" from program participants (p. 148). They reported that while inmates with pets had slightly fewer disciplinary offenses, the severity of the infractions was not affected. However overall, they argue, "it seems clear from some of these preliminary findings that the program has worked to instill in its members a sense of responsibility and goal oriented achievement toward a rewarding vocation" (p. 150). A final treatment effect was the help provided by the participants in society's efforts at controlling the overpopulation of unwanted animals (ibid).

The authors describe the program as providing "a unique opportunity for individuals who have committed heinous crimes to perhaps redeem themselves or at least to show a different side of themselves" (p. 133). Yet they never consider the redemptive or restorative potential of the program they evaluate. The authors do not consider the role of the program within the criminal justice system except to argue that the program should be replicated. And while they note that the program contributes to easing society's burden of unwanted animals, they do not consider the impact of the reparative practices on the participants. As the program provides the opportunity to have a pet while incarcerated there are clear personal benefits to participation. It is unknown whether participants are aware of or acknowledge the potential for their work to serve as a form of restitution in the process of healing the damage their offenses inflicted on society.

The literature's most rigorous research has been conducted on the Wild Mustang Program (WMP) which operated from 1988 to 1992 at a New Mexico prison in partnership with the state Bureau of Land Management. The program not only sought to save and tame wild mustangs, but it also served as a vocational program in the prison, and generated a profit for the facility when the horses were sold to members of the community (Cushing & Williams, 1995). Several themes emerged from the interviews conducted by the researchers. Program participants took on "a very different kind of role than is usually available to inmates" (p. 101). They were caregivers who expressed affection in the name of taming and rehabilitating the mustangs—the goal of their job. The tasks entrusted to them allowed the participants to serve as "their 'own boss' [which] added to the inmates' sense of challenge, accomplishment, and pride in a job well-done. Autonomy is a characteristic that was valuable to the inmates" (p. 101). Program participants reported seeing changes in their fellow participants "who appeared to have developed an increased ability to handle stressful situations. The local administration said that the inmates who were in the program developed an increase in self-esteem and self-confidence as a result of working with the large animals" (p. 103).

The researchers examined a number of psychosocial and behavioral treatment effects. Staff members were asked to indicate whether they felt the program influenced participants' self-esteem, self-confidence, stress, violent behavior, and disruptive behavior. Most reported that the program improved participants' self-esteem (76 %) and increased self-confidence (74%). The researchers point out "a notable minority (40%) of staff cited 'no change' in violent behavior being observed" (p. 104). The authors conclude the program appears to be "wildly successful. However, a somewhat more cautious view is warranted upon realization that most of the basis for the subjective assessment is in the realm of psychological outcomes and these determinations are hardly being made by dispassionate neutral scientists" (ibid).

The program participants' official disciplinary records offer a different perspective of the PAP's treatment effects. Based on this quantitative measure, the researchers concluded that "participation in the WMP is clearly associated with a reduction in the overall number of disciplinary reports and the severity of reports swung away from major to minor" (p. 106). The total number of infractions for participants incarcerated for violent offenses decreased, while the number increased overall among property offenders. However, the increase was for minor offenses; the number of major disciplinary offenses for property offenders decreased. The authors suggest there was a "problem officer" responsible for the increase among a few property offenders (1995). The researchers also note the possibility of an interaction effect with participants who were also attending a substance abuse counseling program. They found that "the total number of disciplinary reports for the inmates who were not in substance abuse counseling is much larger per person" (p. 108).

The researchers acknowledge that their "efforts reveal strong subjective assessments of positive benefits of the program. Given these glowing, if anecdotal, evaluations and...against a backdrop of a good public image," they argue the program should be continued (p. 110). But they omit any discussion of the implications of a prison having a good public image or that a facility would earn one by implementing an innovative and cost-effective program that has a range of beneficial aspects. While they examine recidivism rates they do not consider any theoretical support for why these programs reduce recidivism. As with the rest of the literature in this area, these researchers do not include any discussion of the role of this program within the larger criminal justice system. The program's implications in terms of punishment and justice are not investigated.

In a review of another New Mexico PAP, incarcerated older teenagers were paired with unwanted dogs from a nearby shelter and trained in obedience for three weeks (Harbolt & Ward, 1991). Participants cleaned their dog's kennel, exercised, socialized, and groomed their dog, and learned about dog health and medicine. The researchers analyzed letters written by the participants to their dog's future owner and found the youth demonstrated compassion, were dedicated to their tasks, and gained experience giving and receiving positive regard. For some, it was the first time they had ever known a dog as a pet; their previous experience was with dog fighting or dogs serving as protection.

A more recent compilation of evaluations of PAPs continues to find support for a variety of treatment effects. Inmates at Colorado's Canon City prison reported reduced illegal drug use, increased self-confidence, patience and respect for both people and animals, and said that time seemed to pass faster when working with the horses in the PAP (Lai, 1998). Juvenile offenders who participated in Project Pooch at the Maclaren School of the Oregon Youth Authority adopted a dog from a local animal shelter and trained the dog for adoption by a community member. Administrators report that "all the students who have participated have decreased their number of office referrals, and show improved self-esteem, patience, responsibility, and vocational skills" (ibid, p. 27).

Research conducted in the mid-2000s also supported previous findings (Turner, 2007). The Indiana Canine Assistant and Adolescent Network (ICAAN) founded in Indianapolis in 2001 oversees several PAPs throughout the state where participants train dogs to become service animals for people with a variety of disabilities. At a medium-security facility for men, the researcher conducted interviews with each participant; there were only six men in this small program. Each participant reported the program taught increased patience. Related to patience is improved parenting skills. The inmates believed they could apply the lessons they learned about training dogs to improving how they interact with and mold the behavior of their children. The opportunity to help others was also a theme; a few inmates had relatives with disabilities and reported they felt particularly connected to the purpose of the program. With only six inmates participating in the program, and a facility population of over 1400, being chosen to participate was a source of pride. The unique status of these men as participants also brought with it responsibilities and privileges which added to their self-esteem. With increased assurance came improved social skills. Participants reported more frequently interacting with staff, other inmates, and each other as they had to learn to work together as a team. Having a dog also had a normalizing effect that involved activities any person would engage in outside prison. The dogs were able to bring joy inside a dark place. The final theme from the interviews with the participants was about the calming effects the dogs had on the environment—not only for themselves but for the whole facility (Turner, 2007).

Most recently, a quasi-experimental design was used to evaluate the PenPals program at a minimum-security prison for men in Virginia (Fournier, Geller, & Fortney, 2007). Participants in the treatment group trained shelter dogs for 8 to ten weeks while the control group was comprised of men on the waiting list to participate in the program. Participants received statistically significant fewer institutional infractions and demonstrated statistically significant improved social skills (ibid). As have many before them, the researchers call for a study that utilizes a true experimental design, but note that "it is unlikely prison administrators would allow inmates to be randomly assigned to" a PAP (p. 101). The authors make the insightful suggestion of using a group-randomized research design where whole groups are randomly assigned to treatment or control status, such that institutions with and without PAPs are randomly assigned. They further note the findings from this type of design that used "several different correctional populations and settings would be more generalizable" (p. 101).

The limited international research available reports findings equivalent to those from the United States. In several English and Welsh prisons, cockatiels are bred and cared for by inmates, and aquariums are installed in common areas (Graham, 2000). A review of programs in Scottish prisons found "an increase in the level of communications between prisoners and again between inmates and staff. Visitors seemed more relaxed and stayed longer. They also found that the presence of animals resulted in a reduction of staff stress levels" (Graham, 2000, p. 250). An evaluation of a pilot program in a women's prison in Australia contains one of the only true experiments in the literature (Walsh & Mertin, 1994). Researchers found significant improvements in participants' self-esteem and levels of depression, based on standardized self-report measures, after participation in the program for 6 months (ibid).

A comprehensive review conducted by the executive director of the Delta Society, Linda Hines (n.d.), summarized the animal programs in prison as having the following treatment effects:

> improve socialization
> overcome depression
> decrease suicide
> reduce anger, violence, and drug use
> increase cooperative behavior
> learn team skills
> provide constructive use of time
> reduce stress levels/tension
> learn caring and nurturing behavior
> exercise emotional control
> learn patience
> learn to complete tasks
> experience confidence, self-esteem
> learn responsibility
> experience work ethic
> increase respect for animals and others

A talented dog or horse trainer requires the participant to develop "patience, careful observation, calm assertiveness, and knowing how to effect change through praise, not punishment" (Ormerod, 2008, p. 289). In addition, the effects at the facility-level were identified as: the prison offers a successful and popular vocational program; there is improved inmate behavior and cooperation; the prison has a more positive public image from the media and visitors; and the participants are able to make a positive contribution to the community (ibid).

While there are benefits to the larger community and psychological well-being of the individuals involved, PAPs have also been shown to influence the overall employability of participants (Harkrader et al., 2004). Lai (1998) reports that "one universal aspect of the program is that inmates tend to set and achieve their goals" (p. 14). It appears that PAPs teach participants the basic skills necessary for obtaining and keeping a job, including responsibility, dedication and respect.

Animals have long played a role inside prison, particularly animals that are injured or otherwise unwanted. There are a number of parallels between animals and inmates. Unvalued and unwanted by society, they both experience rejection and stigmatization. Incorporating animals into prison-based programs creates an opportunity for both groups to help each other in a symbiotic relationship that benefits the very society that discarded them. The programs achieve a win-win-win situation.

Given the beneficial physiological, psychological, and social benefits, it should be no surprise that animals have been incorporated into prison life. Despite their increased development, however, few attempts have been made to comprehensively examine PAPs. In a now dated review of the (mostly American) literature published by Correctional Services of Canada, PAPs were found in the United States, Canada, England, Scotland, Australia, and South Africa (Lai, 1998). In addition to using a wide variety of animals, these programs also encompassed a range of program designs as well (ibid). While dogs were most common, this review reported animals used in PAPs included wild animals, farm animals, and other domestic animals such as cats. For example, inmates at Saughton Prison in Edinburgh, Scotland raise fish for developing nations (ibid).

As described, the beginnings of PAPs were generally grass-roots efforts—the simultaneous, if uncoordinated, work of individuals and small groups proposing their ideas to receptive prison administrators across the country. There was no one organized or unified national movement to bring animals to prisons, but clearly these innovators have created more than a passing fluke. They are only now receiving attention on a national level that might unite the various efforts across the country and the globe. Prison-based animal programs are a real trend in prison programming, although it is doubtful if in the early days these innovators knew where their efforts would lead. As evidence described below indicates, there are a growing number of PAPs despite criticism from skeptics and others who complain the programs are too rewarding for the inmates themselves. As time goes on it will only be more difficult for naysayers to remain in denial about the power of interactions between non-human beings and humans.

National Survey

Surveys were sent to the top administrator of each state's Department of Correction in the fall of 2004[1]. The administrators were asked to forward the surveys to the staff members best able to answer the questions. The directors at the individual facilities with PAPs most frequently answered the surveys. Surveys were received from 46 states (92%); administrators from 4 states did not respond: Illinois, Iowa, Louisiana and Texas. Of the 46 states that participated, 10 states' surveys indicated no PAPs were being administered: Arizona, Arkansas, Delaware, Hawaii, Maine, Minnesota, Mississippi, New Hampshire, Rhode Island, and Utah. Surveys from the 36 states that indicated having at least one PAP described 71 designs, or models, of PAPs at 159 sites throughout the country (see Table 4.1). The results provide an initial qualitative and quantitative description of PAPs on the national level.

Typology

The PAPs were analyzed according to the typology based on Hines' (n.d.) presented above (see Table 1.1). The most common program design is the community service model (N=24; 33.8%) which is being implemented at 59 sites (see Table 4.2). In this model, animals (usually dogs, N=19, 79.2% of community service models) are rehabilitated and then adopted out to the community. The model is also used with horses in Kansas, Kentucky, Nevada, and Oklahoma (N=4, 16.7%). One program model in Kansas uses cats. The community service design is being administered at 59 sites.

Service animal socialization programs are the second most frequent type of PAP model being administered (N=15; 21.1%). In this model, participants socialize and begin training puppies which are then sent on to more advanced service animal training (e.g., Seeing Eye dog school, explosives-or drug-detection school). The design is being administered at 34 sites.

Table 4.1 Number of PAP Designs and Sites by State

State	# of PAP Designs	# of PAP Sites
Alabama	1	5
Alaska	1	1
Arizona	0	--
Arkansas	0	--
California	2	2
Colorado	3	6
Connecticut	1	1
Delaware	0	--
Florida	1	1
Georgia	1	1
Hawaii	0	--
Idaho	1	1
Illinois	Missing	Missing
Indiana	2	3
Iowa	Missing	Missing
Kansas	4	4
Kentucky	5	6
Louisiana	Missing	Missing
Maine	0	--
Maryland	1	1
Massachusetts	1	3
Michigan	2	2
Minnesota	0	--
Mississippi	0	--

Missouri	1	1
Montana	2	2
Nebraska	2	2
Nevada	2	5
New Hampshire	0	--
New Jersey	3	3
New Mexico	1	1
New York	3	18
North Carolina	2	3
North Dakota	1	1
Ohio	10	61
Oklahoma	3	3
Oregon	1	1
Pennsylvania	1	3
Rhode Island	0	--
South Carolina	3	3
South Dakota	1	1
Tennessee	1	1
Texas	Missing	**Missing**
Utah	0	--
Vermont	1	1
Virginia	2	5
Washington	1	1
West Virginia	1	1
Wisconsin	2	4
Wyoming	1	1
TOTAL	**71**	**159**

Table 4.2 Frequency of PAP Designs

Design	Frequency	Cumulative Frequency	Percent	Cumulative Percent
Community Service	24	24	33.8	33.8
Service Animal Socialization	15	39	21.1	54.9
Multi-modal	14	53	19.7	74.6
Livestock Care	10	63	14.1	88.7
Visitation	3	66	4.2	92.9
Wildlife Rehabilitation	2	68	2.8	95.7
Other	2	70	2.8	98.5
Vocational	1	71	1.4	99.9
Totals	**N = 71**			99.9%

Note: Percent total does not add to 100 because of rounding.

Multi-modal programs are the third most common type of PAP model (N=14; 19.7%). The multi-modal program models are most commonly a combination of vocational and service animal socialization components (N=4; 28.6% of multi-modal designs). There are also vocational and community service combinations (N=3; 21.4%) and community service and service animal socialization models (N=3; 21.4%). Two programs combine community service, service animal socialization, and vocational components (14.3%). In one program livestock care and community service components are combined (7.1%), and in another visitation and service animal components are combined (7.1%). The two types of animals used in the multi-modal designs are dogs (N=11; 78.6%) and horses (N=3; 21.4%). Multi-modal programs are being administered at 19 sites.

Livestock care programs are the fourth most common type of PAP model (N=10; 14.1%); they are considered prison farms, or institutional agricultural programs. Cattle/cows are being raised at each of the farms (N=10); pigs/hogs are being raised at four of the programs and sheep are being raised at one program. Livestock care programs are being administered at 39 sites. Due both to the sordid history of inmate labor and their very nature—the violent slaughtering of animals—these programs necessitate removal from the PAP typology currently being used in the field.

There are three visitation program models being administered (4.2%). Two of these programs, one at one site in Kentucky and the other at a site in Montana, use dogs and cats; a visitation model at one site in Ohio includes llamas and domesticated deer.

There are two wildlife rehabilitation programs (2.8%). The wildlife rehabilitation models, at one site in Kansas and one site in Ohio, involve local wildlife that has been found injured or abandoned. Animals that have been rehabilitated include rabbits, raccoons, and birds.

Two programs were identified as "other" (2.8%) and both involve participants raising pheasants for release into the wild. One program is located at one site in Michigan where the animals are released onto state property, and the other is at one site in North Dakota where the animals are released onto the prison grounds for handicapped hunters who are brought in and driven around on tractors. However, given the programs' similarity to farm programs that slaughter animals these programs should not be labeled genuine PAPs either.

There is one vocational program (1.4%) at one site in Oklahoma. The program model involves the use of privately-owned domestic horses that are groomed and trained. Participants receive a state technician certificate in equine management.

Types of Animals

The primary animal used in PAPs is dogs (N =47; 66.2%). The community service design (N=19; 40.4%) is the most common model of PAP that incorporates dogs. The second most common design that incorporates dogs as the primary animal is the service animal socialization model (N=15; 31.9%). Eleven dog programs were identified as being of a multi-modal design (23.4%). Two dog programs are visitation program models (4.3%). The 47 PAPs that use dogs as the primary animal are being administered at 107 sites.

The next most common animals used in PAPs are cattle/cows (N =9; 12.7%) and horses (N =9; 12.7%). Cattle/cows are raised for milking and meat in each of these farm or livestock care programs being administered at 33 sites. Of the nine PAP models that incorporate horses, four are community service programs, three are multi-modal, one is a vocational program, and one is a livestock care program model. Four programs involve wild horses that are trained and then adopted out to the community, three involve retired thoroughbred race horses that are rehabilitated and then adopted out, and two involve domesticated horses. The nine PAP models that incorporate horses as the primary animal are being administered at 13 sites.

Two PAPs use pheasants (2.8%), and two programs involve wildlife (2.8%). The two PAPs that incorporate pheasants have models described above as "other." Llamas (1.4%) and cats (1.4%) are the primary animals used in one program model each. Llamas are the primary animal used at a visitation model being administered at one site, while cats are the primary animal in a community service model being administered at one site.

While most programs (N = 64; 90.1%) use only one type of animal, four programs (5.6%) include two types of animals and three programs (4.2%) include three or more types of animals. Of the four programs that use two types of animals, three are farm or livestock care models and one is a visitation program. Of the three programs that use three or more types of animals, two are farm or livestock care programs and one is a visitation model.

The vast majority of animals become involved in PAPs through a shelter, humane society, or rescue organization. Service animal socialization programs get their dogs from a non-profit guide dog agency or a breeder, either purchased or donated. Farm or livestock care programs breed their own animals or purchase them. The four models included in this survey that incorporate wild horses, receive them from the federal Bureau of Land Management (BLM).

Program Characteristics

The earliest program included in this survey was identified as being established in 1885: a livestock care or farm model in Wisconsin. The next four oldest programs (1900, 1920, 1930, and 1981) are also livestock care or farm models. Six programs were established in the 1980s, 14 in the 1990s, and 34 since 2000. The date of establishment was not reported for 12 program models included in the survey.

The size of the PAPs varies. The smallest program has only two inmates participating (a pheasant raising program), while the largest program has approximately 300 participants (a livestock care/farm program). When the five smallest and five largest programs are removed from the analysis, the size ranges from five participants to 70 participants. According to this restricted mean, the average size program has 21.2 participants.

According to the 67 surveys in which the gender of participants was specified, males (N=38; 56.7%) are more likely than females (N=15;

22.4%) to be participants in PAPs. Both males and females participate in 14 (20.9%) program models.

The number of animals currently participating in each program also varies. While the livestock care programs/farms have the largest numbers of animals, the participating inmates generally do not work one-on-one with the animals which eventually go on to be slaughtered. Of the non-livestock care programs/farms, respondents from community service models followed by multi-modal programs indicate having the greatest number of animals currently participating.

The smallest programs are a visitation program with two animals (a dog and a cat which live on the prison's hospice unit), three models (one service animal socialization, one community service, and one multi-modal) each have three dogs currently participating, and six models (three service animal socialization and three community service programs) each have four dogs currently participating.

Since the largest programs (the livestock care/farms) are also among the oldest programs, these are the programs' surveys that report having the greatest number of inmates and animals participating since their start. Of the non-livestock care programs/farms, surveys indicated community service models have the greatest number of inmates and animals having participated since the program began.

Of the 47 surveys that included responses to the question that asked for the number of participants discharged or removed from the program due to rule violation since the program's start, 13 indicated having to remove zero participants (seven community service models, three multi-modal programs, two "other" programs, and one service animal socialization program); five report having to remove one participant (two multi-modal programs, one community service program, and one service animal socialization program), six report having to remove two participants (three community service programs, two service animal socialization programs, and one multi-modal program); and four report having to remove three participants (two service animal socialization programs, one community service program, and one multi-modal program). The respondents from the livestock care/farm program models were again the most likely to report having removed the most participants.

Respondents from most PAP models (N = 43; 60.6%) report working with a non-profit organization that administers the program and provides animals, supplies and training. The organizations are animal shelters, rescue groups (e.g., Greyhound Pets of America), county humane societies, and service animal agencies (e.g., Guiding Eyes for the Blind). As discussed above the four programs that involve wild horses work with the BLM. The livestock care/farm models are the least likely to work with an outside agency. They breed their own animals or purchase them from private companies. Participants most commonly (N=30; 42.3%) are paired with animals 24 hours a day. Nearly half the community service models (N=11 of 23; 47.8%) and service animal socialization models (N=12 of 15; 80.0%) pair participants all day. The number of hours each day that participants work with animals in the multi-modal programs included in the survey ranged from seven (N=3 of 14; 21.4%) to 24 hours (N=7 of 14; 50.0%). According to the surveys from each of the livestock care programs/farms, wildlife rehabilitation and vocational models (N=12; 100%) participants work with the animals for a six- to eight-hour work day. In the two models described as "other" (pheasant raising), inmates work with the birds for two to three hours each day. The time participants spend with animals in the two visitation programs varies. The number of hours participants and animals work together each day was omitted on the surveys of three models.

According to the responses most of the livestock care/farms, visitation and "other" models do not pair participants with specific animals. In the 45 programs (63.4%) where participants are paired with specific animals, the average time they work together is 7.6 months. The length of time a participant works with a specific animal ranges from one to 24 months.

The average time participants remain in the PAPs included in the present survey is 10.8 months. The length of participation ranges from three months to 36 months. The average length of participation indicated on the surveys from the 10 community service models included in the sample is 9.9 months; the surveys of 14 community service models did not contain a response to the question. The average length of participation reported by the administrators of eight service animal socialization models that responded to the question is 11.8 months; seven surveys did not contain a response to the question. The average length of participation reported by the administrators of ten multi-model designs that responded to the question is 15.2 months; four surveys did not contain a response to the question. The average length of participation reported by the administrators of five livestock care/farm programs that responded is 7.4 months; five programs' surveys did not contain a response to the question. The one wildlife rehabilitation program administrator that responded reported an average length of participation of 30 months. The average length of participation in the vocational program is six months. The average length of participation in the two "other" programs is 15 months. The surveys of two of the three visitation programs that included responses to the question indicated no average length of participation as inmates remain in the programs indefinitely (a prison hospice unit and a unit for developmentally disabled inmates).

According to the surveys most programs (N=53; 74.6%) do not have policies that limit the length of time an inmate may participate in the program. Of the six (8.5%) surveys from program models that report having a maximum length of time a person may participate, four of them are community service programs, one is a service animal socialization program and one is a multi-modal program. Overall, the average maximum length of time an inmate may participate in these programs is 15.3 months; the maximum length of participation in these programs ranges from two months to 24 months. The average maximum length of participation for community service models is 12.5 months. In one service animal socialization program participants are limited to a maximum of 18 months in the program. The one multi-modal program that has a maximum length of participation limits inmates to 24 months in the program.

Pre-Participation

Administrators from 26 (36.6%) programs report having no waiting list, while 33 (46.5%) programs have a waiting list and 12 (17.1%) surveys did not contain an answer to this question. Overall, the average length of time an inmate remains on a waiting list is 4.2 months according to the 21 program surveys that specified the average time. There is not a waiting list at either visitation program or the one vocational program. Ten service animal socialization, 10 community service, eight multi-modal, three livestock care/farm, one "other" and one wildlife rehabilitation models have a waiting list. The program models with the longest waiting lists are multi-modal programs (mean = 5.2 months) and service animal socialization (mean = 4.9 months).

Prior to their acceptance into the program the vast majority of potential participants are screened (N=51; 71.8%); prior to their acceptance participants are not interviewed at eight PAPs (11.3%) and 12 surveys (16.9%) did not have a response to the question. Respondents from three of the livestock care/farm programs, three multi-modal programs, one community service, and one visitation program report they do not interview participants before acceptance. Most frequently, program staff (N=36) is involved in the interview process, followed by other prison staff or administrators (N=28) and representatives of the affiliated non-profit agencies (N=18). Respondents from five program models reported including security staff such as correction officers in interviewing potential participants. (More than one person was generally listed on the surveys as being involved with the interview process.)

Surveys from two programs (a multi-modal program and a community service model) indicated staff administers a psychological survey instrument to potential participants. One reported using a specific instrument: *Institutional Basis Psychological Examination*. Three other programs' surveys (two community service models and one service animal socialization program) report reviewing psychological evaluations conducted upon inmates' arrival in the system.

Respondents from 16 programs (22.5%) report that there are no crimes that make inmates ineligible to participate; at 42 programs (59.2%) inmates are ineligible based on the nature of their convictions and 13 surveys (18.3%) did not contain a response to the question. Respondents from neither visitation program, neither "other" program, nor the one vocational program indicated inmates can be ineligible based on their crime. The most common types of crime are crimes against animals (N=25, 59.5%), sexual offenses (N=19, 45.2%), and crimes against children (N=11; 26.2%). (Some respondents listed more than one type of crime.)

Twenty-one (29.6%) programs have no minimum length of time potential participants are required to have remaining on their sentences in order to participate, while 37 (52.1%) program models have minimum sentences, and 13 (18.3%) cases were missing. The minimum sentence ranges from one month to 60 months, while the average requirement for a remaining minimum sentence is 17.3 months and the mode requirement is 12 months (frequency = 13).

Respondents from 53 (74.7%) programs report having additional eligibility requirements. The most common criteria is behavioral (i.e., remaining free from disciplinary infractions) in nature, N=29; 54.7%. At 18 (34.0%) programs a potential participant's work or program history is considered. Requirements pertaining to custody level are in place at 14 (26.4%) programs. Respondents from 12 (22.6%) programs report having educational requirements (i.e., participants have demonstrated a specified level of education). At 9 (17.0%) of programs the level of interest or enthusiasm of a potential participant is considered. (Some respondents' surveys listed more than one additional eligibility criteria.)

Most inmates do not engage in pre-participation training (N = 22; 31.0%). The type of pre-participation training provided varies. Of those programs where an orientation is offered, it most commonly includes videos and/or manuals (N=19, 38.8%). The information included in these pre-program orientations includes basic animal care and safety and program expectations and rules. At other programs (N=9; 18.4%) participants are provided with extended instruction (ranging from eight hours to five-weeks) in animal training prior to program participation. A few programs have trainees shadow current participants or observe the on-going lessons of current participants (N=3; 6.1%).

Training/Education

Most PAPs include on-going lessons or classes related to the animals (N = 44; 62.0%); 15 programs (21.1%) do not include on-going training and 12 (16.9%) surveys did not have a response to the question. Training ranges from less than one hour (a community service program with bimonthly trainings lasting from two to three hours) to 15—20 hours (a service animal socialization program) per week. On-going lessons are most frequently associated with community service programs (N=17 of 19 surveys that included responses to the question; 89.5%) and service animal socialization programs (N=10 of 12 surveys that included responses to the question; 83.3%). According to the surveys of each of the 13 (100%) multi-modal programs participants receive on-going lessons. Inmates at two of nine (22.2%) livestock care/farm programs provide on-going lessons related to the animals. Surveys from one wildlife rehabilitation and one vocational program were returned and indicated participants received on-going lessons. Respondents from both of the two visitation and two "other" programs that were included in the sample reported having no on-going training components.

The vast majority of programs (N=49, 70.0%) do not include a certificate-yielding component. Of the 10 programs (14.3%) that do offer state-recognized credit, the most common type is a state vocational certificate (N=3), followed by a pet care technician certificate (N=2), and veterinarian assistant (N=2). Two programs (a multi-modal program with dogs and a community service program with wild horses) provide community college credit for participation. One program offers a certificate in dog behavior modification and one offers a certificate in dog handling. A livestock care/farm program offers several certificates including groomer and barn boss.

Twenty-four survey respondents (33.8%) reported knowing of former inmates working with animals in the community since being released[2]. The type of program most commonly associated with former inmates working with animals is multi-modal models; 10 of the 14 respondents (71.4%) from multi-modal programs reported knowing of former inmates working with animals in the community. Six of nine respondents (66.7%) from livestock care/farm programs reported knowing former inmates working with animals. Five of the 15 respondents (33.3%) from community service programs reported knowing of former inmates working with animals in the community since being released and respondents from three of 12 (25.0%) service animal socialization programs answered affirmatively. The respondents from the visitation, wildlife rehabilitation, vocational program and "other" programs reported not knowing of former inmates working with animals in the community since being released. Those respondents who reported knowing of former inmates working with animals described a variety of job capacities, including horse trainers on farms and for private individuals, dairy and farm workers, farm managers, and in various capacities at veterinarian's offices, including kennel and vet assistants. One respondent reported knowing of a former inmate working as a manager at a Petco pet supply store.

Seventeen survey respondents (23.9%) indicated that the program includes a job referral or a link to a possible job in the community upon release. A job referral or a link to a possible job in the community upon release is available at five of 12 service animal socialization (41.7%), five of 13 multi-modal (38.5%), three of 17 community service 17.7%), and two of eight responding livestock care/farm (25%) programs. One wildlife rehabilitation program and one vocational program included in the sample provide a job referral. According to 39 (54.9%) surveys the program does not include a link or job referral. The question was omitted in 15 (21.1%) cases.

Funding

Respondents from 37 PAPs (52.1%) report receiving donations while 23 (32.4%) do not receive donations and the surveys from 11 programs (15.5%) did not include an answer to the question. Programs receive donations from staff and inmate and fundraisers, the general public, private veterinarians, and privately owned supply stores including Walmart and PetCo, and PetSmart, and from corporations such as Iams and Purina. Donations of animals, food, supplies and medical services are also received through the humane society, shelter or non-profit organization that administers the program.

In addition, PAPs may collect fees related to the animals; respondents from 20 programs (28.2%) report collecting fees, 38 programs (53.5%) do not receive fees, and the surveys of 13 programs (18.3%) did not include an answer to the question. Money is usually from adoption fees, training/service fees, or sale of livestock. Respondents from five of nine responding livestock care/farm (55.6%), six of 13 multi-modal (46.2%), and seven of 19 community service (36.8%) programs indicated collecting money related to the animals. Fees are collected from one of 10 (10%) service animal socialization programs, and the one vocational program. Fees are not collected from each of the two visitation programs, two "other" programs, and the one wildlife rehabilitation program. While the PAP may not generate money for the facility, the animal trained in the program may earn the administering humane society, shelter or non-profit organization funds.

According to survey responses PAPs also receive funding from additional sources, including grants from public and private agencies, as well as money from the state. Several (N=7) livestock care/farm programs sell agricultural products such as crops, animal products such as eggs and milk, and surplus stock.

Benefits and Limitations

When asked if the respondent would recommend this type of program to other prison administrators, one of 61 would not. Sixty out of 61 respondents (98.4%) reported they would recommend the program; 10 surveys were missing an answer to this question. Follow-up with the facility warden who responded in the negative revealed that he does, in fact, "like the program, but it provides no revenue, so it depends on what you're looking for the program to accomplish" (Personal communication, 4/8/05).

An open-ended question asked respondents about how the program benefits the inmates who participate in it. Overwhelmingly, the most commonly cited benefit is the sense of responsibility instilled from caring for a dependent animal ($f = 10$). The job skills and vocational instruction ($f = 17$) and the ability to engage in meaningful work that is a community service ($f = 16$) were the next most commonly cited benefits for PAP participants. Respondents report that participants learn patience and anger management skills ($f = 14$), and that the program enhances participants self-esteem ($f = 14$). Participation also fosters empathy ($f = 12$), teaches parenting skills ($f = 12$), and improves communication skills ($f = 12$) according to respondents. In addition, participants gain a sense of pride or accomplishment ($f = 11$). Benefits also cited include: instilling a work ethic ($f = 10$), humanizing or calming the facility environment ($f = 8$), increased self-control or improved institutional behavior ($f = 7$), teaching participants relationship skills and trust ($f = 7$), and reducing participant stress ($f = 6$).

An open-ended question asked respondents to identify negative aspects associated with the program—for the inmates, staff, or facility.

Most (N=42, 60.0%) reported no negative aspects associated with the PAP. The most common response provided was staff resistance to the PAP (f = 8). Challenges related to the animals (f = 7), such as people's fear of them and the mess and noise they can create, and a lack of resources, including space and staff, were the next most frequently cited negative aspects of the programs. Constraints or struggles that result from administering a program inside a secure institution (f = 5) were indicated by respondents. Resentment from non-participating inmates (f = 3) and separation of participants from their animals (f = 3) were also indicated by respondents. Finally, jealousy between various program participants (f = 2) and negative press (f = 2) were negative aspects of the programs according to respondents.

A follow-up survey focusing on canine socialization programs was conducted in 2009. Among the administrators from the 39 state DOCs that submitted responses, there were 36 canine socialization programs being administered in 32 states (seven states do not have a canine socialization program being administered in any facility). The results indicated the number of these programs more than doubled over the course of the five years between the surveys. The canines being trained inside prisons are mostly going to people with a variety of physical disabilities including blindness, physical limitations, others who are wheelchair-bound and people with autism. Findings indicate only seven programs have working relationships with local, state, or federal law enforcement agencies. The programs continue in the same manner as those documented in 2004: the prison facility is associated with a non-profit organization that provides the canines; participants usually spend all day with their animals; participants are reported to benefit from the responsibility of caring for an animal in a number of ways including gaining patience, and experiencing positive relationships with not only the animals, but also the prison staff and administrators, and members of the outside community. The sense of restitution and contributing to society is also still being reported.

A Sample of Programs & Partnering Non-profit Organizations

A brief examination of the programs being administered in various states can demonstrate the widespread nature of PAPs. At one of California's most infamous prisons, San Quentin, inmates who are part of the Prison Pup Program train and socialize shelter dogs to increase their chance of adoption. Falling under the auspices of the Colorado Correctional Industries is their Prison Trained K9 Training Program where participants work with dogs to become adoptable pets as well as fill service roles for people in need. Wakulla Correctional Institute in north Florida is a Faith and Character-based facility where inmates attend religious programs and life-skills training classes, and can receive education in language, public speaking, writing, and landscaping (Klinkenberg, 2008). Partnering with Citizens for Humane Animal Treatment, more than 30 men participate in the Paws in Prison program where they socialize abandoned dogs using an eight-week curriculum (ibid). In one of the larger PAPs, Kansas's Safe Harbor Prison Dog Program at the Lansing Correctional Facility, nearly 100 inmates work with abandoned dogs from across the Midwest in a community service-style program. Some states stand out: in Massachusetts inmates at 14 facilities work to socialize puppies that go on to advanced service training; inmates at 15 facilities in North Carolina work with shelter dogs, and a variety of models are being administered at 30 facilities in Ohio.

Animal programs are not limited to publicly funded state and local facilities. The Pen Pal Program is administered at Davis Correctional Facility in Holdenville, Oklahoma, a private medium-security prison for men owned and operated by Corrections Corporation of America, based in Nashville, Tennessee. Many of the dogs are provided by the Pets and People Humane Society of Yukon, Oklahoma. In 1990, the Humane Society began as a visitation program that brought animals to area nursing homes. Today, the non-profit agency is a no-kill humane society that rescues adoptable dogs and cats from public animal control facilities across the state of Oklahoma on the day they would otherwise be euthanized. Animals needing obedience training to increase their chances of adoption are sent to Davis Correctional Facility or to one of their network of foster homes. Two years after its founding, the Society partnered with PetSmart Corporation to hold regular adoption fairs. A year after that, a school visitation program was funded by PetSmart, the Junior Pets and People program, in order to teach children about the importance of spaying and neutering animals and serve as an additional source of fundraising. Supplementing monetary donations, the Humane Society raises funds by operating a thrift store and relies upon donations of animal supplies such as food, toys and linens, in addition to monetary donations (www.adoptatraineddog.com).

Breed-specific PAPs tend to be those that work with greyhounds. In Michigan the Second Chance at Life program is being administered at three prisons. In Indiana three prisons work with greyhounds to socialize them for adoption through the Indy Prison Greyhounds Program. In Florida the Second Chance at Life Greyhound program is administered in a privately run county jail where the dogs stay for 12 weeks working with female inmates (Bogues, 2007). Participation in the program can help women earn good time for earlier release (ibid). As will be described in more detail, young men in New Jersey, in conjunction with Greyhound Friends of New Jersey, work with retired dogs to train them to be domesticated pets. Internationally, greyhound programs have been established in at least four jails in Australia in conjunction with Prison Pet Partnership ("Prisons go to the Dogs," 2008).

Prison-based animal programs are being administered in countries across the globe. England has visitation programs for both males and females using Labradors. At the men's facility, the dogs were brought in "to calm down inmates" (Cotter & O'Shea, 2008). The dogs "are a big hit with the women. They were brought in so they'd have something to focus on other than each other and take a bit of the tension out of the place" (ibid). In other English facilities, long-term inmates are being permitted to keep pets including cats, dogs and birds in an effort to reduce the suicide rate which had hit two deaths per week (Nelson, 2007). New Zealand's dog training program at a minimum security facility was established to help alleviate the great wait for assistance canines in the country (Chisholm, 2007). In Australia, Assistance Dogs Australia is administering socialization programs in several prisons (Dobbin, 2009). Some of the dogs are being trained to work with people with quadriplegia (ibid). At one of Japan's several private prisons, Japan Guide Dog Association administers a puppy socialization program based on U.S. models (Yomiuri, 2007). The prison will also "offer inmates the opportunity to raise a horse—an animal sensitive to human feelings, but difficult to train with the use of force. The program aims to have inmates learn patience and improve communication abilities" (ibid).

A PAP is reliant on its affiliation with a non-profit animal organization, whether a humane society or other type of group. Most often these groups are grass-roots in nature and volunteer-supported and operated. Without the work of the volunteers, whether fundraising, securing veterinarian care, recruiting foster homes or spending time walking dogs or cleaning cages, many PAPs, particularly community adoption programs, would not exist. It is worthwhile to examine several particular programs in order to understand both their variation and similarities.

A larger, more formally organized umbrella agency is Pathways to Hope (www.pathwaystohope.org), a religious-based charity that operates their Prison Dog Project at several prisons across the country and internationally. In addition, they do relief work domestically and in developing nations in places where people have experienced trauma due to war and genocide. Their Prison Dog Project (www.pathwaystohope

.org/prison.htm) operates an assistance dog training program at Downeast Correctional Facility in Bucks Harbor, Maine—a facility that incarcerates both males and females at both the medium- and minimum-security levels. At Sanger B. Powers Correctional Center for men in Wisconsin, assistance dogs are trained for people with physical disabilities. At James River Correctional Center in Virginia, dogs from area shelters are socialized by male inmates to increase their chances of being adopted. At Washington State Correctional Center for women in Gig Harbor, participants train assistance dogs for people with a variety of physical disabilities; another component of the program is the ability to learn formal dog grooming techniques. Inside York Correctional Institution in Niantic, Connecticut, a maximum-security facility and the state's only prison for women, participants train assistance dogs. Women also train assistance dogs at the California Institution for women in Corona, California. A unique program for women is administered at Pocahontas State Correctional Center where participants learn dog grooming and operate a cat shelter. Internationally, Pathways to Hope operates the ConFido Prison Dog Program in Rome, Italy, at the Ribibbia Prison for Women where they both train assistance dogs and socialize dogs from the humane society.

Another national group, National Education for Assistance Dog Services (NEADS) operates the Prison PUP Partnership, an assistance dog training program with over 80 puppies at eight facilities around New England (Mulvany, 2008). Founded in 1979, NEADS is one of the oldest and largest assistance animal training and placement agencies in the country. After approximately 18 months of training in prison, the dog is returned to the NEADS dog training campus at its headquarters in Princeton, Massachusetts. Trained to work with deaf people and those confined to a wheelchair, the dogs learn advanced skills including retrieving dropped items, turning light switches on and off and opening doors. According to NEADS having inmates work with the dogs when they are puppies expedites the training process, enabling them to place dogs with clients at a faster rate (prisonp.tripod.com/neads.htm).

Across the country in Colorado is the Prison Trained K-9 Companion Program (PTKCP), mentioned above, located in a growing number of facilities (www.cijvp.com/serviceproviders/puppy/index .html?intro). The agency is both a community service program that socializes dogs from shelters across the state for adoption as family pets and a service animal socialization program. Dogs have gone on to work in nursing homes, been trained as hunting dogs and received additional training for service work. Another unique aspect of the program is the boarding service where privately owned dogs must stay a minimum of four weeks while they receive obedience training. The program falls under the auspices of the Colorado Correctional Industries which means inmates are paid for their work with the dogs and eligible to earn vocational certification in Canine Behavior Modification.

Animal programs are not limited to adults. Descriptions of juvenile programs are often more focused on the therapeutic effects for the participants, or students. For example, through the Shiloh Project, based in Fairfax, Virginia juvenile offenders and at-risk youth are taught about animal abuse and how to interact with others by socializing and interacting with rescued animals. Working with homeless dogs, the organization seeks to prevent animal abuse through lessons about compassion and respect for all beings (www.shilohproject.org). In Woodburn, Oregon Project POOCH pairs youth with shelter dogs afflicted with behavioral problems and in need of socialization. With obedience training for the dogs the students learn how to control their own behavior and gain control of their own agency by successfully training dogs (www.teacherspetmichigan.org). At Echo Glen Juvenile Correctional Facility in Washington State the at-risk youth work with dogs unlikely to be adopted—training them in the hopes of finding them a permanent home (www.courthousedogs.com/juvenile_detention _centers.html). There is a visitation program at the Bernalillo County, New Mexico Juvenile Detention and Youth Services Center. The program was instituted with the idea that the visiting dogs would improve the morale and behavior of the youth (ibid). Publicly, there is less resistance to having juveniles work with animals compared with adults. Juveniles are often seen as having the potential to reform, while adults have often been given up on. For adult offenders, many see animals as a reward they do not deserve.

While dogs are most common, PAPs are not limited to domesticated animals. As reported in the survey, there are wildlife rehabilitation programs inside prisons. At the Ohio Reformatory for Women in Marysville, participants work with injured or orphaned wild birds, squirrels, opossums, ducks, and rabbits. The program began in 1994 when the Ohio Wildlife Center, a private rescue organization, was so overwhelmed with people bringing in injured animals that they partnered with the prison. Citizens rescue the animals and turn them over to the Ohio Wildlife Center (OWC), and then the animals are sent to the prison for recovery. After lessons on proper diet and treatment, the participants provide 24-hour care which can include hand-feeding birds. Recovered animals are returned to the wild. Due to the success at Marysville facility, the program has expanded to the Marion Correctional Institution, a male facility.

The opportunity to learn equine husbandry by working with horses is often a "powerful, unique experience" for participants at the handful of facilities with these programs (Deaton, 2005). The size and power of the animals, particularly feral horses, can be humbling to participants who may have used force or the threat of force during their lives (Deaton, 2005; Wise, 2003). As described in detail in chapter 2, in cooperation with the Bureau of Land Management (BLM), men gentle and train (also known as halter breaking) wild horses. Due to the size of the animals, the safety of the participants is an important aspect of the programs; individual safety comes from following training protocols. California's wild horse program includes a 90-day program in horse gentling using the "resistance-free method" which does not use force in training the horses. At Colorado's largest prison, in Canon City, participants receive over 150 hours of classroom education in horse care as well as business skills related to the horse business (Deaton, 2005). Horse programs of this type often generate money for the facilities when the horses are sold at auction or adopted out to the community. The other model that uses horses has inmates working with retired racehorses. Young men at the Charles H. Hickey School in Baltimore, Maryland work with retired racehorses. Through the Thoroughbred Retirement Foundation (TRF), juveniles aged 12 to 20 are responsible for all aspects of the horses' care from feeding and grooming, to exercising and watching injury recovery (Deaton, 2005). The program was modeled after a long-running program for men at Wallkill State Correctional Institution in New York which was established in 1983. Similar programs are being administered through TRF at the minimum-security male facility Blackburn Correctional Complex in Lexington, Kentucky and at male facilities in Florida and Oklahoma.

Lest anyone think only progressive, bleeding-heart prison administrators are willing to establish PAPs in their facilities just look to the Maricopa County Sheriff's Office (MCSO) in Phoenix, Arizona. The program is managed by the infamous Sheriff Joe Arpaio, best-known for programs he claims producing deterrence including banning coffee, having inmates live in the hot desert sun in large tent cities, wearing pink underwear and black and white stripped uniforms, and working on chain gangs. In May 2000, the Sheriff converted an abandoned jail into space for animals seized by the Animal Cruelty Investigation Unit. Known as the MCSO Animal Safe Hospice (MASH), the facility houses dogs, cats, ducks, and other animals until their cases have been adjudicated and they can be adopted out to the community. Female inmates care for the animals and engage in work that includes tending to wounds and illnesses, cleaning cages, socialization and teaching basic obedience commands. The MASH facility is air-conditioned and a no-kill shelter, providing care until an appropriate placement can be found (Rhoades, 2001). It may also be surprising that even Rush Limbaugh, the face of political conservatives, has been described as an animal lover (VegNews, 2009, p. 25). He went so far as to record two public service announcements for the Humane Society of the United States: one was speaking out against dog fighting and the other used religion to remind believers of their moral obligation to care for all creatures (ibid).

When animal programs do transpire in prisons, the control and custody of inmates must prevail, even at the cost of an effective program. At one program, a CO treated a PAP participant to a hamburger after a public speaking engagement for school children. The CO, with a flawless record of over 25 years was reprimanded and consequently resigned. The community volunteers and trainers associated with the PAP were so disappointed in the action taken by the DOC that they were no longer willing to work with the facility. As a result, the PAP dissolved (www.pathwaystohope.org/prison.htm).

It is common to hear about prison programs being halted in response to one transgression. For example, a state DOC ended a farming program for juvenile offenders after one absconded while out in the field despite being swiftly and easily captured. Critics will point out examples of parolees who commit crimes as proof of the need to end parole, a very necessary part of the criminal justice system. Without parole the prison system, already operating at full and often times over-capacity, would cease to operate as facilities simply would not have room for additional bodies. Mistakes made in other fields, even those that result in death, do not receive the same knee-jerk terminating response. After a number of women died during routine plastic surgery operations several years ago no one was holding a press conference calling for a complete halt to the procedure. Countless young adults leave our public schools unable to read. Are we shutting down schools across the country? The criminal justice system, particularly our mechanisms of punishment, is unique in its lack of critical thinking and rationality about policies and procedures.

Several years ago it was difficult to find information about the non-profit organizations that created animal programs with prisons. Today, a Google search returns many website addresses. Not only are the non-profits putting out information about their partnerships with prisons, but prisons are also posting information about (and boasting about) their animal programs. Rather than waiting for an article about the good work they are doing for the animals and the community to be written up in a local newspaper, prisons are profiling their programs on their own.

Chapter 4 Endnotes

1. The Federal Bureau of Prisons responded to a request to participate by indicating that the office "does not have the resources to respond to the numerous requests for data" received.

2. It is worth noting that many departments of correction have policies in place that forbid employees from contact with former inmates once they are in the community.

5
Who Benefits and Why:
Theoretical Implications

The national overview of PAPs described in the previous chapter can be complemented by the closer examination of two specific programs. Triangulation, or use of multiple research methods, can decrease the influence of any one method's weakness (Maxfield & Babbie, 2001). Both programs described here are located in the same northeastern state. The data were collected from the stakeholders of the two PAPs and informed by the state DOC employees who completed the national survey for each facility. The first program, in a maximum-security facility for females in the northeast, pairs offenders with puppies that are socialized in preparation for advanced training in explosives detection. The second program, located in the same state, in a medium-security facility for males aged 17-25 in the same northeastern state, pairs offenders with greyhounds rescued from destruction after the end of a racing career (usually 2-3 years) who are socialized for placement as pets in homes in the community. The two programs chosen represent the most common types in the nation: service animal socialization and community service programs.

The question of the effects associated with the programs was informed primarily by interviews with program participants. The programs' directors, responsible for the daily operations of the programs, and the facilities' superintendents and their deputies, as well as the correction officers posted in the units where the PAPs are housed were interviewed as well. Fifteen individual participant interviews were conducted at the female facility and seven individual interviews and a focus group with 14 participants were conducted at the male facility.

Interviews took place in the prison facilities where the programs are located. Interviews with each of the program's 15 participants at the female facility were conducted over the course of two days in a private room in the administration building. Interviews of the program's seven primary handlers at the male facility were also conducted over the course of two days. The first three interviews were conducted in a private room with the program director, a senior CO posted inside. On the same day a focus group with all 14 program participants was conducted in a private room in the basement of the dorm that houses the program participants; the program director was also present for the focus group. The final four interviews were conducted in a private room in the administration building. At each site, the program's director was interviewed before beginning interviews with program participants on the first day as a way to obtain an overview of the program. At each facility, the superintendent and deputy were interviewed in the superintendent's office; this interview took place on the second day of data collection at the female facility and on the first day of data collection at the male facility. Two correction officers were interviewed in front of the program director at the female facility. At the male facility the program director, also a senior member of the custody staff, was the only correction officer interviewed. The executive directors of the two non-profit organizations that administer the PAPs were interviewed over the phone. In addition, program curricula and documents were examined.

The Female Program

The female prison is the only one in the state, comprising minimum-,medium- and maximum-security level facilities on one campus. Here, the PAP is housed in a low-security area of the compound and women are paired with puppies who are socialized in preparation for service work or advanced training in explosives detection. At the time of the interviews in spring 2005, there were 13 dogs and 22 inmates participating, 15 as primary handlers and seven back-up handlers. Among the 15 primary handlers interviewed, ages ranged from 24 to 50 years-old. Seven participants identified themselves as white, five as black, and one each as Hispanic, Native American, and biracial. The average length of program participation was 22.4 months and ranged from six to 60 months.

The Puppies Behind Bars (PBB) program began at the female facility in March 2001. The program is administered by PBB, a non-profit organization with the purpose of training prison inmates to raise puppies for work as assistance dogs and explosive detection canines (www.puppiesbehindbars.com). Puppies Behind Bars was established in July 1997 by Gloria Gilbert-Stoga, the agency's president. The program was initiated at Bedford Hills Correctional Facility, New York State's only maximum-security prison for women. Today PBB is in operation at six sites, in both male and female state prisons in New York and New Jersey. A program in Connecticut is located at the Federal Correctional Institution in Danbury. The organization has placed nearly 900 dogs; in addition to aiding people with disabilities, PBB has placed canines with the federal department of Alcohol, Tobacco, Firearms and Explosives, and the New York Police Department Bomb Squad. It is not uncommon for the law enforcement officers paired with dogs trained inside through PBB to return for a visit to express their thanks, share stories, and remind the participants what they have achieved with their hard work.

Activities

Participants rise each day at 5:30 am; the dogs are fed and exercised in the enclosed yard attached to the side of the dorm for approximately one hour. The dogs then accompany their handlers to work or school for approximately two hours. While the prison conducts its count, the participants and their dogs are in the dorm, and then there is another one hour recreation period. The dogs return to school or work with their handlers for two hours in the afternoon and after their evening meal they receive one more hour of recreation. Participants attend a weekly eight-hour class that focuses on various aspects of training and health, taught by PBB's two dog trainers.

Staff

The program is overseen by the facility's administrators with additional primary duties; the facility's Administrator and the Assistant Administrator were responsible for bringing the program to the facility and assume the role of the program's administrators. The director of the program since April 2005 is the Administrator's Executive Assistant who is responsible for the day-to day operations of the program.

Pre-Participation Assessment.

Participants are referred to the program when they write to the administration and express interest. In order to be selected for the program, an applicant must have at least two years left on her sentence and be eligible for minimum custody status, as well as be participating in other types of programs (educational, vocational, employment). In addition, participants can not have been convicted of a sex offense or a crime against a child. Applicants must also be infraction- or charge-free for one year prior to applying. Inmates need not be incarcerated for a specified length of time before they can participate. In over four years, one participant has been removed from the program due to rule violation. All participants begin as trainees, who are not assigned to a specific dog and instead are responsible for general clean-up and similar least pleasant duties. Trainees progress to alternate handlers and then are assigned their own dog as a primary handler. Progress is determined in part by vacancy so the time spent as a specific status varies. The three DOC employees meet with the executive director of PBB communicate with each other frequently, but not according to any set time frame.

Program participants are with their dogs 24 hours a day and often swap dogs so they get accustomed to a variety of people and settings. Program completion for the inmate participants is when they leave the facility. Dogs spend approximately 16-18 months in the program when they are tested for their suitability for explosive-detection work. Program success for the inmate participants is having their dogs go on to specialty training and then on to work in law enforcement in the U.S. and overseas. There are several rewards or incentives in place to encourage program participation and completion. Having the dogs is a reward itself for the inmate participants. These inmates also have their own cells. The informal rewards, such as the psychological and social benefits identified in the interviews with participants, should also be noted. While the program clearly utilizes more rewards than punishments, termination of participation will result for those found to have engaged in a serious infraction. (Infractions are divided into two types: minor, a pink slip and serious, a blue slip.)

In addition to their activities with the dogs, each participant is required to keep a journal of the dog that will go to the dog's handler. The journal includes pictures, nail and fur trimmings, and information such as a favorite toy or activity. It also tracks the dog's progress in training, socialization, and health. The program's two outside trainers are able to discuss vocational opportunities with participants. Records on program participants are kept by PBB, not the facility.

Program participants are somewhat segregated from the general population. They live in their own dorm, on the minimum-security campus of the facility, which also houses a limited number of non-participants. Most participants also work with non-participants during the day in programs or through employment.

People from outside the facility also play roles in the program. Participants' family members cannot play a role in the program. While the dogs are permitted to accompany participants on visits, participants' families cannot serve as weekend sitters who take the dogs out on visits or furloughs. The program participants receive lessons in dog training and care from the program's two trainers who are volunteers with and trained by PBB.

Post-Program

The program provides no aftercare services. The state's policy prohibits employees from contact with those released from custody. There is no tracking procedure in place to monitor participants after completing their participation. While the executive director reported that she will provide a reference if asked, "we are not in the job placement business." The program collects data on participant progress and punishments and violations received by participants. The program does not collect data on participants' placement in outside agencies. The administering non-profit organization maintains records regarding the progress of the dogs, but extensive or comprehensive files are not kept on program participants. This agency stresses the importance of adhering to a code of ethics surrounding the care of the dogs and participation in the program, in general. The program has demonstrated stability and strength in terms of its funding and community support.

Part of the wide-spread success of PBB is the nature of its boards of directors and advisors; both groups are comprised of people with significant power within New York State's prisons, and people with significant wealth. Puppies Behind Bars has a board of directors that includes the current and immediate past Commissioner of New York State Department of Correctional Services, and a board of advisors that includes Libby Pataki, the wife of New York's former Governor, George Pataki, and Henry A. Kissinger and his wife Nancy. The organization has received national attention, being profiled on The Oprah Winfrey Show and in The New York Times. The actress Glenn Close has also worked with the organization with the women at Bedford Hills Correctional Facility.

Support/Cooperation

The program's primary collaboration is between PBB and the state's DOC. PBB has partnerships with Iams and the Animal Medical Center, a nonprofit veterinary hospital in Manhattan. All program materials are provided by PBB. The state provides the space and the labor and is adequately supported by PBB and receives sufficient funding. The program enjoys an excellent relationship with the prison's administration, according to both sides. The state's central DOC administration is supportive of the program. According to interviews and observations, the vast majority of the facility's staff members are supportive of the program. Those unsupportive of the program have not had a significant impact on its operation. For example, a member of the custody staff assigned to the dorm identified the dog's choker collars as a security risk and had them prohibited from being used in the dorm.

There was one significant change made in the program operations since it was first implemented. After September 11, 2001 the demand for explosive-detection canines from law enforcement greatly increased. The agency currently works with the New York Police Department (NYPD) Bomb Squad and the Bureau of Alcohol, Tobacco and Firearms (ATF).

The staff of the current program is small. The program's director is also the executive assistant of the facility's administrator with a variety of other responsibilities. The two trainers who teach the weekly lessons are volunteers of the administering non-profit, the executive director of which is highly involved with the program in at-least monthly site visits. All involved with the program at this level appear qualified and bring a diversity of training and experiences to their work. They have also been relatively stable, with the program director having recently been given the position.

Interview with Administration

Origins of the Program

The researcher met with the Administrator (sometimes referred to as a warden) and Assistant Administrator, who are both notably committed to the program and involved. The interview was started by asking how the Administrator first heard about PAPs and how she went about trying to bring the program to her facility. She reported that she was approached by a member of the community with a proposal for a community service program where shelter dogs would be socialized and adopted out. Unsure that was the type of program she wanted, the Administrator contacted Gloria-Gilbert Stoga, the president of PBB. The Administrator, Assistant Administrator, and security Captain visited the PBB program at Bedford Hills Correctional Institution, a maximum-security facility for women in New York. Research, or leg-work on the part of several facility correction officers uncovered other types of programs, but "the proven track record" of PBB was something "we could take to the unions."

The Administrator acknowledged facing challenges in implementing the program. The CO union had concerns about "the nature and personalities of the dogs." Union officials were also concerned with "health issues" associated with inspections in medical, vocational, and food service areas. Officers wanted to know where the dogs would go and where they would be prohibited from going. In addition, could inmates with job assignments in areas like food service still participate in the program? As summarized by the Administrator: "So there were questions that needed to be answered before we could go forward."

It might seem impossible to imagine anyone given the opportunity to leave prison who would not take it. There is anecdotal evidence of PAP participants who decided to remain incarcerated to be able to continue in the program. When asked, the administrators were unable to identify any participants who turned down a transfer to a half-way house in order to maintain their participation. During interviews with the participants, two women reported forfeiting the opportunity to leave the facility.

Program Goals
The Administrator was asked to identify the goals of the program. First, she said, "we're giving back to the community." The program, she said, matches the Department's "focus on transition and victims". Another goal, she said, is to benefit the participants who "develop trust, love, and confidence" and foster "growth and pride". The Administrator noted that the program is also an opportunity for "the community to recognize the value of people who are incarcerated."

The Administrator was asked to describe how the program measures success. First, she identified the program's retention – in five years, only one person has been removed for a disciplinary charge, second, the number of dogs working in agencies and overseas, and third, the number of women participating in the veterinarian assistant certificate program and working with animals once released. Asked to identify any changes they have seen in the participants, the Administrator first noted that there has been no recidivism among the program participants. She said she has seen the women "rise above their limitations" as well as become less aggressive. The Assistant Administrator was quick to report that he sees "staff who never smile, smile at the dogs." In a separate conversation, the program director noted that "the facility greatly supports the program; these dogs change the whole place; everyone who works here loves to see the dogs." Both Administrators agreed that they see the participants put their own needs aside and cooperate for the sake of the dogs and to remain in the program. They also both agreed that the most positive aspect of the program is the growth of the women who participate. However, meeting specific criminogenic risks were not discussed.

Challenges
The Administrator was asked how other prison administrators react when they find out she has a PAP at her facility. She said the reaction is generally positive, while "some say, 'good for you, but keep it there.'" Corrections is a naturally order-centered bureaucracy and having dogs in a facility presents possible challenges for the staff in maintaining the control that must remain the first priority.

The Administrator provided examples of the sort of negotiation and flexibility that are necessary to maintain this program. When the dogs first arrived, there was a universal impulse to feed them. When PBB representatives told the participants to stop feeding the dogs 'people food' the women were then faced with a situation where they possibly had to tell COs they could not feed the dogs. The Administrator made feeding the dogs against facility policy and now everyone knows not to feed them. In order to avoid a possible conflict of interest, another decision was made to prohibit facility employees from serving as PBB volunteers who take the dogs out weekend furloughs.

The administrators were asked to identify any negatives associated with the program. The Administrator first mentioned the time commitment that can be required by the program, but acknowledged that this is the case "with any progressive program". She said there is a perception that the inmates in A Cottage are favored by staff and administrators, but that "it is because of our commitment to this program." She also said there is jealousy between the participants based on whose dogs are most successful or learn the quickest.

Suggestions for Improvement
The Administrators mentioned needing a more grassy area for the dogs to be exercised; the current yard at the side of the dorm has sparse grass and is mostly dirt. The Administrator also said she would like the participants to have more job opportunities (currently, participants cannot be employed in food service). She noted that she has "talented women working as porters [basic clean-up crews in a prison]."

Other
The administrator acknowledged the need for a program such as this for the women locked in maximum-security but said the compound "is not conducive to it. There is too much idle time and there are no single cells."

When asked if she would be interested in bringing a horse program to the facility the Administrator balked. She said the stable would require an additional security post and mentioned the difficulty of disposing of horses when they die.

The Administrator mentioned that she is allergic to dogs. Despite needing to wash her hands after any contact with the animals, the Administrator sought this program and continues to provide it with necessary resources and support. Sadly, she recalled having to recently put down her two Yorkshire Terriers (a low-allergy breed).

Upon leaving the facility, the Assistant Administrator informed the researcher that the fact that all 15 primary handlers spoke with me "is indicative of the program". He went on to say that the researcher "would never," for example, get all the participants of the Therapeutic Community drug treatment program at the facility to participate in an interview.

The Male Program

The second program, in a medium-security facility for males aged 17-25 in the same northeastern state, pairs offenders with greyhounds rescued from being destroyed after the end of a racing career (usually 2-3 years) who are socialized for placement as pets in homes in the community. "The Greyhound Program," as it is known at the facility, has been in operation since May 2002. The program is administered by Greyhound Friends of New Jersey (GFNJ), a non-profit organization with the purpose of finding homes for ex-racing greyhounds (www.greyhoundfriendsnj.org). GFNJ was incorporated in 1995 by Barbara Wicklund, the agency's founding director; today the president is Linda Lyman. The prison program, only one of the ways in which the agency trains dogs, is the only canine socialization program for men in the state and has had over 250 dogs graduate and find homes. At the time of the interviews, there were seven dogs and 18 inmates participating: seven primary handlers, seven back-up handlers, and four trainees. Individual interviews with each of the seven primary handlers and a focus group with 14 participants were conducted at the facility. Among the seven primary handlers, the average age is 25.6 years and ages ranged from 21 to 33 years old. Six participants identified themselves as Hispanic and one as Black. The average length of program participation was 18.1 months and ranged from nine to 36 months.

Greyhound Friends of New Jersey was established after Barbara and her husband Al, adopted a greyhound from Greyhound Friends of

Hopkinton, Massachusetts, an organization that took retired greyhounds (generally two to three years of age) from racetracks throughout New England to prevent their destruction by finding them homes. The Wicklunds were so taken with their former racer that they wanted others to know the experience of living with a greyhound. Within years, Barbara and Al's offer to expand the Massachusetts organization to New Jersey grew into its own agency. Today the greyhounds come from racetracks and other greyhound rescue groups from across the country when these other agency's kennels are at capacity and a dog is at risk of destruction if temporary placement is not found.

The life of a racing greyhound is not that of a domesticated pet; their lives are generally limited to the track and a holding crate. They have never seen stairs or lived in a house. Upon arrival at GFNJ, many dogs are fostered in homes for a period of socialization and/or recuperation if suffering from a broken leg or other racing injury. The prison program is another place dogs are socialized to increase their chance of adoption. There is a $235.00 adoption fee to adopt a dog from GFNJ. As the organization is maintained by a core of approximately 100 volunteers in the greater New Jersey area, donations and grants are a necessity. Further evidence of its grass-roots nature can be seen in the types of functions regularly held throughout the year to raise funds, including two reunion picnics, a winter holiday craft sale and other fund raisers. On weekends volunteers participate in "Meet and Greets" where potential adopters can spend time around the dogs and ask questions. Greyhound Friends of New Jersey places more than 250 dogs each year in adoptive homes. The agency's philosophy is, "Accept these greyhounds in need of a safety net, regardless of gender, size, color or age. There is a home out there for every one of them; it's our job to find it" (www.greyhoundfriends nj.org).

Activities

Participants rise each day at 5:45 am and go out with their dogs for a brief walk. The dogs are then fed and walked at 7:30 am for approximately 15 minutes. The dogs are then either in the handler's room or the kennel, dependent on the weather, while the participants are at work or school. After the participants eat lunch the dogs are outside for a walk or a run in the yard. Then they are back in the room or out in the kennel in nice weather. At approximately 4 pm the dogs are fed and walked again and then they are in the room or kennel until 8:45 when they go for their last walk. Participants attend a weekly one-hour class that focuses on various aspects of training and health, often featuring an outside speaker. Presentations are videotaped for future participants to view.

Staff

The program is voluntarily staffed by facility employees with additional primary duties; all current staff members have been with the program since its inception. The director of the program is a Senior CO; he is responsible for the day-to day operations of the program. The program administrator is also the Assistant Superintendent of the facility. In addition, the facility's Administrator is involved with the program. While the director's current vocation is a CO, he also has professional experience working with dogs. He breeds dogs for sale and leads hunts (for birds using dogs), and his wife owns a kennel for dogs whose families are vacationing. While in the military, this CO worked with a 'perimeter dog' and has previously worked with a 'bite dog' (used for cell extractions) with the state DOC.

Pre-Participation Assessment

Participants are referred to the program when they write to the Assistant Administrator and express interest. In order to be selected for the program, an applicant must have approximately one year left on his sentence, not have been charged with animal or child abuse, and not be gang-affiliated. The program director also weighs heavily the information he obtains from the applicant's housing unit officers, teacher and/or boss.

In addition, applicants must be infraction- or charge-free for six months to a year, depending on the severity. Inmates need not be incarcerated for a specified length of time before they can participate. In three years, one application has been refused, with the ultimate decision belonging to the program director. During this same time period, one participant has been removed from the program due to rule violation. There are program materials, such as a handbook and a video library, for inmates when they begin their participation. All participants begin as trainees, who are not assigned to a specific dog and instead are responsible for general clean-up and similar least pleasant duties. Trainees progress to back-up handlers and then are assigned their own dog as a primary handler. Progress is determined in part by vacancy so the time spent as a specific status varies. The three state DOC employees meet with Barbara Wicklund once each month or as needed to discuss the program and participants.

Program participants spend up to approximately 18 hours each day with their dogs. Program completion for the inmate participants is when they leave the facility. Dogs are eligible for adoption after passing the American Kennel Club Canine Good Citizen Test.

Program success for the inmate participants is preparing their dogs for adoption, through socialization and behavioral training, in approximately eight weeks. There are several rewards or incentives in place to encourage program participation and completion. Having the dogs is a reward itself for the inmate participants. These inmates also have their own cell and are each issued a second locker in which to store their personal items (some of the dogs are prone to eat what is left out, e.g., hairbrush, slippers, radio, etc.). In addition, GFNJ sponsors a party for the program participants where outside food (i.e., pizza and sandwiches) is served twice each year, in the summer and during the winter holiday season. The informal rewards, such as the psychological and social benefits identified in the interviews with participants, should also be noted. While the program clearly utilizes more rewards than punishments, termination of participation will result for those found to have engaged in a serious infraction. (Infractions are divided into two types: minor, a 'pink slip' and serious, a 'blue slip'.)

In addition to their activities with the dogs, each primary handler is required to keep a journal of the dog that will go to the adopting family. The journal includes information such as what the dog likes to eat and play with and what she may be afraid of. It also tracks the dog's progress in training, socialization, and health. The program director and the weekly speakers discuss vocational opportunities with participants. The director of GFNJ is also available to discuss vocational opportunities. The program director has confidential files of the program participants, and the inmate coordinator keeps files on the dogs, including their medical histories, and the inmates, including their progress in the program.

Program participants are somewhat segregated from the general population. They live on the first floor, in single cells, of one of the facility's several cottages. Non-participants live in the dorm on the second floor. The cottage shares one day area. Most participants also work with non-participants during the day.

Participants' family members can play a role in the program. The dogs are permitted to accompany participants on visits they receive. In addition, one participant's mother adopted a dog from the program. Several staff members have adopted dogs as well.

Post-Program

The program provides no aftercare services. State DOC policy prohibits employees from contact with those released from custody. There is no tracking procedure in place to monitor participants after completing their participation. The non-profit agency's executive director reported setting up job interviews for several former participants released on parole. Employment has been obtained for released participants at a dog daycare center and a kennel affiliated with the program. She reported the placements have been successful.

Support/Cooperation

The program's primary collaboration is between GFNJ and the state DOC. GFNJ has partnerships with other rescue groups, pet supply stores, and a variety of community groups; a large part of the agency's work is weekend "meet and greets" off facility grounds to get the adoptable dogs exposure in the community. All materials are provided by GFNJ. The state DOC provides the space and the labor, is adequately supported by GFNJ, and receives sufficient funding. The program enjoys an excellent relationship with the prison's administration, according to both sides. The state's central DOC administration is supportive of the program and is responsible for the addition of the weekly speaker component of the program. However, there are political constraints imposed on the program by COs who do not support the program. Members of this contingent have impacted the program. A senior member of the security staff had the dogs prohibited from entering any facility building (such as the main administration building or school) except the dorm where participants are housed.

There have been changes made in the program operations since it was first implemented. An event relayed to the researcher by the program director provided as an example of the dynamics of the environment in which the program operates. Another senior member of the custody staff prohibited the dogs from wearing booties (worn for a paw injury) with a camouflaged design; the employee told the program director (also a member of the security staff) the booties had to be fluorescent in color because the camouflage posed (an unspecified) danger.

The positive aspects appear to greatly outweigh any negatives. The program has a strong positive relationship with the community. There has been significant positive press given to the program by both TV and print media. The current program appears to target, if indirectly, most of the criminogenic needs or risks identified by the literature. The program is multi-modal, employing no one specific treatment approach. Again, the corrections department does not consider this program's rehabilitative effects for the participants the primary goal; the program is of a voluntary community service nature. The program utilizes more rewards than punishments; again, participation in the program is considered a reward in itself for most participants. Release from the program generally coincides with release from the institution; while the executive director of the administering non-profit will serve as an employment reference, the program does not offer specific re-entry services.

While the majority of program participants reported feeling they can talk to and provide feedback to one or more of the staff members or the inmate assistant, there is no formal feedback process. The program's success is primarily based on the number of dogs that are adopted. The facility administration also pointed to the retention rate and enthusiasm among participants as evidence of how well the program is functioning. Anecdotally, they believe there is no recidivism among participants, but there was no formal tracking after release. Given that the rehabilitative effects for participants are not a goal, their lack of measurement is not a surprise.

The program director reported keeping personal records on the progress of both the participants and the dogs, but the facility does not. The administering non-profit agency stresses the importance of adhering to a code of ethics surrounding the care of the dogs and participation in the program, in general. The program has demonstrated stability and strength in terms of its funding and community support.

The level of political constraints for this program appears to be minimal. The administrator of the facility reported being supported by the state's central DOC administration. He reported having to navigate resistance from the prison's security staff union before the program was implemented. The program director reported still facing resistance from a few specific individuals on the security staff but indicated that their impact on the operations of the program is minimal.

Origins of the Program

The researcher met with the Administrator, Assistant Administrator, and the Senior Correction Officer who is responsible for the day-to-day operations of the program. The interview was started by asking how the Administrator first heard about PAPs and how he went about trying to bring the program to his facility. He reported that one of the facility's teachers, who has a rescued greyhound, saw an article about a similar program in a greyhound magazine and brought the article to him. He called "a few" greyhound rescue groups and the executive director of GFNJ, Barbara Wicklund "immediately returned my call to say she was interested." When asked if he could identify a person who particularly advocated for the program he indicated that the program director "jumped right in to volunteer."

The Administrator acknowledged facing challenges in implementing the program. The Commissioner of the state's DOC had "safety and security concerns" as well as "misinformation about the dogs." In addition, the unions and some staff members had concerns "about dog bites and messes." The Administrator recalled that "the security staff hassled me over it, saying, 'This is a prison, what is he doing?'" The Administrator characterized employees as "probably 60-40 in favor of it" when first presented with the idea. Now, though, "they are 90-10 in favor of it." He conceded that "there are still a few hold-outs who just don't think dogs belong in a prison." Despite that, though, COs have adopted dogs from the program and the Administrator reported that COs want to work on the unit now. The nay-sayers "have been proven wrong; it is routine now," he said. When asked, the three were able to identify one participant who turned down a reduction in his security level to "full minimum status," which would have allowed him to move to a half-way house, in order to remain in the program.

Program Goals

The Administrator was asked to identify the goals of the program. First, he said, is to rescue dogs, second to train inmates in responsibility and self-discipline and caring for others, and thirdly, to educate inmates in career options. The Administrator was asked to describe how the program measures success. First, he identified the lack of injuries, second, the number of adoptions (99 since May 2002), and third, the "changes we see in [participants'] behavior, attitude, and self-control." Asked to identify the changes he has seen in the participants, the Administrator referred to his previous response and added that "the program teaches caring and responsibility as well as self-discipline."

Challenges

The Administrator was asked how other prison administrators react when they find out he has a PAP at his facility. He acknowledged that "they're interested, and inquisitive, and think it is a little crazy too.

Philosophically, it is a change in the routine, and safety has to always remain paramount." He went on to say that this type of program "requires flexibility on the part of the administration and the custody staff," since, he said, "most programs won't work without the support of custody." His last statement refers to the influence of Correction Officer unions on prison policies and procedures. The officers' union ensures the work conditions of the members who are public employees with a contractual agreement with the governmental agencies that operate the facilities. Any changes in those conditions, such as with the addition of a new program or a change in how officers are mandated to complete their work, must be approved prior to being implemented. Throughout the United States state and local departments of correction are, like many governmental agencies, largely dependent on the success of their staff and employees rather than the administrators at the top. The officers' unions determine which programs can be administered.

The group was asked to identify any negatives associated with the program or if there was anything they would change about the program. The program director said that there is not enough staffing for the program and the varying training levels of the dog-inmate pairs can cause tension. The Administrator acknowledged that "guys have to defend the dogs sometimes from the other inmates who will insult their dogs for being so skinny." The Administrator went on to report name calling that included "crack-smoking dog," "dope-shooting dog," and "AIDS dog".

Suggestions for Improvement

The three agreed that they would like increased opportunity for the dogs' socialization and movement. The dogs are with the inmate population as much as possible, such as in the day room, but according to the Administrator, "there are 'institutional constraints'" and "some inmates fear the dogs." [The researcher later found out that the Administrator was alluding to an incident with a senior member of the security staff who was posted in the administration building and managed to get the dogs banned from the building. Dogs are now only permitted inside the cottage where the participants are housed. During warm months the dogs are outside in caged runs during the day while their handlers are in programs or working. During the winter the dogs remain in the primary handler's cell on the first floor of the dorm.] The Administrator went on to note that "the dogs are with the inmates more than they would be with an owner in the real world where someone is out of the house for 9 or 10 hours a day." Finally, there was agreement with the Administrator who pointed out that "there is a lot of separation anxiety around the dogs' adoptions. We replace the dog right away; I have seen guys near tears."

Program Comparison

The two programs examined in the research presented above had similar strengths and weaknesses and several key differences when compared to each other. The female program is more intense and includes more lessons in animal training and offers the opportunity to become certified in animal care through correspondence school. Another strength of the female program is that it is one of several sites administered by this non-profit organization; the model specific to this agency has been practiced for several years prior to being put into place at the current prison. The male program faces significant staff member changes when the program director and executive director of the administering non-profit retire.

The two programs also include common characteristics unique to PAPs. Participants in the male program keep journals that follow the dogs when they are adopted; written in their own words, it allows participants to share the goals he and the dog reached together and what he has learned about the dog's unique personality, such as any likes or dislikes. The puppy books created by the participants in the female program follow the growth and development of the dogs through pictures and samples of the dogs' first nail clippings and puppy fur from groomings, and also go with the dogs when they leave. These books serve as an opportunity for the participants to demonstrate their knowledge about a dog they have dedicated a significant amount of time and energy to. It also serves as a tangible, lasting connection between the participants and the dogs, thus reinforcing a new, pro-social relationship.

The two programs also have strengths not often found in correctional programs and are unique to PAPs. Prison-based animal programs may be among the most cost-effective programs to administer inside a correctional facility. All supplies are generally provided by the administering non-profit agency and the facility is responsible for providing the labor and the space. Few correctional programs are the source of such positive media attention or able to encourage positive relations with the community. Community members and recipients of the animals, whether law enforcement officers or families with children, also "become more aware of the broad range of issues faced" by incarcerated people and can "gain deeper insights into the crime-related challenges faced by offenders, victims, communities, and justice agencies" (Holsinger & Crowther, 2005, p. 329). While PAPs provide a range of benefits most correctional programs can hope, at best, to positively impact the individual participants.

The interviews with program stakeholders regarding program effects revealed further confirmation for many of the findings regarding psycho-social benefits previously reported. Supporting the work of Arkow (1998), most participants of both programs reported learning to get along with and trust each other as they worked together with shared responsibilities aimed at common goals. Similar to Moneymaker and Strimple (1991), most participants in these two programs reported having a more positive outlook on life since they began the program. These researchers and others, including Cushing and Williams (1995), also found evidence of participants experiencing improved self-worth and increased self-esteem. The vast majority of both the male and female participants in the current study reported feeling more positive about themselves and feeling more worthwhile as a result of their work with the dogs. Increased self- confidence and patience, found in an evaluation of a wild mustang program (Lai, 1998), was also reported by most of the male and female participants in the current study. The results are also consistent with the findings of Cushing and Williams (1995). As in their work, many of the current sample of participants noted that being entrusted with the dogs was significant or meaningful and contributed to their sense of accomplishment and of being able to take pride in their hard work.

The data collected for the current study indicate support for the findings from a review of Scottish PAPs. According to Graham (2000) the programs were found to increase communication among inmates and between inmates and staff members. While a number of participants from both sites of the present study reported increased interactions with their fellow inmates, a nearly even number did not. Many did report more positive interactions with some staff members. The Scottish study found visitors stayed longer and many participants in the current study told of including the dogs on visits and in discussions during phone calls with family members. Also in concordance with Graham (2000) is the finding that the animals were associated with reduced levels of staff stress. Staff and administrators at both program sites reported the overall support of and enjoyment from the dogs.

The data from the male facility support findings reported by Harbolt and Ward (1991) who examined a community service program with incarcerated older teenagers. Those researchers found that the youth demonstrated compassion, were dedicated to their responsibilities, and had gained experience giving and receiving positive regard. The male participants in the current sample also consistently demonstrated compassion and dedication to their work. They also noted the therapeutic effects of having a dog with them inside prison.

The effect on vocational skills noted by Harkrader et al. (2004) and Lai (1998) was supported by the current research. Participants and stakeholders alike reported that the programs instilled a sense of responsibility in participants. Responsibility was also commonly reported in the national survey included in the present project. At the female facility, participants with at least a GED and 18 months left on their sentence are able to take a correspondent course in Veterinary Assistant paid for by the non-profit that administers the program. Administrators reported that five participants have taken advantage of the offer. Two participants reported currently pursuing the certification.

The two programs examined in the present study reported lower rates of participant discharge from the program than that found by Moneymaker and Strimple (1991). One participant of the 30, or 3.33%, who have participated in the female facility's program was removed for disciplinary violation. The male facility reported an even lower number of participants discharged, one of 63, or 1.59%. Moneymaker and Strimple (1991) found 12% of participants removed in their examination of a prison pet adoption program.

The sociological and more large-scale effects of PAPs reported in the literature (see Harkrader et al., 2004; Lai, 1998) were found in the present examination. Positive community relations and positive press was reported as a benefit by administrators of both facilities. The sense of engaging in positive work and of serving the community was also raised by administrators from both facilities. Both programs also affected larger social issues, the demand for working dogs at the female facility and the rescue of dogs that would have otherwise been destroyed at the male facility.

The academic literature lacks discussion of challenges to implementing PAPs. Administrators and staff members at both facilities acknowledged facing challenges to implementation. Concerns from union members, those allergic and fearful of dogs, and those who argued that dogs just don't belong in prison had to be addressed at both sites. Administrators and supportive staff members helped spread a positive message about the programs. Interviews from both sites indicated that today most staff members support the programs even while some refuse to be impressed by the lack of problems and relative success of the program. No one interviewed expressed concern that the programs might be in jeopardy because of these non-supporters.

Prior research has not considered the effects of these programs on non-participants nor how non-participants treat or regard those in PAPs. Participants at the male facility were particularly vocal about being made fun of or harassed by inmate not in the program. During interviews participants told of being taunted by those who see them as weak and needing a dog for protection. They also reported others making fun of the dogs for being skinny; greyhounds are exceedingly different from the pit bulls inmates are familiar with in the cities where they are from. Some male participants indicated that others see them as privileged. Female participants also reported problems with jealousy from non-participants and with a few staff members who assume the participants feel they are special or better than other inmates and go on to remind them they are not.

Previous studies have not considered the role of the facility administrators. Both top administrators interviewed in this study acknowledged the progressive nature of the programs as well as the mixed reactions they face from other administrators who learn of the program. With additional research regarding the numerous benefits of PAPs more acceptance of the programs will hopefully follow. It will become more difficult to justify the notion that animals just don't belong in prisons if PAPs are shown to be positive, cost-effective measures that bring with them benefits for participants, staff members, and the community at large.

It is necessary here to identify a key characteristic of both programs studied. Neither program required changing, nor more importantly, adding to staffing needs. The need to satisfy security demands, in terms of staffing levels is basic to prison operations. Here, neither program required adding a new post or position charged only with overseeing PAP activities. Both programs are housed in dorms already staffed with security. The dogs are not housed in an area requiring additional staffing. For example, one administrator said a horse program would not be feasible at the facility because the stable and necessary fields would require additional security posts. Dogs, on the other hard, are housed in the dorm's cells and cared for and exercised in a small yard adjacent to the dorm.

The results of the present research also include findings not previously reported. Most notable is the data indicating a large number of female participants who reported positive physiological effects. Two-thirds lost weight (and half of them lost over 20 pounds each) and nearly half reported sleeping better for the first time since being incarcerated. One woman's thirty-year dependency on Insulin to control her Diabetes abated within three months of participation, and by sustaining lower blood pressure she has been able to reduce this dose of medication too. Another woman's debilitating back-injury has improved as a result of her increased activity. And yet another woman stopped taking anti-depressants since starting the program.

Some of the findings from previously reported research were not supported by the present investigation. Since the current study did not ask about illegal drug use prior to program participation, it is not known if participation positively impacted, or reduced, drug use. Hines (n.d.) reported that there was evidence of decreased suicide among PAP participants. The present study did not ask about suicide ideation but respondents overwhelmingly reported the positive effect the dogs have on their mood. Also, while PAPs can serve as a source of revenue at some facilities, the two programs examined here do not generate money.

The self-report nature of the data collected revealed differences between the participants based on gender. The interviews with the females were longer in duration and were generally more relaxed than the interviews with the males. The female interviewer sensed the male participants were not comfortable during the interviews. Half of the interviews were conducted with the program director in the room, and the other half were conducted in a private office belonging to a superior administrator. There are a number of additional possible influences, including participants did not understand the true nature of the inquiry, they saw the researcher as a DOC employee deserving deference, or they may have been reacting to some characteristic or behavior on the part of the researcher. The females may have appeared more comfortable speaking about their participation because they have been interviewed before by representatives of the press. The females were also significantly older than the males interviewed. The females were generally more verbal and better able to express themselves as compared with the males.

It is necessary to also note the distinctions between the nature of the two programs that may contribute to the variability in the self-reported findings. The program at the female facility is larger and has been operating for more than a year longer than the male program. The program at the female facility is also in operation at four other sites in two other states. It has a Board of Directors that includes the state's former governor's wife and the state's former commissioner of correctional services. Funding is not a reported concern. The female participants are with their dogs for more time during the day, usually all day, while the male participants are not with their dogs while they work an eight-hour day. Female participants work with the same dog for up to 18 months while male participants work with a specific dog for four to six months. The female program has more regular lessons for the participants and the training is more challenging and advanced. The female program also offers the opportunity to earn a vocational certificate at no charge. Overall, the female program model has undergone greater testing and review and is more formal and financially stable.

A strength of the data collection process for this research question was that it allowed for direct observations of the program stakeholders and activities. Bouffard and colleagues (2003) point out that "techniques that allow evaluators to observe the operation of the program first-hand, rather than relying on stakeholders' report or understanding of the operations, will provide" more accurate information (p. 152). A limitation of the data is the size of the sample. The total number of participants interviewed is small, but it is currently the largest in the literature. Another strength is that due to the relatively small size of these programs it was possible to include most program participants from each site in the sample.

How do we explain that even more recent works in this area continue to avoid a discussion of the programs' theoretical implications or the broader issues surrounding our ideology of punishment? The United States' growing number of PAPs may be indicative of a trend away from the retributive and vengeful policies generally relied upon in this country. But counter-indicative of any trend is our continued punitiveness with policies that include life sentences for minors, mandatory minimums, and the increasingly vengeful policies that govern sex offenders. The place of PAPs, then, within our current approach to criminal justice remains unexplored.

Theoretical Implications

An alternative to the treatment-punishment dichotomy is based on the concept of transformation or desistance which differs from rehabilitation in a number of ways. "Rehabilitation seeks to change the way a person behaves; transformation changes how a person thinks. Rehabilitation looks to the past; transformation is future oriented. Rehabilitation often occurs externally; transformation originates from within" (LIFERS, 2004, p. 63S). It is also significant that "the aim of rehabilitation is to restore the individual to some former state that may or may not have worked for the individual in the first place. Transformation, on the other hand, works to completely transform the person's way of thinking" (p. 64S).

Hans Toch argued this transformation in self is encouraged by participation in what he calls "altruistic activity" or "activity designed not for profit or gain but to assist some underprivileged people who stand in manifest need of assistance" (2000, p. 270). Similarly, the strengths-based approach to corrections outlined by Maruna, LeBel and Lanier (2004) refers to this idea as generative activity which allows "convicts and ex-convicts to make amends, demonstrate their value and potential, and experience success in support and leadership roles" (p. 140). Participating in these types of activities can provide "a sense of purpose and meaning, allowing them to redeem themselves from their past mistakes, and legitimizing the person's claim to having changed" (p. 133). The growth that can result can lead the offender to reject his "past offender identity" and adopt "a new identity and a new self and a new set of goals" (Toch, 2000, p. 276).

It is this new sense of self that Maruna (2001) argued is key for desistance because in order to "desist from crime, ex-offenders need to develop a coherent, prosocial identity for themselves" (p. 7). He found that desisters had changed or repaired their ideas of self and argued that desisters must not only be able to explain their reform in terms of their experiences to others, but also "perhaps more importantly, ex-offenders need to have a believable story of why they are going straight to convince *themselves* that this is a real change" (p. 86, italics in original). The "recovery story" or "redemption script" created by ex-offenders often establishes them as good or conventional and through the "help of some outside force, someone who 'believed in' the ex-offender, the narrator is able to accomplish what he or she was 'always meant to do.' Newly empowered, he or she now also seeks to 'give something back' to society as a display of gratitude" (p. 87). Maruna, LeBel, and Lanier (2004) found desisters often adopted a role as a wounded healer, having experienced "the transformation of identity from victim to survivor to helper" (p. 142). The concept of the participant as helper will be discussed further in chapter 6.

This remainder of this chapter argues that the development of relationships—between prisoners and their dogs, and prisoners and other humans—is at the core of such success. Research suggests that a new view or sense of oneself is necessary for successful transformation or desistance from crime. Successful desistance from criminal activity, or "making good" (Maruna, 2001), may be dependent on a changed self-identity. It has been argued that this new prosocial sense of self requires both social reaction and personal experience (Maruna, LeBel, Mitchell, & Naples, 2004).

Prison-based animal programs may affect how a person labels him/herself and is labeled by others. Inmates may engage in a process of assigning the animals with which they work a human-like identity, similar to that of traditional pet owners (Sanders, 1993; Alger & Alger, 1997). Once established, this unique relationship may then result in the prosocial re-labeling of ex-offenders. The animal is viewed by participants in such a way as to influence their sense of self, and at the same time, participants are viewed differently by both themselves and others because of the relationship with the animal. Included in this chapter are data based on two programs in one northeastern state: one is housed in a maximum-security facility for women, and the other is located at a facility for young men who are often serving their first adult (versus juvenile) state sentence.

The present research describes how PAP participants undergo self transformation from their relationships with the dogs. First examined is the extent to which PAP participants attribute a human-like identity to the dogs, which in turn is able to influence their self concept. Based on Bogdan and Taylor's (1989) research on humans and Sanders (1993) extension to human-animal relationships, PAP participants are found to assign four aspects of selfhood to program dogs by perceiving them as thinking intelligent beings, as individuals, as emotionally giving, and as having a social role. Second examined is the extent to which these relations with dogs affect a new self-identity as a result of both personal experiences and feedback from others. A process of re-labeling appears to occur whereby participants come to perceive themselves as non-criminal or rehabilitated, and others—both humans and the dogs—treat the participants as such. Finally, the implications of the findings for facilitating desistance from crime are briefly outlined.

Selfhood in Others

Several contemporary theorists have described the process by which humans attribute identity to other humans, even when their interactions lack a verbal, shared language. Bogdan and Taylor (1989), for example, have studied how nondisabled people, in the course of interacting with severely disabled people, define the latter's humanness and define the other as a human with a unique self. According to Bogdan and Taylor (1989), "the nondisabled view the disabled people as full-fledged human beings. This stands in contrast to the dehumanizing perspectives often held by institutional staff and others in which people with severe disabilities are viewed as non-persons or sub-human" (p. 138).

Bogdan and Taylor identified four aspects of the nondisabled person's perspective that enable the maintenance of a human identity for the severely disabled person. There is a spectrum of the extent to which people are neurologically damaged, specifically, the authors use the example of someone in a vegetative state. First, the nondisabled person attributes thinking to the disabled person. Despite usually significant physiological limitations, the disabled person is regarded as intelligent, even if unable to fully communicate thoughts. Second, the disabled person is viewed as an individual with a unique personality comprised of likes and dislikes, feelings and motives, a life history, and a physical appearance. Third, the nondisabled person regards the disabled person as reciprocating or contributing to the relationship. In addition to companionship and the opportunity to meet others in the community, the nondisabled person may derive a "sense of accomplishment in contributing to the disabled other's well-being and personal growth" (Bogdan & Taylor, 1989, p. 144). Finally, the disabled person is given a social place and regarded as a "full and important member" and participates in the "rituals and routines of the social unit" (p. 145).

Sanders' (1993, 2000) research extends that of Bogdan and Taylor to human-animal relationships. He found that through "routine, intimate interactions with their dogs, caretakers come to regard their animals as unique individuals who are minded, empathetic, reciprocating, and well aware of basic rules and roles that govern the relationship" (1993, p. 207). According to Sanders, the same four features identified by Bogdan and Taylor are used by people to construct a subjective identity for their pets. Pet owners attributed thinking to the animals and regarded their animals as intelligent and having free-will. Frequently, they cited "their dogs' play activities, and the adjustments they made while being trained. The dog's purposive modification of behavior was seen as indicating a basic ability to reason" (1993, p. 213). Pet owners also viewed their dogs as individuals with "unique personal tastes. Informants typically took considerable pleasure in talking about individual likes and dislikes in food, activities, playthings, and people" (pp. 215-6). In addition to the "subjective experiences" described above, pet owners reported that "they frequently understood their relationships with the animals as revolving around emotional issues. ...One indication of the intensely positive quality of their relationship with their animals were the owners' perceptions that their dogs were attuned to their own emotions and responded in ways that were appropriate and indicated empathy" (p. 218). Given the value placed on the relationship, it should be no surprise that dog owners reported "they actively included their animals in the routine exchanges and the special ritual practices of the household" (p.

219). Sanders thus concluded that the preceding are "categories of evidence used by dog owners to include their animals inside the ostensibly rigid but actually rather flexible boundaries that divide minded humans from mindless others" (p. 221). It should be noted that Alger and Alger (1997, 2003) extended Sanders' findings on dog owners to cat owners and found a similar process of viewing cats as minded actors.

Dog as Thinking, Intelligent Being

Unlike traditional pet ownership, the main purpose of the relationship in the PAPs is the training of the dogs. For the female participants, successful training meant the dogs will go on to specialized explosives training; for the male participants the dogs will be adopted by families. The participants' discussions of their dogs reflected this focus. Many participants were enthusiastic about describing their dog's intelligence and special skills. Through their participation, the women have learned that the dogs have innate abilities; the dogs were bred specifically to excel at their training and are usually the offspring of previously successful working dogs. One female participant told how her dog progressed through the program more quickly than any other dog, which she attributed to his nature as a particularly gifted and intelligent creature, and denied she had any special ability as a trainer.

Participants believe that their dogs have free will and claim to control their own behavior in light of their animals' perceived independence. More than half of the female sample said they were less angry and more patient as a result of their participation. "I was angry," said one woman, "and this is slowing me down and has taught me to be calm. We go at the pace of the puppy." Three male respondents also reported increased impulse and/or emotional control. For example, according to one participant, "I think before I react. I'll think 'Why is the dog acting that way?' and then I do something." In recognizing the intellectual abilities of the dogs the women have themselves become more thoughtful aware beings.

Dog as an Individual

Program animals are regarded as unique creatures by participants. All keep records of their dogs' individual progress. Women create a "Puppy Book" that follows the dog's development from a puppy and accompanies the dog upon leaving the facility. The book contains samples from the dogs' first nail clipping and grooming as well as the dogs' baby teeth and pictures of them dressed for various holidays (e.g., Christmas and Easter) and in paper birthday hats during celebrations. During a tour of the participants' dormitory where they live with the dogs, two participants proudly shared their Puppy Books with the researcher. One woman commented that the books are much like the baby book she kept as a new parent. In the program at the male facility, participants keep a written journal about their dogs that is given to the adopting family. Participants include information such as how the dog progressed with training, the dog's favorite toys and tricks, and any behavioral quirks, such as chewing certain objects, that the dog may still possess. In addition, during interviews at both facilities, participants consistently introduced the researcher to the dog after introducing themselves.

Other comments from the participants also demonstrate how they view the dogs as unique, individual beings for whom they want to do their best. Sounding as a mother wanting the best for her child, one woman described her efforts to "bring my dog to her full potential." A male participant noted he saw other guys in the program "get concerned for the dogs." One of the young men also said "you feel mature taking care of something else." One of his fellow participants followed up by adding "the dog depends on you and you look out for the dog. You take care of the dog and then yourself." Continuing with the idea of protecting the dogs, a participant said, "The dogs have been hit before but [no one is going to] they're not gonna do it again." Another participant agreed when he said "we share concern over the dogs. We are overprotective with the dogs." This was echoed by a female participant who said "You have to put you last and the puppy first."

Dog as Emotionally Giving

There was agreement that the dogs provided emotional support to the participants. According to one female, "To come to a place with no hope or joy and get unconditional understanding is amazing." Another said, "He doesn't criticize me or talk back or want to pick a fight. No matter what I say, here is here for me." Another woman described her relationship with her dog as "better than any I'll have with a person." Approximately half of all respondents identified the companionship of the dog as the major benefit of participation.

Participants reported that their interactions with their dogs help alleviate their depression or improve their mood. As one woman emphatically stated, "These puppies make me happy." According to another participant, "I have my 'jail days' when I'm depressed and angry but I see that little face and the wagging tail and they're happy to see you and it just can't be a bad day." Another said the program has given her "happiness and a purpose to life." The ability of the dogs to fulfill participants' emotional needs was demonstrated by the woman who reported that she no longer gets "upset with my kids for not writing enough; I just talk to my best friend here [referring to the dog]."

The male program participants reported receiving similar emotional support from the dogs. One male participant reported that, "I took Anger Management and Behavior Modification Therapy but they weren't as helpful as this program. I can show real emotion toward the dog. I have better sessions with the dog than I do with the doctor I see here in therapy. I'm more comfortable with the dog." Another male participant said, "I let my barrier down with the dogs because they're not gonna judge me." According to another male participant, "I will talk to him after a tough call with my daughter; it definitely helps with stress." And another said simply, "I talk to my dog—she is better than a person." Thus, participants from both programs indicated having emotional needs met through their interactions with their dogs.

Dog as Having a Social Role

Participants support the idea that the dogs they work with take on social roles in their lives. They recognized their dogs' ability to serve as social facilitators; participants told of increased communication with fellow participants, other inmates, and staff and administrators regarding their dogs. According to one female participant, other women "will ask about your dog when you wouldn't usually talk to them." Participants in both programs reported conversations about the dogs' health and training progress as common topics. Another female related that, when she was seen walking the prison grounds without her dog, who was recuperating in the cell after being spade, "everyone was asking where she was. They were all worried about her, and if something bad had happened to her." This participant also said that others "all greet her before me when we're walking around grounds." Describing increased interaction with facility staff and administrators, one woman said "we talk more about the dogs and they'll ask how they're doing. I talk to them about her health and stuff." In addition, the dogs increase communication between participants. Among the female participants, one woman said, "We share concern over the dogs." A male respondent noted, "We have more trust with each other in the group." A second participant reported that "we get along for the dogs. If you took the dogs away we wouldn't be a community." Another participant agreed and said that "Without the dogs we wouldn't talk to each other as much."

Participants also reported the dogs had positive effects on their relationships with family members. One woman said, "My family loves it. I talk to them about the dogs on the phone. My mom always asks me about them. My family focuses on the dog when they come visit. They're proud of me and they see the changes in me." Another reported that her children are "less anxious about me being locked up. They get to see the dog when they visit and they'll even request a specific dog for me to bring." Male participants also reported that their families are interested in the dogs and they discuss the dogs with their families. According to one, "When my family calls me they check up on the dogs and me."

Another indication of the extent to which the dogs take on social roles for participants is the sadness they anticipated when their dogs leave the facility. "I do experience sadness with the program. It is tough to leave them; it's like separating from my kids all over again," according to one woman. (As with most programs, the two programs included here work to quickly pair the participant with another dog.)

Re-labeling

Prison-based animal program participants assign their dogs a human-like social identity. This newly constituted human-animal relationship may transform inmates' sense of self. Maruna, LeBel, Mitchell, and Naples (2004) refer to this new self-definition as re-labeling, which they contend is necessary for successful desistance from crime. They argue that desistance depends on a two-step process involving both social feedback and personal, or agentic, experiences. The first stage, or primary desistance, refers to any break or interruption in criminality, while the second stage or secondary desistance occurs when the individual comes to assume the role of a transformed or changed person.

Maruna et al (2004) propose that secondary desistance may best be achieved when the desisting person's change in behavior is acknowledged by others and mirrored back to the individual. They go on to note that the source of this new, prosocial label is significant and might be most effective when coming from authority figures. The authors suggest that "if the delabeling were to be endorsed and supported by the same social control establishment involved in the 'status degradation' process of conviction and sentencing (e.g., judges or peer juries), this public redemption might carry considerable social and psychological weight for the participants" (p. 275). In PAPs, prisoners have been carefully chosen to participate in a rewarding opportunity where prison staff and administrators and members of the community interact with participants as responsible and worthy of the chance they have been given. As a result of participating in the program, prisoners can receive feedback from others that reflects the transformed self-identity they experience internally.

To examine whether PAP participants' relationships with program dogs lead to re-labeling or development of a pro-social identity, evidence was gathered to see if they received feedback from others who recognized such change and if they regarded their own efforts in the PAP as having brought about this change. According to participants, they were treated differently by those around them; interactions with prison staff and administrators indicated they recognized the participants as reformed. Participants also identified their own efforts in the process of redefinition; they reported having experiences that supported a changed self-concept.

Social Feedback

More than half of the participants reported receiving better treatment from the staff since entering the program. According to one woman, "The COs treat us differently because we're doing something special and worthwhile. We get a little bit of respect." Another participant indicated that "the dog makes me different from other inmates and I'm in better standing with the officers. I've been complemented by officers who had been tough on me before." Another participant said COs "treat you more humanely; you're not just a number."

Family members also served as a source of positive feedback for many participants. One woman said, "My family loves it. I talk to them about the dogs on the phone. My mom always asks me about them. My family focuses on the dog when they come visit. They're proud of me and they see the changes in me." Another participant indicated that her family members have "come to admire what I do. I work hard whether it is freezing or hot outside. They admire my dedication and see I have gone above and beyond what I need to do in here."

Participants are aware that, in this process of change, others' views of them are important, as demonstrated by the woman who said "raising dogs for law enforcement means a lot. Being an inmate doesn't make us evil." Another participant may have captured the essence of the 'looking-glass self' when she noted that "this gives me more credibility with others on my journey to being a whole and trusted person again."

The prison's director and deputy director confirmed the participants' reports of how staff members viewed them. Asked to identify any changes she has seen in the women, the director said they "develop trust, love, and confidence" and that participation fosters "growth and pride". She stated that she has seen the women "rise above their limitations" as well as become less aggressive. She also noted that the program is an opportunity for "the community to recognize the value of people who are incarcerated." Both the director and the deputy director agreed that participants put their own needs aside and cooperate for the sake of the dogs, as well as to remain in the program. They also concurred that the most positive aspect of the program is the personal growth of the women who participate.

Agentic Experiences

Participants claimed they achieved emotional growth as a result of their involvement in the program. More than half of the sample said they were less angry and more patient as a result of their participation. "I'm more relaxed and not as tense," said one woman. "I was angry," said another, "and this is slowing me down and has taught me to be calm." Several participants said the program has led them to be more aware of their emotions and more connected to those around them. One woman reported, "I have seen an enormous change in my emotions. Before, I didn't show much emotions. I'm not a people person. But the dogs make my emotions more active. I worry about them if they are hurt during play or whatever. It is truly a big breakthrough for me." Another woman acknowledged being more emotionally engaged, stating "I was a drug addict out there so my feelings were all bottled up. This is opening up pathways for me to tell my family things I couldn't before. I tell them what I'm feeling now."

Most participants reported having increased pro-social interactions with those around them because of their involvement in the program. One woman said she has become "more outgoing. I am less nervous reading out loud in group. I've come out of my shell and can be open with people I don't know." A number of respondents indicated that they have dog-focused interactions with other inmates, facility staff, and administrators with whom they would not have interacted prior to their participation. "Before I stayed to myself," said one, "now I'm more apt to talk to people about the dogs."

The continual effort, and therefore sense of agency, required of their participation was an obvious theme of the interviews. One woman said, "We have to keep personality issues outside the program. We have to work together for the dogs. We have to have common courtesy for each other." Another declared she "wouldn't jeopardize her [dog's] training for anything. You have to set aside your feelings. You have to put you last and the puppy first." Comments indicated an awareness that their efforts with the program are connected with benefits they will later receive. One woman described the program as "a tremendous life lesson. I'm trusted with something alive. We've lost trust being in here and to get it back we'll do this hard work."

Participants also gained a sense of empowerment. One woman reported knowing, "I can get through anything. As uncomfortable as life can be, it is bearable. I can achieve anything I want to." Another said she learned "I'm not as stupid as I was always told I was. I have a lot to offer, to the community and to other women in the program, and to the dogs too." Another participant said she learned "to voice my opinion and not be a carpet. I say what I want people to know."

Finally, participants claimed that they experienced positive physical changes, as a result of their program involvement. Nearly everyone reported having lost weight since starting the program. A striking account came from a participant who said, "I gained over 100 pounds in county [jail awaiting trial] and I've lost most of it from the walking and exercise I get from the dogs." An additional four participants reported having lost between 34 and 60 pounds each. Most of the women also reported they are more active now and have more energy. "I used to lay around a lot in max. Here you're constantly busy," said one woman. According to another, "My energy is where it used to be. You're with them for 24 hours a day, being active. It's a great feeling." Almost half the group said they sleep better as a result of their participation. One woman extolled, "I sleep great. I'm physically exhausted. I'm healthier. It's a good clean, tired feeling." Another reported, "I have no more sleepless nights." In addition, one woman said she is "off anti-depressants" since beginning the program. Another participant reported that she had struggled with diabetes since age 12, but that, "within three months of being in the program my blood sugar stabilized at 180. I haven't used insulin in three months. Medical [staff] here and my family can't understand it. My blood pressure is lower too." While not everyone can achieve such results from participation in a PAP, it is worth noting that the potential for such change exists.

Discussion

Data presented above support the idea that a process of identity formation occurs among PAP participants similar to that occurring in the pet owners studied by Sanders (1993) and Alger and Alger (1997). Two processes characterize the experience of PAP participants; their relationships with dogs influence how they view themselves and how others view them. The new self-definition that can result from their participation may promote criminal desistance, which has been theorized to require a transformation or re-labeling.

What is it, in particular, about PAPs that might make for this transformation? The non-verbal nature of the social interactions people have with animals is often used to dismiss this type of contact as less valuable and/or legitimate than interactions between people. However, contemporary evidence establishes an intersubjectivity between animals and people irrespective of language. Specifically, there are a number of human subpopulations that have been previously ostracized or considered deviant by the dominant culture, including people with disabilities and those institutionalized in prisons and hospitals, whose members may be particularly able to benefit from the unique, non-verbal type of interactions that take place with animals. It is this very lack of language that may facilitate the relationships developed through PAPs. In fact, it may be that interactions not reliant on a common language are of particular benefit to prison inmates who often have long histories of people's words being used to reject and punish them. That is, without language to offend or cause harm, interactions between people and animals can feel less judgmental and therefore more therapeutic for incarcerated people. Indeed, prison inmates and animals may even be regarded as sharing a history of being excluded from the category of "human." As Sanders (1993:210) reminds us "'primitives,' African Americans, and members of various other human groups routinely have been, and continue to be, denied the status of human...and studies of interactions in total institutions...are filled with descriptions of the 'dehumanization' of inmates by staff members, principally on the grounds that the inmates do not possess the requisite level of mind."

Further, the human-animal relationship inside prison appears to support a new, non-criminal label, applied by both the individual participants and others. While primary desistance is any cessation in criminal activity, Maruna et al. (2004) argue that both reactions from others and personal experience are needed for the transformation that occurs with secondary desistance. It is worth noting that because participation is contingent on maintaining a clean institutional record, participants in these programs are actively demonstrating desistance, albeit while still incarcerated. There is evidence here that the changes in self and others' perceptions that are necessary for successful desistance from crime can occur during participation in a PAP.

The data presented in this chapter indicate that PAPs have ranging policy implications. As the ability of animals to influence a person's self-hood has become more widely recognized, animals should increasingly be included in treatment programs aimed at people with a range of psychosocial needs. Beck and Katcher (1996) point out that it is "when people face real adversity, affection from a pet takes on new meaning" (p. 38). Few in our society face the level of hardship experienced by many of the over two million people incarcerated in our prisons and jails. While we have only just begun to examine the extent of the effects experienced by PAP participants, we already know that not only do the inmates benefit, but so too do the animals and those they go on to serve in the community as well (e.g., Strom, 2006). It is difficult to identify other programs being administered in prisons today that can also claim to create a win-win-win situation.

Limitations

Lawrence and colleagues point to a "range of methodological limitations [that] preclude any assessment of *direct* and *unequivocal* beneficial effects of prison programming" (2002, p. 4). The present study also suffers from these limitations. The most significant limitation of the proposed study is its quasi-experimental nature. Because there is no control or comparison group to which the PAP participants are compared, it is not possible to conclusively attribute any reported treatment effects to the program. Further, linking the positive outcomes to specific program components presents a challenge, particularly in multi-modal programs such as the ones included here (Lawrence et al., 2002).

Selection bias of the program participants threatens the validity of the findings. Because participants must fit a number of eligibility requirements, the nature of those eligible may be systematically different from those ineligible. If participants are not typical of inmates in general, any program effects may actually be due to the inherent characteristics of those chosen to participate. The selection criteria result in what Maxfield and Babbie (2001) refer to as "*creaming*—skimming the best risks off the top. Creaming is a threat to validity because the low-risk persons selected ...may be most likely to succeed, yet they do not represent the jail population as a whole" (p. 166). Prison-based animal programs may restrict participants based on the type of offense for which they are incarcerated, for example, limiting participants to those inmates who have not been convicted of a crime against a child or a violent crime with a weapon. In general, program participants are also thought to be more motivated than those who do not participate in programs (Lawrence et al, 2002). Participant motivation is therefore regarded as a "characteristic of programs [that] tends to confound almost all program evaluations because those who participate are different from general population inmates" (Lawrence et al, 2002, p. 8).

Much of the data regarding treatment effects were not collected from objective measures. For example, interviews with program staff asked about their experiences with the program and the changes they have witnessed. Program participants were asked to report their subjective experiences as well. The reports regarding the physical effects of participation, such as measurable weight loss and changed medicinal schedules, are more objective than the reports regarding the psycho-social effects. The most objective measure of change is from participants' official disciplinary records, previously recognized as compromised.

The size of the sample should also be considered. While most of the universe of the two program participants was included in the sample, the total number of individual interviews, 22, is still relatively small. But given how few total participants exist, the current sample size may be considered adequate. The sample size, the limited amount of time spent at each facility, the presence of the CO during the first group of individual interviews and the focus group at the male facility, are each limitations that could be considered to stem from the difficulty of "gaining entry to prisons and other hard-to-access criminal justice organizations" (Trulson, Marquart, & Mullings, 2005, p. 451). The lack of control over the study environment or conditions of data collection "should hardly cause surprise...[given] that those who supervise and manage the kept do not initially welcome scholars and other outsiders into their institutions to poke about for largely self-serving research interests" (ibid, p. 457). As a result of this ever-present "institutional fear of outsiders" (ibid), "research within the field of corrections is rarely easy or uncomplicated" (Patenaude, 2004, p. 69S). Despite the challenges, however, qualitative research conducted inside correctional institutions captures "what quantitative researchers often miss, through no fault of their own, the richness of meaning, depth of understanding, and flexibility that are hallmarks of qualitative research" (p. 70S).

6
Emerging Ideas in Punishment

Given the relatively recent development of prison-based animal programs and the lack of a standardized method of administration or organized network of the myriad local programs that exist, it is unclear where these programs fit within the larger prison programming literature—or, for that matter, where they fit within the fields of criminology and criminal justice in general. Some would argue this uncertainty is not limited to PAPs but to criminal justice and punishment techniques in general: "we have a few ideas, we are making progress; however, we have yet to attain the status of a mature, evidence-based, and evidence driven science. We lack consistent, proven diagnostic instruments; [and] we lack a definitive body of knowledge" (Eskridge, 2005, p. 305). Again we see this hybrid, or ambiguous nature, of punishment. Therefore, this chapter will begin by examining a few examples of contemporary trends in how researchers are thinking about justice and the prison experience, followed by examples of what could be considered alternative prison programs.

In one area of study within the treatment literature researchers argue successful programs are those that focus on so-called criminogenic behaviors or risk factors, such as antisocial personality factors including impulsiveness and risk-taking; antisocial/pro-criminal attitudes; criminal associates and a lack of pro-social associates; substance abuse; poor problem solving skills; and high levels of anger or hostility (Andrews, 1995). Non-criminogenic needs, which have not been found to be associated with criminality include self-esteem, feeling alienated, and improving the neighborhood in which a person resides (ibid). There are two types of criminogenic needs that put people at increased risk of offending: dynamic risk factors which can be changed and static risk factors that cannot be changed. Static risk factors include a person's previous criminal history and experience with substance abuse; dynamic risk factors include antisocial attitudes, problem-solving skills, and levels of hostility. Programs that target these needs or behaviors have been found to more effectively reduce criminality, as compared to programs that do not target criminogenic factors. In fact, the authors found that "the targeting of noncriminogenic needs was associated with null effects of treatment or even increased reoffending" (Andrews & Bonta, 2003, p. 86).

One program that seeks to target the risk factors discussed above is an Australian program known as the Good Lives Model (GLM) of offender rehabilitation (Whitehead, Ward, & Collie, 2007). The approach seeks to instill offenders with "the competencies (internal conditions) and opportunities (external conditions) to implement" plans of change. As described by the interview data presented in chapter 5, PAP participants report the benefits of gaining useful skills and the opportunities for emotional, physical, and even vocational growth.

Restorative Justice

While not necessarily treatment, an alternative response to crime is restorative justice where criminal activity is viewed as harming not only a given victim but the larger community and the offender as well. As a result, all three groups of stakeholders should be included in a collective reaction to the offense; this stands in contrast to the traditional American approach to criminal justice that includes the offender with the victim virtually removed from the process and replaced by the state. Prison-based animal programs, specifically community service and service animal socialization models, include what can be viewed as restorative activities. Restorative justice or restorative practices have been offered as an alternative to the retribution versus treatment dichotomy that has dominated criminal justice (Bazemore, 1998). While lacking an agreed upon definition, the orientation has been traditionally conceived of as a process where the victim, the community, and the offender come together to collectively decide on a resolution (Shapland, 2003). Shapland (2003) argues for broadening this definition to include a variety of approaches with either a restorative process, a coming together, or a restorative outcome, one with a future-looking quality. And while Bazemore (1998) maintains that a restorative approach "necessarily involves victim and community," it may be "symbolically if not always actively" (p. 770). The restorative nature of any one specific practice or response to crime is a matter of degree according to McCold and Wachtel (2003). Thus, the omission of specific victims from PAPs does not necessarily preclude them from congruence with a restorative justice paradigm.

Prison-based animal programs incorporate the compassionate response called for by restorative justice practitioners (Harris, Walgrave, & Braithwaite, 2004) in a number of ways. The administering agency entrusts the animals to the participants, and the animals in turn provide unconditional love (arguably, better than compassion) to the participants. Intentionally avoiding a concrete definition, Van Ness (2003) has proposed 23 basic principles that "address particular programmatic expressions of restorative justice" (p. 166). More generally, Maruna and LeBel (2003) define the strengths-based or restorative paradigm as calling for "opportunities for ex-convicts to make amends, demonstrate their value and potential, and make positive contributions to their communities" (p. 97). According to them, this approach "would ask not what needs to be done to a person in response to an offense, but rather what the person can accomplish to make amends for his or her actions" (p. 98). A significant component of their approach is based on the idea of "the therapeutic power of helping" (p. 99). The helper principle "simply says that it may be better (that is more reintegrative) to give help than to receive it" (ibid). Hans Toch (2000) refers to this idea as altruistic activity.

There are many programs that allow inmates to engage in activities that provide them with the opportunity to provide restitution through their efforts. At Angola Penitentiary men restore bicycles and build toys for under-privileged children (Bertuca, 2005). In Wisconsin, maximum-security inmates also build birdhouses for conservatory groups and rocking horses for Head Start programs (Tischler, 1998). In Maine, juveniles convicted of serious offenses can participate in the Blanket Program where they learn to crochet blankets and hats (Germani, 2007). The blankets are donated to day-care centers, homeless shelters, and retirement homes, and according to one participant create a time and space to "calm down" (ibid).

The "sharp differences in opinion on how restorative justice should be delivered" allow for PAPs to be compatible with restorative practices (Shapland, 2003, p. 195). The second of Van Ness' (2003) 23 principles of restorative justice is a restorative outcome which includes "restitution, community service and any other program or response designed to accomplish reparation of the victim and community, and reintegration of the victim and/or the offender" (p. 166). Similarly, Shapland (2003) takes note of the growing "examples of penal outcomes and initiatives which also use the rhetoric of restorative justice but tend to ignore the ideas of 'coming together' and 'collective resolution'" (p. 198). Community service or work is an approach included in England and Wales' reparation order under the Crime and Disorder Act of 1998 where neither the victim nor the community is involved in a cooperative decision regarding the tasks assigned (ibid). Maruna and LeBel (2003) contend a restorative approach should include "community service work [that] is voluntarily agreed upon and involves challenging tasks that could utilize the talents of the offender in useful, visible roles" (p. 98). They go on to recommend "projects in which offenders visibly and directly produce things the larger community wants" as a way to both "build stronger communities, and carve channels into the labor market for the offenders engaged in them" (ibid). For researchers who view restorative practices as more than the traditional coming together of community, offenders, and victims, reparations in the form of community service or work not necessarily related to the offense or the victim, as with PAPs, can be considered part of restorative practices.

Creative restitution, developed by psychologist Albert Eglash, is an idea that dates back to the 1950s (Mirsky, 2003). He sought an alternative to what he considered the criminal justice system's lack of "humanity and effectiveness" (p. 1). According to this expanded interpretation of restitution, "an offender, under appropriate supervision, is helped to find some way to make amends to those he has hurt by his offense, and to 'walk a second mile' by helping other offenders" (p. ibid). In an early paper, Eglash outlined five characteristics of creative restitution:

1) It is an active effortful role on the part of an offender....Restitution is something an inmate does, not something done for him, or to him.
2) This activity has socially constructive consequences....Being constructive, restitution may contribute to an offender's self-esteem.
3) These constructive consequences are related to the offense.
4) The relationship between offense and restitution may be reparative, restorative.
5) The reparation may leave the situation better than before the offense was committed (pp. 1-2).

Therefore, other than his third criteria, PAPs are congruent with Eglash's definition of creative restitution. In addition, PAPs display each of his characteristics of creative restitution that distinguish it from traditional compensation:

1) It is any constructive act.
2) It is creative and unlimited.

3) It is guided, self-determined behavior.
4) It can have a group basis (p. 2).

Eglash has theorized that the creative restitution process would "provide a gateway to comfortable relations with others" (p. 2). In transforming how the offender relates to others, the concept includes an assumption of some change or rehabilitation that has taken place within the individual.

Another type of restorative practice that may be infused with rehabilitation is Bazemore's (1998) concept of "earned redemption" which "requires a sanctioning approach that allows offenders to make amends to those they have harmed to earn their way back into the trust of the community" (p. 770). It also "does imply some tradition of societal mercy and some basic level of community capacity to forgive, if not forget, the actions of offenders once they have made reparation" (p. 785). Central to this "relational rehabilitation" (Bazemore, 1998, p. 787), as well as to restorative justice practices in general are the emotional dynamics involved in the process (Harris, Walgrave, & Braithwaite, 2004). Because a community's response to crime impacts how offenders see themselves, a restorative response creates an opportunity where "respect for the offender can be expressed because he or she has had the courage to confront his or her responsibility and this might have been difficult" (Harris et al., p. 203). Therefore, irrespective of the offense, others still treat the offender with dignity. What is hypothesized to follow is that, "while defects in the self, in the ethical identity of the person, are revealed by the offense and its condemnation, these defects in a mostly good self can be repaired. Through their compassion supporters are saying "'you are not irredeemably bad and that is why we are standing beside you'" (ibid). Compassion as a reaction to crime "assists the worse of us to put our best self forward" (p. 204).

Braithwaite (2005) argues shame acknowledgement is necessary to prevent future crime. Then there can be a paradigm "shift from a blame culture to a learning culture" (p. 289). Mercy and learning encourage what he refers to as active responsibility, as opposed to the passive responsibility associated with traditional criminal justice responses to crime. According to Braithwaite, "passive responsibility means holding someone responsible for something they have done in the past. Active responsibility means taking responsibility for putting things right into the future" (p. 291). The redemption that he reasons will follow may aid in the desistance from crime, or enable what Shadd Maruna (2001) refers to as "making good."

Prison-based animal programs provide offenders with the opportunity to make reparations for the damage their crimes caused society at large. Through participation offenders recognize their responsibility for their actions while at the same time they engage in a self-healing process. Restoration comes from this acknowledgement and truth-telling. It is crucial to note that the process requires forgiveness on the part of society as well; there can be no bystanders—all members of society are harmed by crime and therefore must participate in restoration. The cycle of harm, punishment as retaliation and continual stigmatization and suffering is interrupted when all parties seek to transform bad into good. Restorative justice requires the building of a bridge of good- will based on trust and a need to heal. A moment to teach and learn from each other is created when a process of forgiveness is allowed to proceed. In PAPs participants acknowledge they have responsibilities to society and through their work they attempt to break from their past and transform themselves. Restorative justice and PAPs specifically are forward-looking—that is they are oriented toward the future and the potential good that can be accomplished; the programs give both people and animals a second chance. As one participant of an Illinois PAP remarked of her work with her poodle-partner, "'I'm trying not to look back,' she said. 'My success with Gracie [the poodle] is helping me look forward'" (Quintanilla, Feb. 11).

Critique of Restorative Justice

The restorative practices orientation has been criticized for limitations similar to the treatment orientation that acts on offenders, removing their agency from the process. Restorative justice, with vague notions of when redemption is earned, can be perceived as being done to offenders (McCold & Wachtel, 2003). While the offender may be included in restorative practices, "often the decisions about what the offender 'needs' are made in the absence of knowledge about or reference to the research or professional knowledge of 'what works'" (M. Kay Harris, personal communication, 7/31/05). In addition, the process by which offenders are held responsible or accountable "can result in offenders being treated as objects in the quest for public safety rather than as moral subjects with their individual worth" (Harris, 2005, p. 321). Despite these criticisms however restorative justice is an enlightened alternative to criminal justice.

Prison-based animal programs, as restorative practices, generally escape these criticisms. Because PAPs are not specifically designed with offender rehabilitation or transformation in mind, the role of the inmates can be diminished or dismissed; they may be viewed as simply carrying out the larger, animal-centered goals of the program without considering the restitution and redemption they are creating. Most often, however, the work of the program participants is recognized by the people of the non-profit organization, prison facility, and the recipients of the animals. It is this acknowledgement of the hard work and discipline of the participants that makes the programs in part so unique. The bad people who committed offenses against society come to be seen as having renewed regard for the very public they harmed.

Alternative Programs

The growing number and wider acceptance of PAPs can be viewed as paving the way for other programs that at one time would not have even been considered appropriate for the prison environment. Whether they are alternative, unique, enlightened, or all three, there are numerous prison programs that stand out from what is thought of as traditionally found inside prisons. Prisons, irrespective of some nuances, have remained starkly similar over the past 250 years. Emerging ideas threaten the status quo and attempt to bring more humanity to one of our most inhumane institutions. Non-traditional programs demonstrate the ability of change, however incremental, to occur even inside prison. As emerging ideas continue to take hold we see the continuation of the fight against the treatment-punishment dichotomy.

Under the guise of the growing environmental trend prisons across the country are taking steps to go green. In Washington, inmates work composting leftover food and coffee grinds, which creates a soil used to grow organic vegetables in the facility's small farm. Inmates also raise bees and recycle shoes that are turned into playground turf. At a facility in Oregon inmates recycle old prison uniforms into diaper bags distributed at women's shelters and dog beds for animal shelters. Bees are also being raised at this facility (Le, 2008).

Parolees can be found engaging in farm-like work in one of Chicago's economically depressed neighborhoods. The Sweet Beginnings program teaches ex-offenders the skills involved in beekeeping, landscaping, and food processing retail sales (A.P., 2006). The pay ranges from $7 to $9 an hour, none of the participants has returned to prison, and workers are employed during training; they engage in tasks such as painting hive boxes which does not require advanced skills. One participant, who has completed training despite being illiterate, said, "At one time, I'd see a bee and kill it. Now I've got a love for bees....They're sort of like people in the streets" (ibid). While working as a beekeeper, he is attending literacy classes and is being trained in other vocations.

In California, men attend the Marine Technology Training Center in Chino and are being taught skills that will allow them to work at off-shore and deep-sea jobs (Kandel, 2008). The jobs the graduates of the intensive diver's training program become eligible for jobs that pay excellent wages and provide the men with real opportunities to economically sustain themselves upon release. In North Carolina men can attend barber school where they can earn a certificate in a field considered recession-proof (Shaffer, 2008). The men are in class 8 hours each day, studying the history of barbering, skin texture and how to match a hair cut to the shape of a person's face (ibid).

There are also increasing numbers of programs that focus on the existential, internal experience of humanhood—irrespective of incarceration. In recent years, the positive effects of yoga have become accepted by the mainstream and its practice is no longer seen as hokey or something only hippies do. It should not be a surprise then that yoga is being brought inside prisons. In Oregon, women participate in a yoga program administered by a non-profit organization that teaches the practice at substance abuse clinics, homeless shelters, and prisons (Etter, 2006). For the women who participate yoga has taught them to react in a more peaceful manner. One participant reported the skills she has learned have taught her to better tolerate the stressful environment of prison and remain calm. Much like PAPs the programs are very popular and have waiting lists to participate. Having the volunteers give their time and effort demonstrates that the women have value and are worth investing in. People from the community "care about them and want to help them succeed. This is an example of community support; they are building bridges back into the community with this program" (ibid).

Lest anyone assume yoga is only for women, yoga classes are being taught at San Quentin State Prison, one of California's most notorious institutions (Portis, 2009). Classes are led in both the medium-security unit and the life-sentenced unit for 250 men in 18 classes—at no cost to the prison. Through the Insight Prison Project, founder James Fox teaches "mindfulness practices…meant to reconnect students with their bodies, and one of the common by-products of those practices is a new desire to take responsibility for past actions—in this case criminal behavior" (ibid). Fox has established Prison Yoga Project, a non-profit organization designed to bring yoga to prisons across the country. "For many inmates, the yoga class is the first opportunity they have had to develop emotional and spiritual awareness" (ibid). He is also at work on an instructional book so students can practice in other prisons and places where classes are not offered as well as once they are released. While reducing idleness in the prison yoga also instills skills that the participants can take with them back to the community and apply to their lives outside prison.

A meditation program for inmates was recorded in a 2007 documentary, "*The Dhamma Brothers*" which chronicles a 10-day retreat held in complete silence in a maximum-security prison near Birmingham, Alabama. The program was administered in an attempt to reduce the men's stress level and bring a sense of calm to the facility. The Director of Treatment for Alabama Department of Correction reported that the participants were better able to control their anger and the first group to complete the course reduced their disciplinary infractions by 20 percent (Joiner, 2007). Even after the official course was completed the men continued to meditate on their own. The program was suspended for four years when the prison chaplain expressed concern about the inmates practicing Buddhism which would threaten his own congregation (ibid). When the prison's administration changed the program was reinstated. For the meditation teacher "it was a miracle that this happened in the Deep South in one of the worst prisons in the country" (ibid.)

Transcendental Meditation (TM) is an approach to conscious mindfulness that has been taught around the world. Sitting in calm silence for 20 minutes twice each day has been found to bring about a range of treatment effects according to hundreds of scientific studies in hundreds of institutions in over 25 countries over the past 30 years (Anklesaria & Lary, 1992). A benefit of following this program is that it is standardized—it is (supposed to be) administered in the same way anywhere it is taught; this allows for evaluation at many sites. Also, there is a global network of practitioners that ex-offenders can connect with upon release from incarceration. The only cost of the program is the yoga mats (about $10-12 each) since the lessons are led by volunteers.

There are other programs that teach skills that may not necessarily lead to employment upon release, but do promote institutional behavior modification and contribute to a more positive prison environment. In Utah, men can teach and learn how to play musical instruments (Burger, 2007). What began with an inquiry from nearly 20 experienced musicians has expanded to nearly 400 who practice guitar, piano, sound mixing, song writing, and music theory and practice inside the prison's chapels on donated equipment (ibid). Monthly recitals and the peer-education of the skills bring inmates together. The inmate-manager of the program's equipment noted that "people may come to practice with a scowl, but they leave with a smile, and they bring that back to the cellblock" (ibid). The corrections lieutenant who runs the program with the prison's chaplain says this leads to a safer prison for both inmates and staff.

Religious programs are not new to prisons—the first penitentiaries were about penance and asking for forgiveness. As discussed, the only reading material available to inmates at Eastern State Penitentiary was the Bible. Perhaps the largest organized religion-based group was founded by Charles Colson who was incarcerated in 1974 for obstruction of justice related to the Watergate scandal. After serving months of a one to three year sentence, Colson was released. By 1976 he had formed Prison Fellowships, an organization that brought churches of all Christian denominations together for outreach to offenders and ex-offenders, as well as crime victims and their families. In 1979 he established Prison Fellowship International with over 100 chapters (http://www.pfm.org/Bio.asp?ID=43). It can be difficult to study the effectiveness of participating in a religious program while incarcerated given the wide variety of activities considered religious. While a full review of the research is beyond the scope of this project, many studies have found inmates who study religion have fewer disciplinary problems (O'Connor & Perreyclear, 2002) and are less likely to return to prison (Johnson, 2004). A contemporary concern, however, is inmates using prison as an opportunity to convert others into practicing radical or fundamentalist versions Islam (Smith, 2004).

Creative programs are certainly not limited to the U.S. In France, 194 inmates and 124 COs participated in 1,500 miles of the 2009 Tour de France (BBC News, 2009). The inmates had sentences ranging from five to 10 years. The inmates had to bicycle in a pack and were not permitted to sprint away from the pack. At the end of each day, each of the team's 17 stopovers occurred in a town with a prison or jail so they could be locked in for the night. Prison officials believe participation in the race instilled team work and helped increase inmates' self-esteem. Officials "want to show them that with some training, you can achieve your goals and start a new life" (BBC, 2009). According to one inmate, participating in the bicycle race is a unique opportunity to experience a change from the daily routine and monotony of life in prison. He even hoped that if the ride went smoothly and the members of the group followed all the disciplinary rules it could contribute to an earlier release on parole.

A country known for its role as the center of the 1700s era renaissance, Italy's sophisticated culture can even be seen in its approach to prison programming. Theater programs are being administered in nearly half of Italy's 205 prisons (Povoledo, 2009). The most renowned theater company is "the Compagnia della Fortezza, the theater company named after the Medici-era fortress that houses the Volterra jail" (ibid). Not simple plays or pieces from popular culture, once each year for the past 21 years the theater company produces a piece of "experimental, impossible theater" (ibid). The 2009 show "'Alice in Wonderland: A Theatrical Essay on the End of Civilization'—is loosely based on Lewis Carroll's masterwork, but the text weaves in soliloquies from other authors, in this case Shakespeare (predominantly Hamlet) but also Genet, Pinter, Chekhov, and Heiner Muller" (ibid). The men incarcerated in the maximum-security prison strut and pranced while "wearing outlandish costumes with oversize hats and wigs, and boots with 15-centimeter heels from a Milanese store that caters to drag queens" (ibid). For the theater director, who worked as an actor with avant-garde groups prior to working with the inmates, his motivation has never been "driven by notions of psychological assistance or therapy or social reform; it's always been about theater….It's not about giving the inmates an outlet or a recreational break. It's work" (ibid). According to the inmates who volunteer for the program, as both actors and behind the scenes, thy have gained self-respect as well as new-found interest in theater. There are inmates who have been transferred to the prison for the sole reason of participating in the program as well as inmates who have turned down early release to remain in the program. However, as in so many prisons in the U.S overcrowding and budgetary restraints leave the program in jeopardy. Also like in U.S. prisons the fate of this program is always at risk; while the director acknowledges "'It's all been a bit of a miracle'….he doesn't take anything for granted. 'Just one gust of wind and this could all topple,' he said. 'And that would be a real shame" (ibid).

Unique prison-based programming illustrates the range of creativity and thoughtfulness some are bringing behind prison walls. Connected to the criminal justice system, but outside prison walls, the work to help animals continues. "Pit bulls and Parolees," a show aired on the Animal Planet channel, is an ideal example of this trend. The show profiles Tia Maria Torres and her Villalobos Rescue Center, the country's largest rescue facility for pit bulls (www.animal.discovery.com/tv/pitbulls-and-parolees/about-the-show). Torres is nationally recognized for rehabilitating pit bulls. Matching her participants (parolees) to the clients (bit bulls) provides an added synergy to the work. She recognizes that "not many are willing to give a second chance to these parolees, but I have. And now the 'bad boys' of society meet the so-called 'bad boys' of the canine community, and boom! Just like that—they create magic together. They bring out a side of each other that's sweet, warm and unbelievably touching" (ibid). It is worth noting that at one time pit bulls, known as the "nanny dog" for their kind, gentle nature with children, were among the most popular breeds in America. Today they are viewed as threatening and associated with violence and criminals. For the average American, pit bulls are so closely tied to crime it seems they are inseparable. However the dogs reflect their owners and behave in ways that have been reinforced over time. Dogs trained to fight will fight, but they have to be exposed to those conditions—pit bulls are not born bad (as some would argue is the same as people). But the dogs are generally "viewed as unadoptable, with many shelters automatically deciding to put them down" (ibid). One of Torres' goals is to combat "stereotypes against both pit bulls and parolees" and to make people think twice before they judge this breed and the men at her ranch who help save them" (ibid).

Perhaps Michael Vick[1], the National Football League superstar, celebrity endorser for Nike, multi-millionaire who pleaded guilty to dog fighting conspiracy in federal court in December 2007 and later state dog fighting charges could have benefited from the science classes taught in the Boulder County Jail in Colorado. A professor of animal behavior and conservation biology teaches inmates in what has become the most popular class. Professor Bekoff believes "one reason the course is so popular is that many prisoners find it easier to connect with animals than with people....They trust and empathize with animals in ways they don't with humans" (Bekoff, 2009, p. 20). Bekoff has found many inmates have a false sense of the violence between animals hunting their prey; he emphasizes "there is also a lot of cooperation, empathy, and compassion" in the animal kingdom (ibid). Often many inmates come from dangerous streets to live in jail, another potentially violent environment, so he uses applicable examples such as teaching how wolves, which live in packs, learn to co-exist and help each other. Bekoff has found that "science and humane education help the inmates connect with values that they otherwise would not have" (p. 21). The attitudes necessary for humanity are also taught to younger people in order to prevent incidences of animal abuse. Through the Humane Education Ambassador Readers program, volunteers read choices from "a carefully selected list of picture books about people and animals. The goal is to help children develop the empathy for other creatures that prevents animal cruelty and promotes responsible care of pets" (Lombardi, 2009). As the Vick case tragically demonstrates, a spectrum of people can benefit from being exposed to such ideas[2].

Also occurring outside prison walls are unique alternatives to prison. One such program is Changing Lives Through Literature (CLTL). The program was established in 1981 in Massachusetts but is being used in states including Texas, a place not known for its enlightened approach to criminal justice. Rather than prison, offenders are sentenced to probation and a condition of that probation is that they join a reading group. A study of the first cohort of program graduates found a 19% rate of reoffending compared to 42% of people who did not go through the program (Barker, 2010). While literacy is often a problem among the population most likely to go to prison, those with low levels of reading skills can still participate in the program and be assigned to a group comprised of people with similar abilities and read short stories rather than novels, or attend a group where passages of a novel are read aloud and then discussed. The single-sex groups are comprised of up to 30 people and led by an academic, a probation officer, and often another criminal justice representative such as a judge. The books are chosen to reflect the issues some of the offenders may be facing. For example, a group reading John Stuart Mill's *On Liberty* may examine topics including power, freedom, and harm. A group reading Ernest Hemingway's *The Old Man and the Sea* can explore the fisherman's persistence despite facing numerous obstacles. The program is now being expanded to England where reading groups will take place both inside and outside prison.

Other Roles for Dogs Inside Prisons

An inevitable outcome of the increasing numbers of working canines is the increase in the number of dogs that will be used for work inside prisons. One evolving trend that needs additional study is the use of canines by DOCs to detect contraband. Supplementing mechanical devices used to identify metal weapons and physical searches to find smuggled illegal substances, DOCs are increasingly relying on canines to discover cell phones and tobacco which are currently the most popular items being brought inside (Morse, 2008). The dogs are trained to detect the smell of the phone's lithium battery which has a unique smell. In the follow-up survey, while not specifically asked, four state DOCs noted they keep a cadre of canines for use as detection tools. Even shelter dogs have been trained for this type of work. The cell phone trade inside prisons has been referred to as "one of the most severe security issues" for prisons and jails across the United States (Thompson, 2009, April 14). Canines are also being trained to detect tobacco—contraband in the ever-growing number of facilities that have prohibited smoking and other tobacco products.

Cell phones are a particularly dangerous type of contraband for a number of reasons. Inmates can use phones to "run criminal enterprises, threaten witnesses and warn fellow inmates about the movements of correctional officers" (Morse, 2008, p. B01). Gang members can continue to manage drug dealing on the street or could order a contract killing from inside prison. As with all contraband phones are smuggled in by visitors, contractors working inside the prison, and prison staff. The phones are very valuable and can be sold between inmates for hundreds of dollars. And as phones continue to get smaller it becomes easier to hide them. In Virginia dogs have found phones stuck in jars of peanut butter as well as phones wrapped in plastic and stored in toilets. A variety of breeds can be trained to detect phones. In Maryland, the first dog trained was a springer spaniel who already worked at the facility detecting illegal drugs; the state also has several Belgian malinois. In a demonstration that tested the dogs in several different scenarios, they only once failed to detect the phone within 30 seconds (Morse, 2008).

The practice is international. The Prison Service of England has drug and phone detection dogs at every major prison in the country. The dogs are even able to detect if a person has come into contact with illegal drugs before the visit. Prison employees are subject to being searched, or sniffed, as well as visitors ("Jail Dog Boost," 2007). Ireland also has a detection dog and handler team at each of the prisons ("Dogs Unleashed," 2008). Before the dog teams were stationed at each prison there was great resistance by the inmates (Cunningham, 2007a). At least three dogs have had hits placed on them by inmates who have circulated pictures of the dogs to visitors (ibid). In one jail there was a riot protesting the hiring of a dog. Overall, prison visits are down more than 30% at facilities with dog teams (ibid). The record number of seizures has angered inmates. In some facilities, handlers have been threatened not to confiscate anymore phones (Cunningham, 2007b). While the dogs are kept in a secure area when not working, handlers are vulnerable when not working and on public streets. In a greatly embarrassing incident for prison officials, an inmate called into a radio show from inside one facility (ibid). Clearly, once in a while, a dog is going to miss, but visitors can be clever in their attempts to smuggle in contraband. A number of prisons both in the U.S. and other countries have reported "parents knocking babies on to the floor to cause a distraction when the drug dogs come through" (Norman, 2007, p. 24).

Scotland has also adopted the dog sniffing method as their prison population grows to unprecedented levels (Howie, 2008). Drugs have become an increasing problem inside facilities as they are smuggled in more with ingenuity. Scotland officials have found drugs hidden in orange and banana peels which look like trash, thrown on to prison grounds. A dead bird was also thrown in over the perimeter fence stuffed with drugs (ibid). At another facility where damaged bicycle frames were donated to be refurbished drugs were found inside bicycle frames and tires (Davidson, 2008). Even SIM cards that have been smuggled in can be used to make trades between inmates. The problem goes beyond Euro-America and is a growing challenge for Chinese prison officials as well (Chan, 2007). Dogs are being used to detect cigarettes, drugs, cell phones, and even home-brewed hooch or alcohol inmates make by fermenting fruit and rice (ibid). Just like here, China uses springer spaniels, Labrador retrievers, and beagles. The dogs are donated by the public, purchased from overseas, and rescued from shelters (ibid).

Since 1986, Idaho has employed a "sentry dog program" that has dozens of large, aggressive dogs patrolling the perimeter of the prison between an inner and outer-most fences (Boone, 2009). While the dogs are rescued from shelters where they would be put down for their aggressive nature, they are not socialized as in traditional PAPs. According to one prison official, "those same instincts that make them a bad pet make them good sentries" (quoted in Boone, 2009). Officials cite the benefits of the dogs: they are cheaper than human officers, more accurate than technology that can be evaded, and better than human officers in the dark or fog. They believe the dogs have a deterrent effect since no one has escaped from the prison since 1986, or even tried since the early 1990s (ibid). While no inmates have been injured, unsecured dogs have bitten dog handlers. Dogs have not been a preferred tool used by law enforcement to control people since the civil rights era when the police and demonstrators engaged in public and violent confrontations. The dogs became associated with racist and excessive police tactics (ibid).

The work of canines in prisons extends beyond searching perimeters and detecting contraband. An unfortunate trend of dogs in prisons has recently emerged. While most of us have seen the now all too familiar photographs of inmates at Abu Ghraib being threatened by large barking dogs, it seems the Americans imported the practice. Dogs are used to scare and even bite inmates at prisons in five states: Connecticut, Delaware, Iowa, South Dakota, and Utah. Both Arizona and Massachusetts prohibited the practice in 2006 (Human Rights Watch,

2006). Dogs are used primarily for cell extractions—removing an uncooperative inmate from a prison cell. The type of dogs used for cell extractions are often German Shepherds or the similarly-looking Belgian Malinois—both are large breeds that usually weigh more than sixty pounds and stand at least two feet high. The dogs are trained to apprehend or bite and release on command (ibid).

The dog's barking upon arrival at the cell is supposed to intimidate the inmate to comply with the order to "cuff up" or allow himself to be cuffed by turning his back to the cell door and getting on his knees. The order allows staff members to enter the cell with more assurance of their safety. If there is still no compliance the cell door is opened and the handler will have the leashed and pulling dog enter the cell. The dog is supposed to remain leashed at all times, but there have been reports of dogs being let loose on inmates in their cells (Human Rights Watch, 2006). According to an Iowa corrections official, "[The dogs are] taught a deep—a full-mouth bite. The dog opens his mouth real wide and gets as much as [he can] whether it's a thigh or whatever in his mouth" (quoted in Human Rights Watch, 2006, p. 5-6). Arizona had a different procedure when using dogs in cell extractions. There the dog would enter the cell, bite down on the inmate, and then the dog handler would pull both the dog, with the inmate still in his mouth, out of the cell.

The dogs are supposed to be used only when all other options, including verbal and chemical methods (i.e., smoke bombs or other exploding devices), have been exhausted. Corrections officials who support the use of dogs in cell extractions say the dogs prevent injury to staff and are cheaper than more advanced technology. They also report not being aware of anyone receiving serious injury such as losing a finger or ear. Injuries are usually limited to puncture wounds, unless the inmate attempts to pull away from the dog which can cause tearing to the skin (ibid). Not all corrections officials approve of the methods, however. Some urge use of the safest method—simply waiting out the inmate until he complies with orders. According to the Human Rights Watch report, "Cruel and Degrading: The Use of Dogs for Cell Extractions in U.S. Prisons" (2006), the United States is the only country known to allow the use of dogs for this purpose which continues to remain a relatively well-kept secret.

Conclusion

There are countless programs being administered ad-hoc inside prisons today. Unfortunately, there is no comprehensive network for administrators and volunteers who lead similar programs. Knowing what others are doing and what may or may not have worked for them could increase program effectiveness and save time and resources by eliminating the need to try tactics that have not been found to be successful. While enlightened and hopeful, these grassroots efforts have been criticized for their lack of consistency.

There are academic researchers who argue programs like the ones described above, including PAPs, are examples of "correctional quackery" (Latessa, Cullen, & Gendreau, 2002, p. 43). They define quackery as any treatment that is not based on what we know about the causes of criminality and past evidence of the approaches that have been found to change behavior. Among the list of 16 "questionable theories of crime" the authors identify are:

> "Offenders need to get back to nature" theory.
> "Offenders lack discipline" theory.
> "Offenders have low self-esteem" theory.
> "Offenders need to have a pet in prison" theory.
> "Offenders need a better diet and haircut" theory.
> "Offenders (females) need to learn how to put on makeup and dress better" theory.
> "Offenders (males) need to get in touch with their feminine side" theory.

However, the authors deliberately simplify PAPs and other alternative programs—and they are programs, not theories. A theory is an explanation for a phenomenon, not an experience or a treatment. The programs are dismissed for being grounded in a "common sense" approach and are criticized for not having a greater impact on recidivism (Gendreau, Smith, & Theriault, 2009). But we know recidivism is a complex phenomenon and requires more than the skills or resources a person can acquire from any one treatment. To out-right dismiss PAPs as useless is short-sighted and rigid. No one is saying a PAP is a total cure for all of an inmate's problems, but instead contains mechanisms that can help offenders. Programs have goals and can be implemented to achieve outcomes other than recidivism. Prison-based animal programs can effectively create safer living and working conditions by exerting institutional control. Rather than risk losing privileges such as participating in the program inmates are more likely to stay out of trouble while incarcerated, which as discussed above can be an indication of criminal desistance. In addition many PAPs also lead to social benefits outside the prison walls. Those who point fingers at any treatment that does not completely transform a person can easily publish academic research articles about the program's failure; based on unrealistically sweeping standards nothing will ever work. Every treatment program that has ever been administered inside prison has started as a so-called alternative program. Giving inmates access to only the Bible, having inmates live in silence, treating their mental illnesses, literacy classes, and instituting work furloughs began as new and untested programs at one point. In fact prison itself has been one big experiment (perpetrated on those we care least about). Punishment began as biblical-like revenge. Then it became public and corporal in response to the demons that possessed you. We tried humiliation when we lived in small villages where everyone knew each other and religious purity was paramount. We did not separate men from women and children from adults when we started to lock people in buildings for their crimes. People with mental illness were neither acknowledged nor medically treated. Today we have the hodgepodge, or what some might call mess, we created over the course of these hundreds of years.

So what does work? Some of us believe some improvement is better than none (and isn't it?). We all have to start somewhere and be newly experiencing something—the day one, if you will—be it sobriety, managing your anger, acting with greater compassion towards others, or believing you can shake off that inmate label. People and the reasons they end up in prison are complex, therefore it is only logical to believe that any effort designed to help people would also need to be multi-faceted. Participating in a PAP may affect one or two areas of a person's life while incarcerated, and another program affects additional so-called criminogenic characteristic. It is the totality of the prison experience that shapes the person we release back into society. And if the prison experience can include participating in a PAP then we have an opportunity to positively influence people before they return to society.

Prison-based animal programs appear to be a leader in the growing trend of prison administrators accepting new and innovative programs despite their inconsistency with traditional notions of punishment that make penology "an exercise in separation, categorization, exclusion, isolation, and reification" (Arrigo & Milovanovic, 2009, p. 9). The programs build upon evolving ideas in criminology that question what has been practiced on the people inside prison; while often forgotten, the 2.3 million people behind bars are still human beings. One promising approach that builds on the ideas of doing good and desistance is the re-examination of "conceptions not of who or what offenders are judged to be, but on who or what people can become given the right conditions" (Halsey, 2010, p. 368). The idea really is at the core of penal reform for many of us. I hope PAPs can be part of the (hopefully) coming revolution in penology—one that recognizes that "being human means to make a difference in/to the world, to act on it, to interact with others and together to transform the environment and ourselves;...it is becoming (mutating, evolving, transforming) and not merely existing" (Arrigo & Milovanovic, 2009, p. 28).

The point of this work has been to illustrate that PAPs, rooted in a long and complicated history of prison programing, have already shown great potential but their full capability is yet to be known. The programs' praxis has been developed at a significantly faster rate than theoretical explanations—which are overdue. However, the confines of prisons make research extremely difficult. Also many people who study criminology and criminal justice as well as other members of the public do not believe in the benefits that can come from human-animal interactions—despite supporting research. As a result, there are multiple forces working against the further development of PAPs. But as researchers who have argued for the intelligence and sentience of animals are increasingly being validated, I have hope that so too will PAPs. The only way to encourage the necessary change is to begin with a "flash of light, a poetic spark, a fleeting epiphany, a coupling moment" (Arrigo & Milovanovic, 2009, p. xix) that challenges the machine that is the criminal justice system which is comprised of an "ensemble of categories, discourses, practices, and institutions concerned with enforcement of the sociocultural order" (p. 11). Reform is clearly long overdue.

Chapter 6 Endnotes

1. The case of Michael Vick reinforces both enforces stereotypes about pit bulls as well as people associated with the dogs. His farm in Virginia was the headquarters of "Bad Newz Kennels," an organization owned by him and two co-defendants which hosted dog fights and participated in a multi-state circuit. His story encompasses a number of this book's themes. But Michael Vick also creates a moral dilemma for many. If we want a more humane and less punitive criminal justice system then we would have to offer Vick the chance to provide restitution and make amends. But many people want increased punishments for crimes against non-human animals. Some of us want both and so our ideas about redemption and forgiveness for vile acts get tested. However, a discussion of the incongruence between these stances raises points that are beyond the scope of this book.

2. Just across the line of the law there is another group of tough guys working to rescue neglected and abused animals. Rescue Ink, a Long Island, New York-based organization demonstrates the range of people involved in animal issues. Upon first sight the members of the group may raise eyebrows, similar to initial ideas of stereotypical big, mean inmates caring for, loving and becoming emotionally attached to animals. The men of Rescue Ink are a "group

of tattooed motorcycle-riding tough guys on a mission to save animals in danger" (www.rescueink.org/media). In another parallel to PAPs, "some have violent and turbulent pasts, complete with run-ins with the law, but all are seeking redemption, and solace in their mission to save animals from human abuse" (ibid). Averaging 100 calls each week these men, among them a former NYPD detective, a club bouncer, and a security guard "confront alleged animal abusers, rescue fighting dogs, investigate stolen animals and (firmly) encourage owners to give up their pets if it is in the best interest of the animals" (ibid). Their unique "in your face" approach to fighting animal abuse and neglect has spawned their own book and TV show on the National Geographic Channel.

With an out of control problem of animal abuse and neglect plaguing this country, no tactic is off limits; for the members of Rescue Ink their only limitation is remaining within the bounds of the law. Their zero tolerance approach to animal abuse and neglect drives them "to convince people to do the right thing...[and] we can be very convincing, we'll even buy animals if that's what it takes to get them away from abusers" (ibid). Today they have a national network of people affiliated with the group who support the mission. Recognizing that policy change is necessary to support the grass roots efforts of everyone involved in animal rescue their animal advocates program members contact elected officials at the local, state, and federal levels to fighting stronger protection laws and additional funding for rescue organizations.

7

The Future of Animals in Prison

So we must ask ourselves what can benefit prison inmates both during and after their time spent incarcerated. What is good for society? And what, dare I ask, is beneficial for animals? Is there one answer common to each of these questions? I believe there is: prison-based animal programs. Underlying these tangible benefits is the United States' history of social, economic, and political racial segregation that sinisterly parallels our treatment of animals. There is a synergy created when one examines the similarities between prison inmates and animals, particularly stray and abandoned animals. Both groups are unwanted by society and are put in places (prisons and shelters, respectively) where they are contained until deemed worthy of release by society, or put to death. Neither the overpopulation of unwanted animals nor the mass incarceration of disproportionately poor men of color is an issue of priority to most people. Indeed, people who are concerned about animals are often told by cynics to worry more about all the humans, generally of their own country, who suffer. (There was a backlash to the "Save the Whales" bumper sticker campaign a number of years ago when cars with "Save the Humans" stickers began appearing.) "Oh, you're an animal person," is a common way to dismiss those who are concerned about the welfare of non-human beings. People involved with issues of incarceration are often derided as "inmate lovers." After all, most argue, prisoners did something terrible and deserve to be incarcerated not protected.

Prison-based animal programs are generally considered volunteer work and not part of the rehabilitative services provided by a prison facility. Yet the programs clearly have rehabilitative potential. There has been no discussion by practitioners or researchers regarding whether the current classification as volunteer work is most appropriate. The role of PAPs within the workings of prisons has not been sufficiently determined. Recommendations about policy are therefore premature given the lack of agreement about where PAPs fit within contemporary notions of justice and punishment and their relatively to other prison programs. Prison-based animal programs seem to reflect what Shapland (2003) refers to as the "cafeteria tendency in sentencing (a bit of retribution, a bit of rehabilitation and perhaps a scoop of reparation)" (p. 201). The programs address a hybrid of reasons for punishment (Hannah-Moffat, 2005).

Participation may be an example of what Johnson (2002) conceptualizes as "mature coping," inside prison. It may be that PAPs can serve as part of the foundation necessary for the field's contemporary ideas of desistance and transformation as described by Maruna (2001) and Sampson and Laub (1993). Indeed, participation appears to alter criminal trajectories, at least for the current and former participants of the two programs studied here. The notion of "animal capital" has been conceptualized as having the resources to develop a "meaningful, non-exploitive companionship with animals" (Irvine, 2004, p. 66). The resources Irvine identifies include "knowledge about behavior, nutrition, health, history, breed characteristics, training, and the variety of things that can enrich animals' lives.… [and] a rapport with animals based on an active interest in their emotions, communication, and cognition" (ibid). It may be that animal capital, as a type of social capital, can influence desistance over the life time. Or having "a qualitatively different kind of relationship with animals" (p. 67) may contribute to the redemption script described by Maruna (2001) and discussed above.

The fast-paced growth of PAPs demands further empirical investigation of these programs. A true experimental research design may be able to connect pre- and post-program differences to PAP participation. Longitudinal studies are needed to determine the long-term effects PAPs may have on recidivism and future offender behavior. Treatment effects also need to be reliably identified through multiple studies of a variety of program models. Prison-based animal programs that work with animals other than dogs should be systematically studied for comparison to dog programs. Industrial farm programs probably do not have the same types of effects as associated with more traditional PAPs. As mentioned above, livestock care/farm programs should be studied independently from other PAPs. Another question is whether facilities with PAPs differ systematically from facilities that do not. For example, do prisons with the programs offer more treatment or re-entry or vocational programs than others?

Future research should also be concerned with questions about how to best match participants with programs; that is, would a certain model of PAP be more effective with some populations than others? Perhaps working with animals that participants can identify with would result in stronger effects. Might battered women particularly identify with abused dogs and produce additional effects that would not be seen if participating in, for example, a livestock care/farm program? Feral cats or wild horses which require patience and control when working with might reach troubled youth better than, for example, retired racehorses. The timing of a PAP intervention, whether as a youth or an adult, should also be examined for varying levels of effectiveness.

Anecdotal evidence has found that even the prospect of participating in PAPs can affect institutional behavior. Future research could examine why applicants are willing to change their behavior and meet various criteria including remaining misconduct-free or completing other programs for the opportunity to participate in PAPs. What does the possibility of participation hold for these individuals?

Prison-based animal programs may also be found to promote change on a philosophical level for participants. Participation can encourage increased awareness of animals as sentient beings whose lives have value, like humans. Discussions of free-will and consciousness could spark personal reflection that could be formally incorporated into the program through reflection papers or group sessions.

It is important to note that PAPs are not without their critics. Analyzed through the lens of Foucault's *Discipline and Punish: The Birth of the Prison* (1975), PAPs not only train inmates to be docile bodies but non-human animals as well. The very strengths and benefits of PAPs discussed throughout this book only increase the power of the prison to control or discipline inmates. Having control over inmates, the first priority of a prison, is made all the easier under the guise of sweet, innocent animal programs. Prison-based animal programs empower the state in what some might consider an insidious manner.

Perhaps ironically, it is the growing demand for dogs to work with criminal justice agencies that has helped drive some of the growth in the dog-training industry[1]. While many participants reported feeling positively about being able to make a contribution to society, the government's willingness to accept an incarcerated person's help in training an explosive-detecting dog but not allow him or her to have a government job when released may seem contradictory to some. Programs involving inmates and animals may also send a message to the public that being incarcerated is enjoyable or easy; there is danger in making prison cages appear golden. Criticism about the programs does not stem only from the inmate empowerment perspective but from the victims rights perspective as well.

Some oppose PAPs on the grounds that it is too rewarding for the participants; incarcerated people should never experience happiness or pleasure according to this line of thinking. However this outlook is clearly short-sighted and vengeful. Prison-based animal programs are administered to people whose punishment is to be deprived of their liberty and segregated from society; PAPs do not violate these conditions. Caring for a dog inside prison does not restore freedom or return the participants to their friends and family. In helping to relieve the stress of the prison environment, including the physical and emotional isolation, participation in a PAP can open unique pathways to change.

We know that the cycle of violence often predicts that those who are treated badly will go on to treat others badly. Excessive force, the use of dogs for cell extractions, and extreme overcrowding are just some of the conditions creating a dangerous, but more importantly violent and detrimental, environment inside prisons. Prisons do not work—they never have. Over the course of the hundreds of years that we have had prisons in this country we have continued to have crime. Nearly two-thirds of all inmates are released back into society each year and their experiences inside shape who they become.

There is also criticism of the use of service animals in general on physical grounds. Service animals are isolated from others of their kind, are confined in involuntary work, and prevented from living as they naturally would. At the same time an increasing variety of animals are being used to assist people with an increasing variety of disabilities. The University of Denver recently established the Institute for Human-Animal Connection where researchers are studying how cats can help war veterans with Post-Traumatic Stress Disorder (Kollus, 2009).

Unlike American media, we can see criticism of the programs in foreign press that often includes reaction from victims' advocacy groups and those who oppose the programs. In Ireland, an unnamed prison official was angry that two notorious offenders, nicknamed the Scissor Sisters because they dismembered their victims, had access to the Labradors brought in through a visitation program. He "raged: 'The whole thing is a joke, the prison is a holiday camp....When the inmates aren't sunbathing or whooping it up they are playing with their pets" (quoted in Cotter and O'Shea, 2008). Clearly the official's irritation caused him to exaggerate the program—the dogs brought in for visits were not the women's pets. From my own experience in America, there is no sunbathing at maximum-security prisons. In England, a prison instituted a program that gave inmates the opportunity to care for animals so as to reduce the twice per week suicides. A representative of the Victims of Crime Trust was asked for his reaction to the program. He "blasted: This is nonsense. When people go to prison they forfeit rights and having cats and dogs makes a mockery of the whole system" (quoted in Nelson, 2007). In New Zealand, the Corrections Department was considering instituting a service dog training program. A professor of Sociology from Canterbury University called the program impractical. "'There is a lack of appropriate people in New Zealand's prisons,' he said. You'd have to hand-pick your trainers. You might get one or two dogs out of it. The dog might get out into the real world and be completely bamboozled'" (quoted in Chisholm, 2007). Clearly this professor was not familiar with the research literature on PAPs. There is always an application process potential participants must undergo. There is also ample evidence that the lure of the program will encourage inmates to reform their behavior for the chance to participate and then remain trouble-free to remain in the program.

No one has investigated why the popular media coverage of domestic PAPs does not include naysayers. Perhaps the programs' demonstrated success here has prevented non-supporters from coming forward. We know correction officer unions have presented roadblocks and victims' rights groups might have reason to complain as noted in the foreign press, but it is hard to criticize programs that help meet the need for assistance canines for returning war veterans. Our national need for assistance dogs for people with disabilities was overwhelming before the war, now the demands are even more difficult to fill. No one can deny prison inmates have the time to devote to the very precise work required to train these dogs. And the dogs that come out of prison programs have been shown to be as well and better trained than those trained in homes by outside volunteers who have less time to spend on the dogs' important initial instruction that provides the foundation for their advanced training. Programs that assist in making abandoned animals more adoptable are also providing a desperately needed community service. The restitution the inmates' participation represents is simply undeniable.

In this book, I have highlighted a key contemporary development in prison programming. I have also pointed out the empirical and possible theoretical basis for giving these programs further serious consideration. In doing so, I have examined the evolution of prisons, reviewed the historical development of prison programming, and considered the origins of PAPs. The book does not aim to be conclusive, but rather to be persuasive that these programs deserve genuine consideration for their multi-dimensional potential to benefit. Many consider imprisonment to be a form of death, civil death, but PAPs are an example of how incarcerated people can continue to grow, heal, and transform even while hidden behind the walls where society has placed them.

Conclusion

Some cynics would refer to dogs and prison inmates as throw-away populations. Be sure, it is not a coincidence that the populations these programs bring together— (sometimes) unwanted animals and society's least desirable people—have the potential to greatly benefit each other. Both groups are discarded by a society that cares not what happens to them and prefers they be kept out of sight. But homeless animals and prison inmates are members of our society, a society some would argue created them and hiding and ignoring them has neither aided neither nor society.

And on a final note about punishment, we need to pay attention to preventing crime, not simply reacting to it. Our system is focused on the back-end, so to speak; we need to heavily invest in the front-end and bring to an end the socioeconomic conditions that perpetuate crime and feed the highly flawed punishment machine. We need to invest in our nation's children, our schools and our inner cities. People need jobs that provide livable wages. Community-based interventions are a better investment than prisons; harm-reduction programs are the better way to combat substance misuse, not incarceration, and definitely not by waging a war on drugs which is really just our government at war with its citizens (and affecting and targeting certain groups of people, but that is another book). We have gotten nowhere with decades of misguided criminal justice policy. If the issue was medicine and not crime and a medical treatment being used had levels of failure similar to those of the criminal justice system we would immediately stop the use of that response to the disease. The extent of the lack of plain common sense when it comes to our criminal justice system is astounding— overwhelming, really. We are desperately overdue for sound reason and judgment to drive the future of this country's criminal justice system. Not a small undertaking, it may, in fact, take a revolution in penology (see Arrigo & Milovanovic, 2009).

Charles Siebert, author of *The Wauchula Woods Accord: Toward a New Understanding of Animals* summarizes (to the extent this topic can be summed up) what I have tried to get across in this book:

> The degree to which we humans will finally stop abusing other creatures and, for that matter, one another, will ultimately be measured

by the degree to which we come to understand how integral a part of us all other creatures actually are (p. 80).

This book begins with several quotations that summarize the sentiments described above. One of the characteristics of a noted quotation is that it stands the test of time and remains true over decades and perhaps hundreds of years. Another characteristic is the ability of a limited number of words to succinctly capture human nature. In his 1862 novel, *The House of the Dead*, the great Russian writer Fyodor Dostoevsky said, "The degree of civilization in a society can be judged by entering its prisons." He was describing the conditions in a remote Siberian labor camp where prisoners were dying of tuberculosis, frostbite, and exhaustion. I have spent countless hours inside a number of American prisons; I have read inmate and employee ethnographies of their own experiences; I have viewed and read Nazi concentration camp survivors' accounts, and I have seen pictures from Abu Ghraib and Camp X-Ray in Cuba. Although he was writing in the middle of the 19th century his words stand true today. It is believed that in discussing the morality of vegetarianism in the 1930's Mahatma Gandhi said, "The greatness of a nation and its moral progress can be judged by the way its animals are treated" (http://www.ivu.org/history/gandhi/). In the 1780's Immanuel Kant's essay on man's duties toward animals he wrote, "He who is cruel to animals becomes hard also in his dealings with men. We can judge the heart of a man by his treatment of animals." Today we have research that verifies the link between animal abuse and violence toward people (see Hensley and Tallichet, 2009; Petersen and Farrington, 2007; Schlesinger, 2001). Between 1883 and 1885 the German Philosopher Friedrich Nietzsche wrote *Thus Spoke Zarathustra: A Book for All and None*, a novel about philosophy and morality. In it he included, "Man is the cruelest animal." Enough said.

Bibliography

About pit bulls and parolees. Retrieved December 22, 2009 from http: //animal.discovery.com/tv/pitbulls-and-paolees/about-the-show.

Adams, J. (2007). *Wounds of returning: Race, memory, and property on the post-slavery plantation.* Chapel Hill, N.C.: The University of North Carolina Press.

Alger, J., &Alger, S. (1997). Beyond Mead: Symbolic interaction between humans and felines, *Society and Animals, 5, 1,* 65-81.

American Wild Horse Preservation Campaign. (n.d.). A Study in Mismanagement. July 28, 2009 from http://www.wildhorsepreserv ation.com/resources/study.html). Retrieved July 28, 2009.

Andrews, D. A. (1995). The psychology of criminal conduct and effective treatment. In J. McGuire (Ed.), *What works: Reducing re-offending,* (pp. 35-62). Chichester, England: Wiley.

Andrews, D. A., & Bonta, J. (2003). *The psychology of criminal conduct* (3rd ed.). Cincinnati, OH: Anderson.

Angola: The Farm. (1998). Directors/Producers Jonathan Stack, Liz Garbus. Gabriel Films.

Anklesaria, F., & Lary, S. (1992). A new approach to offender rehabilitation: Maharishi's intergraded system of rehabilitation. *Journal of Correctional Education, 43, 1,* 6-13.

Arkow, P. (1998). *Pet Therapy: A Study and Resource Guide for the Use of Companion Animals in Selected Therapies,* (8th ed.). Stratford, NJ: Author.

Arluke, A. (2011). How animal assisted activities help at-risk and incarcerated children and young adults, *Journal of Social Issues,* forthcoming.

Arrigo, B. (2009). *Revolution in penology: Rethinking the society of captives.* Lanham, MD: Rowman & Littlefield.

Baker, A. (2008, Feb. 2). New operation to put heavily armed officers in subway. *The New York Times.*

Barker, A. (2010, July 21). Novel approach: reading courses as an alternative to prison. *The Guardian.* Retrieved July 28, 2010 http://guardian.co.uk /society/2010/jul/21/texas-offenders-reading-courses.

Barry, D. (2010, August 10). In the rearview mirror, Oklahoma and death row. *The New York Times.* Retrieved August 11, 2010 from http://www .nytimes.com/2010/08/11/us/11land.html.

Batson, K., McCabe, B., Baun, M., & Wilson, C. (1998). The effect of a therapy dog on socialization and physiological indicators of stress in persons diagnosed with Alzheimer's disease. In C. Wilson and D. Turner (Eds.), *Companion Animals in Human Health,* (pp. 203-215). Thousand Oaks, CA: Sage.

Baun, M., & McCabe, B. (2000). The role animals play in enhancing quality of life for the elderly. In A. Fine (Ed.), *Handbook on Animal-Assisted*

Therapy: Theoretical Foundations and Guidelines for Practice, (pp.237-251). San Diego, CA: Academic Press.

Bazemore, G. (1998). Restorative justice and earned redemption: Communities, victims, and offender reintegration. *American Behavioral Scientist, 41,* 768-813.

BBC News. (2009, June 4). Penal tour de France pedals off. Retrieved June 15, 2009 from http://news.bbc.co.uk.go/pr/fr/-/2/hi/europe/8082354.stm.

Beck, A., & Katcher, A. (2003). Future directions in human-animal bond research. *American Behavioral Scientist, 47,* 79-93.

Beck, A., & Katcher, A. (1996). *Between Pets and People: The Importance of Animal Companionship.* W. Lafayette, IN: Purdue University Press.

Becker, M. (2002). *The Healing Power of Pets.* NY: Hyperion.

Beckett, K. (1997). *Making Crime Pay: Law and Order in Contemporary American Politics.* NY: Oxford University Press.

Bekoff, M. (2009, March 21). Jailhouse study is time well spent. *New Scientist,* p. 20-21.

Berger, J. (2008, June 1). Prison puppies. The New York Times, p.1. New Jersey Weekly Desk.

Bertuca, T. (2005). Inmates rehabilitate toys at Angola. Retrieved June 7, 2005 from www.corrections.com.

Blackmon, D. (2008*). Slavery by Another Name: The Re-enslavement of Black Americans from the Civil War to World War II.* NY, NY: Doubleday.

Bogdan, R., & Taylor, S. (1989). Relationships with severely disabled people: The social construction of humanness, *Social Problems, 36,* 135-148.

Bogues, A. (2007, July 18). Jail or death? Jail wins for dogs. St. Petersburg Times (Florida).

Boone, R. (2009, March 29). Prison employs dangerous dogs. Retrieved July 14, 2009 from www.philly.com/philly/hp/news_update/20090329 _Prison_employs_dangerous_ddogs.html.

Bosworth, M. (2002). *The U.S. federal prison system.* CA: Sage.

Braithwaite, J. (2005). Between proportionality and impunity: Confrontation, truth, prevention. [The American Society of Criminology 2004 Sutherland Address.] *Criminology, 43,* 283-305.

Braithwaite, J. (1989). *Crime, Shame and Reintegration.* NY, NY: Cambridge University Press.

Brasic, J. (1998). Pets and health. *Psychological Reports, 83,* 1011-1024.

Brower, C. (2004). The Lives of animals, the lives of prisoners, and the revelations of Abu Ghraib. *Vanderbilt Journal of Transnational Law, 37,* 1353-1388.

Brown, S., & Katcher, A. (2001). Pet attachment and dissociation. *Society & Animals, 9, 25-42.*

Bureau of Land Management. (2009, July 27). What we do. Retrieved July 28, 2009 from http://www.blm.gov/wo/st/en/prog/wild_horse_and_burro /What_We_Do.html.

Burger, D. (2007, Dec 28). Prison music school: Inmates are finding outlet is creating tones and tunes, *The Salt lake Tribune.* Retrieved January 9, 2008 from www.sltrib.com/news.

Burton-Rose, D. (1998, May/June). 'Volunteer' prison labor. Originally appeared in Dollars and Sense Magazine. Retrieved July 1, 2009 from www.monitor.net/monitor/9807a/copyright/prisonvolunteer.html.

Butterfield, F. (1995, July 16). Idle hands within the devil's own playground. The New York Times (Week in Review; The Nation).

Cable, G. W. (1885). *The Silent South*. NY, NY: Scribner's.

Center for the Interaction of Animals and Society (CIAS) located at the University of Pennsylvania's School of Veterinary Medicine (www .research.vet.upenn.edu/cias/Home/tabid/1889/Default.aspx)

Chan, K. (2007, Oct. 19). Sniffer dogs to put prisoners on hold. South China Morning Post. p. 1.

Chisholm, M. (2007, Sept. 25). Prisoners may help train mobility dogs. The Dominion Post (Wellington, New Zealand). p. 3.

Christianson, S. (1998). *With liberty for some: 500 years of imprisonment in America*. Boston: Northeastern University Press.

Christie, N. (2000). *Crime control as industry*, 3rd ed. NY: Routledge.

Chisolm, M. (2007, Sept. 25). Prisoners may help train mobility dogs. The Dominion Post (Wellington, New Zealand), p. 3.

Connelley, W., Conklin, N., & Gordon, R. (1993). Can prison farming be profitable? The case of Arizona Correctional Industries, *Agribusiness, 9*, 257-279.

Conniff, K., Scarlett, J., Goodman, S., & Appel, L. (2005). Effects of a pet visitation program on the behavior and emotional state of adjudicated female adolescents. *Anthrozoos, 18*, 379-395.

Conover, T. (2000). *Newjack: Guarding Sing-Sing*. NY, NY: Random House.

Corson, S., Corson, E., & Gwynne, P. (1975). Pet facilitated psychotherapy. In R.S.

Anderson (Ed.), *Pet Animals and Society*. London: Bailliere Tindall.

Cotter, N., & O'Shea, F. (2008, Sept. 1). Barking mad. The Sun (England).

Cullen, F., Sundt, J., and Wozniak, J. (2001). The Virtuous prison: toward a restorative rehabilitation (pp. 265-286). In *Contemporary Issues in Crime and Criminal Justice: Essays in Honor of Gilbert Geis*. NJ: Prentice Hall.

Cunningham, J. (2007a, Aug. 29). Gangsters order hit on a prison drug dog. The Mirror (Ireland).

Cunningham, J. (2007b, Oct. 7). We'll kill prison dog handlers. The News of the World (England).

Currie, C. (2006). Animal cruelty by children exposed to domestic violence. *Child Abuse and Neglect, 30*, 425-435.

Currie, E. (1998). *Crime and Punishment in America*. NY: Henry Holt and Company.

Cushing, J., & Williams, J. (1995). The wild mustang program: A Case study in facilitated inmate therapy. *Journal of Offender rehabilitation, 22*, 95-112.

D'Alessio, S., & Stolzenberg, L. (2002). A multilevel analysis of the relationship between labor surplus and pretrial detention. *Social Problems, 49*, 178-193.

Deaton, C. (2005). Humanizing prisons with animals: A closer look at "cell dogs" and horse programs in correctional institutions. *The Journal of Correctional Education, 56*, 46-62.

Davidson, L. (2008, July 11). We'll sniff out cell phones. Daily Record (Scotland).

Delta Society (1998). *Animals in Institutions*. Renton, WA: Delta Society.

Dogs Unleashed (2008, July 16). The Sun (England).

Du Bois, W. E. B. (1903/1990). *The Souls of Black Folk*. NY, NY: Vintage

Books.
Earley, P. (1992). *The Hot House: Life Inside Leavenworth Prison.* NY: Bantam Books.
Easkridge, C. (2005). The state of the field of criminology: Brief essay, *Journal of Contemporary Criminology, 21,* 296-308.
Etter, S. (2006, June 14). Living yoga, calming corrections. Retrieved from www.corrections.com on June 15, 2006.
Fine, A. (Ed.) (2000). *Handbook on Animal-Assisted Therapy: Theoretical Foundations and Guidelines for Practice.* San Diego, CA: Academic Press.
Flores, D. (2008, Summer). Bringing home all the pretty horses. *Montana: The Magazine of Western History, 58, 2,* pp. 3-21.
Foucault, M. (1975). *Discipline and Punish: the Birth of the Prison.* New York: Random House.
Fournier, A., Geller, E., & Fortney, E. (2007). Human-animal interaction in a prison setting: Impact on criminal behavior, treatment progress, and social skills. *Behavior and Social Issues, 16,* 89-105.
Franklin, A., Emmison, M., Haraway, D., & Travers, M. (2007). Investigating the therapeutic benefits of companions animals: Problems and challenges, *Qualitative Sociology Review, 3,* 42-58.
Freeman, R. (2000). How labor fares in advanced economies. In Jerome Skolnick and Elliot Currie (Eds.) *Crisis in American Institutions* (11th ed). Boston, MA: Allyn and Bacon.
Friedman, L. (1993). *Crime and punishment in American history.* NY: Basic Books.
Gaes, G., Flanagan, T., Motiuk, L., & Stewart, L. (1999). Adult correctional treatment. In *Prisons: Crime and Justice: A Review of Research.* Michael Tonry and Joan Petersilia (Eds.). p 361-426. Chicago, IL: University of Chicago Press.
Garland, D. (2001). *The Culture of Control: Crime and Social Order in Contemporary Society.* Chicago, IL: The University of Chicago Press.
Garrity, T., & Stallones, L. (1998). Effects of pet contact on human well-being: Review of recent research. In C. Wilson & D. Turner (Eds.), *Companion Animals in Human Health* (pp. 3-22). Thousand Oaks, CA: Sage.
Gendreu, P., Smith, P., & Theriault, Y. (2009). Chaos theory and correctional treatment: common sense, correctional quackery, and the law of fartcatchers. *Journal of Contemporary Criminal Justice, 25,* 384-396.
Gerber, J., & Fritsch, E. (1995) Adult academic and vocational correctional education programs: A review of recent research. *Journal of Offender Rehabilitation, 22(1/2),* 119-142.
Germani, C. (2007, Nov 21). Juvenile offenders start life over with a crochet hook, *TheChristian Science Monitor.* Retrieved November 28, 2007 from www.csmonitor.com/2007/1121/p20s01-ussc.html.
Gilmore, P. (n.d.). Made in the U.S.A. ...by Convicts. Retrieved July 1, 2009 from http://lpa.igc.org/lpv24/lp3.htm.
Goodman, P. (2009). *A Variegated Penology? Using the History of California's Penal Labor Camps to Better Understand the Nature of Punishment.* Unpublished dissertation.
Gorczyca, K. Fine, A., & Spain, C. (2000). History, theory, and development of human-animal support services for people with AIDS and other chronic/terminal illnesses. In A. Fine (Ed.), *Handbook on Animal-Assisted*

Therapy: Theoretical Foundations and Guidelines for Practice (pp. 253-302). San Diego, CA: Academic Press.

Grabosky, P. & Shover, N. (2010). Forestalling the next epidemic of white-collar crimes. *Criminology and Public Policy, 9,* p. 641-654.

Graham, B. (2000). *Creature Comfort: Animals that Heal.* Amherst, NY: Prometheus Books.

Greenwood, P., Model, K., Rydell, C., & Chiesa, J. (1996). *Diverting children from a life of crime: Measuring costs and benefits.* Santa Monica, CA: RAND.

Grometstein, R. (2008). Prison-based animal training programs: Towards a theoretical model. Unpublished paper presented at the Nov. 2008 annual meeting of the American Society of Criminology, St. Louis, MO, Nov. 12-15, 2008.

Hannah-Moffat, K. (2005). Criminogenic needs and the transformative risk subject: Hybridizations of Risk/Need in Penality. *Punishment and Society, 7,* 29-51.

Halm, M. (2008). The healing power of the human-animal connection. *American Journal of Critical Care, 17,* 373-376.

Halsey, M. (2010). *Revolution in penology: Rethinking the society of captives,* by B. Arrigo & D. Milovanovic. NY, NY: Rowan & Littlefield. [Book Review] *Punishment & Society, 12,* 367-382.

Harbolt, T., & Ward, T. (2001). Teaming incarcerated youth with shelter dogs for a second chance. *Society & Animals, 9(2),* 177-182.

Harer, M. D. (1995). Prison education program participation and recidivism: A test of the normalization hypothesis. Washington, DC: Federal Bureau of Prisons.

Harkrader, T., Burke, T, & Owen, S. (2004, April). Pound puppies: The rehabilitative uses of dogs in correctional facilities. *Corrections Today, 66, 2,* 74-60.

Harland, A. (1996). *Choosing correctional options that work: Defining the demand and evaluating the supply* (Ed.). Thousand Oaks, CA: Sage.

Harris, M. K. (2005). In search of common ground: The importance of theoretical orientations in criminology and criminal justice. *Criminology and Public Policy, 4,* 311-328.

Harris, N., Walgrave, L., & Braithwaite, J. (2004). Emotional dynamics in restorative conferences. *Theoretical Criminology, 8,* 191-210.

Hart, L. (2000). Psychosocial benefits of animal companionship. In A. Fine (Ed.), *Handbook on Animal-Assisted Therapy: Theoretical Foundations and Guidelines for Practice,* (pp. 59-78). San Diego, CA: Academic Press.

Hensley, C., & Tallichet, S. (2009). Childhood and adolescent animal cruelty methods and their possible link to adult crimes. *Journal of Interpersonal Violence, 24,* 147-158.

Hines, L. (n.d.). Overview of animals in correctional facilities. In Delta Society (Ed.), *Animals in institutions* (1998). Renton, WA: Delta Society.

Holder, E. (2010, July 13). Attorney General Eric Holder Speaks at the Project Safe Neighborhoods Annual Conference. Retrieved July 21, 2009 from http://www.justice.gov/ag/speeches/2010/ag-speech-100713.html.

Holsinger, K., & Crowther, A. (2005). College course participation for incarcerated youth: Bringing restorative justice to life. *Journal of Criminal Justice Education, 16,* 328-340.

Howe, F. (1913, Nov. 28). Letter to the Editor: Ohio's prison farm: education and outdoor work to supplant the cell block. *The New York Times*.

Howie, M. (2008, Aug. 23). Five drug busts every day in prisons – and it's the tip of the iceberg. The Scotsman (Scotland). p. 10

Human Rights Watch (2006, October). Cruel and Degrading: The Use of Dogs for Cell Extraction in U.S. Prisons. Retrieved July 29, 2009 from http://www.hrw.org/sites/default/files/reports/us1006webwcover.pdf.

Hutchinson, S. (2006). Countering catastrophic criminology: Reform, punishment and the modern liberal compromise. *Punishment and Society, 8,* 443-467.

Irvine, L. (2004). *If you tame me: Understanding our connection with animals.* Philadelphia, PA: Temple University.

Jacobsen, T. (2009). The political economy of prison labor. Retrieved July 1, 2009 from www.sharedsacrifice.us/May28Jacobsen_Prison_Labor.html.

Jacobson, M. (2005*). Downsizing Prisons: How to reduce crime and end mass incarceration*. NY, NY: New York University Press.

Jail Dog Boost. (2007, Nov. 18). The News of the World (England).

Johnson, B. (2004). Religious programs and recidivism among former inmates in Prison Fellowship programs: A long-term follow-up study, *Justice Quarterly, 21,* 329-354.

Johnson, R. (2002). *Hard time: Understanding and reforming the prison* (3rd ed.). Belmont, CA: Wadsworth.

Johnson, R., & Chernoff, N. (2002). "Opening a vein": Inmate poetry and the prison experience. *The Prison Journal, 82,* 141-167.

Joiner, W. (2007, Sept. 13). Staring at death, and finding their bliss, *The New York Times.*

Kandel, J. (2008, Feb 25). Prisoners endure diver's training program, *Daily News Los Angeles*. Retrieved February 27, 2008 from http://www .dailynews.com.

Katcher, A., & Wilkins, G. (1993). Dialogue with animals: Its nature and culture. In S. Kellert & E. O. Wilson (Eds.), *The biophilia hypothesis* (pp. 173-197). Washington, D.C.: Island Press.

Kellert, S., & Wilson, E.O. (Eds.). (1993). *The biophilia hypothesis*. Washington, D.C.: Island Press.

Kollus, B. (2009). A Calming presence, *Cat Fancy, 52, 5,* 42-45.

Klinkenberg, J. (2008, Aug. 31). Leading the way. St. Petersburg Times (Florida). p. 1E.

Lafer, G. (2003). The politics of prison labor: A union perspective. In Tara Herivel and Paul Wright (Eds.). *Prison Nation: The Warehousing of America's Poor* (pp. 120-128). NY: Routledge.

Lai, J. (1998, April). *Pet Facilitated Therapy in Correctional Institutions*. Prepared for Correctional Services of Canada by Office of the Deputy Commissioner for Women. Available at http://www.csc-scc.gc.ca.

Latessa, E., Cullen, F., & Gendreau, P. (2002). Beyond correctional quackery – Professionalism and the possibility of effective treatment. *Federal Probation, 66,* 43-50.

Lawrence, E. (1993). The sacred bee, the filthy pig, and the bat out of hell: Animal symbolism as cognitive biophilia. In S. Kellert & E. O. Wilson (Eds.). (1993). *The biophilia hypothesis*. Washington, D.C.: Island Press.

Lawrence, S., Mears, D., Dubin, G., & Travis, J. (2002, May). *The practice and promise of prison programming*. Washington, D.C.: The Urban Institute.

Lee, D. (1987). Companion animals in institutions. In P. Arkow, (Ed.), *The Loving Bond: Companion Animals in the Helping Professions*, (pp.23-46). Saratoga, CA: R & E Publishers.

Lichtenstein, A. (1996). Twice the Work of Free Labor: The Political Economy of Convict Labor in the New South. London: Verso.

L.I.F.E.R.S. Public Safety Steering Committee of the State Correctional Institution at Graterford, PA (2004). Ending the culture of street crime. *The Prison Journal, 84*, 48S-68S.

Lillis, J. (1994). Prison education programs reduced. *Corrections Compendium, 19*, 1-4.

Linden, R., & Perry, L. (1982). The effectiveness of prison education programs. *Journal of Offender Counseling Services and Rehabilitation, 6*, 43-57.

Lipsey M. (1992). Juvenile delinquency treatment: A meta-analytic inquiry into variability of effects. In T. Cook, H. Cooper, D. Cordray, H. Hartmann, L. Hedges, R. Light, T. Louis, & F. Mosteller (Eds.). *Meta-analysis for explanation*, (pp. 83-127). NY: Russell Sage Foundation.

Lipsey, M. (1995). What do we learn from 400 research studies on the effectiveness of treatment with juvenile delinquents? In J. McGuire (Ed.), *What works: Reducing re-offending*, (pp. 63-78). Chichester, England: Wiley.

Liptak, A. (2009, Nov. 24). Right and left join forces on criminal justice. *The New York Times*, p. 1A.

Liptak, A. (2008, April 23). Inmate count in U.S. dwarfs other nations'. *The New York Times*, p. 1A.

Lipton, D., Martinson, R., & Wilks, J. (1975). *The Effectiveness of correctional treatment*. NY: Praeger.

Litwack, L. (2009). *How Free is Free? The Long Death of Jim Crow*. Cambridge, MA: Harvard University Press.

Lombardi, L. (2009, Dec. 12). Books teach kids to be kind to pets. *The New Jersey Star Ledger*. Retrieved on December 30, 2009 from http://www.northjersey.com/community/pets/news/79114897.html.

Mallon, G. (1994). Some of our best therapists are dogs. *Child & Youth Care Forum, 23 (2)*, 89-101.

Martinson, R. (1974). What works? Questions and answers about prison reform. *Public Interest, 35*, 22-45.

Maruna, S. (2001). *Making good: How ex-convicts reform and rebuild their lives*. Washington, D.C.: American Psychological Association.

Maruna, S., & LeBel, T. (2003). Welcome home? Examining the 're-entry court' concept from a strengths-based perspective. *Western Criminology Review, 4*, 91-107.

Maruna, S., LeBel, T. & Lanier, C. (2004) Generativity behind bars: Some "redemptive truth" about prison society. In E. de St. Aubin, D. McAdams & T. Kim (Eds.) *The Generative Society*. Washington, DC: American Psychological Association.

Maruna, S., LeBel, T., Mitchell, N. & Naples, M. (2004). Pygmalion in the reintegration process: Desistance from crime through the looking glass, *Psychology, Crime & Law, 10*, 271-281.

Math sets dog free in challenge to BSL. (2009, July 28). Retrieved August 6, 2009 from http://www.animallawcoalition.com/breed-bans/article/995.

Maxfield, M., & Babbie, E. (2001). *Research methods for criminal justice and criminology* (3rd ed.). Belmont, CA: Wadsworth.

McCold, P., & Wachtel, T. (2003). In pursuit of paradigm: A Theory of restorative justice. [Paper presented at the XIII World Congress of Criminology, August 2003, Rio de Janiero, Brazil.] Available at www.restorativepractices.org.

McCulloch, M. (1983, Oct. 27-28). Pet Therapy—An Overview. *Proceedings, The Human-Pet Relationship International Symposium, Vienna*, p. 25-31.

McCollum, S. (1994). Prison college programs. *The Prison Journal*, 74, 51-61.

McGuire, J. (2002). Integrating findings from research reviews. In J. McGuire (Ed.), *Offender rehabilitation and treatment: Effective programs and policies to reduce re-offending*, (pp. 3-31). Chichester, England: Wiley.

McGuire, J. (1995). Preface. In J. McGuire (Ed.), *What works: Reducing re-offending*, (pp. xi-xiii). Chichester, England: Wiley.

McKelvey, B. (1935). Penal slavery and southern reconstruction. *Journal   of Negro History, 20*, 153-179. Cited in Weiss 2001.

McMurran, M., & Hollin, C. (1995). Series preface. In J. McGuire (Ed.), *What works: Reducing re-offending*, (pp. ix-x). Chichester, England: Wiley.

Mears, D., Lawrence, S., Solomon, A., & Waul, M. (2002, April). Prison-based programming: What it can do and why it is needed. *Corrections Today*, 66-71, 83.

Mirsky, L. (2003). Albert Eglash and creative restitution: A Precursor to restorative practices. Available at www.restorativepractices.org

Mitchell, K. (2007, July 11). Farms get help from inmates, *Denver Post*. Retrieved from www.denverpost.com July 23, 2007.

Moneymaker, J., & Strimple, E. (1991). Animals and inmates: A Sharing companionship behind bars, *Journal of Offender Rehabilitation, 16*, 133-152.

Moore, S. (2009a, Aug. 5). California prisons must cut inmate population. Retrieved August 11, 2009 from www.nytimes.com

Moore, S. (2009b, Aug. 5). Federal Judges Order California Prisons to Reduce Inmate Population by a Quarter. Retrieved August 11, 2009 from www.nytimes.com.

Morse, D. (2008, July 10). Dogs' new trick: Find cellphones. The Washington Post. p. B1.

Moss, D. (2008, Dec 12). Nonviolent inmates are lending a hand, *Courier-Journal*. Retrieved January 13, 2009 from www.courier-journal.com.

Mulvany, L. (2008, April 6). Putting puppies on the right path: Prison program preps dogs to help disabled. The Boston Globe, p. 3.

Nash, K. (1998, May 11). Prison: Employment opportunities of the future. *Computerworld.*

Nelson, N. (2007, Sept. 30). Pets for jail birds: Exclusive cats and dogs for lags in bid to stop suicide behind bars. The People (England) p. 31.

Nightingale, F. (1860/1969). *Notes on nursing*. NY, NY: Dover.

Nimer, J., & Lundahl, B. (2007). Animal-assisted therapy: A meta-analysis. *Anthrozoos, 20*, 225-238.

Norman, K. (2007, Dec. 28). Dogs' prison role is not to be sniffed at! South Wales Echo. p. 24.

O'Connor, T., & Perreyclear, M. (2002). Prison religion in action and its influence on offender rehabilitation, *Journal of Offender Rehabilitation, 35, 3/4,* 11-33.

O'Neil, J. (2004, June 22) Vital signs: An epileptic child's best friend. *The New York Times,* F6.

Ormerod, E. (2008). Companion animals and offender rehabilitation—experiences from a prison therapeutic community in Scotland. *Therapeutic Communities, 29,* 285-296.

Oshinsky, D. (1996). *Worse than slavery: Parchman Farm and the ordeal of Jim Crow Justice.* NY: Free Press.

Paluch, Jr., J. (2004). *A Life for a life: Life imprisonment: America's other death penalty.* Los Angeles, CA: Roxbury.

Parker-Pope, T. (2009, Dec. 14). The Best walking partner: Man vs. dog. *Well* (Blog). Retrieved December 16, 2009 from http://well.blogs.nytimes.com /2009/12/14.

Patenaude, A. (2004). No promises, but I'm willing to listen and tell what I hear: Conducting qualitative research among prison inmates and staff. *The Prison Journal, 84(Suppl.),* 69S-91S.

Peter, S. (2006, Nov. 28). Dogs do time to earn good behavior: Canines and inmates benefit from training. USA Today. p. 9D.

Petersen, M., & Farrington, D. (2007). Cruelty to animals and violence to people. *Victims & Offenders, 2,* 21-43.

Piper, H., & Myers, S. (2006). Making the links: Child abuse, animal cruelty and domestic violence. *Child Abuse Review, 15,* 178-189. Retrieved from www.thepetpress-la.com/index.html.

Petersilia, J. 2003. *When Prisoners Come Home: Parole and Prisoner Reentry.* NY, NY: Oxford University Press.

Portis, S. (2009, Nov. 5). Bolinas man brings yoga behind bars. Retrieved November 6, 2009 from www.ptreyeslight.com/cgi/latest_news.pl?record = 415.

Povoledo, E. (2009, July 22). Maximum security and a starring role. The New York Times. Prisons go to the dogs. (2008, April 24). Herald Sun (Australia).

Pugliano, B. (2009, Dec. 26). *The New York Times,* p.1.

Quigley, W. (1996). Five hundred years of English poor laws, 1349-1834: Regulating the working and nonworking poor. *Akron Law Review, 30,* 73-128.

Quinn, P. (2004). *Paws for Love.* Exeter, NH: Townsend.

Quintanilla, R. (2008, Feb. 11). Dog training in women's prison helps inmates and the clients who get companion, Chicago Tribune. Retrieved from www.chicagotribune.com.

Rafter, N. (2009). *Origins of Criminology: A Reader.* NY, NY: Routledge.

Raftery, I. (2010, June 23). Keeping a best friend, over a co-op's objections. *The New York Times.*

Raspberry, W. (1984, June 20). Cellblock businesses. *The Washington Post,* p. A21.

Raspberry, W. (1983, Aug 19). Afraid to change our prisons. *The Washington Post,* p. 23).

Research Center for Human-Animal Interaction (ReCHAI), housed at the University of Missouri's College of Veterinary Medicine (www.rechai .missouri.edu).

Rhoades, R. (2001). Prison Dog Programs. http://www.petfinder.com/how-to-help-pets/prison-dog-programs.html retrieved July 5, 2009. Originally published in ASPCA *Animal Watch*, Summer 2001.

Ross, R., Antonowicz, D., & Dhaliwal, G. (1995). Something works. In R. Ross, D. Antonowicz, and G. Dhaliwal, *Going Straight: Effective delinquency prevention and offender rehabilitation,* (pp. 3-24). Ontario, Canada: Air Training & Publications.

Rotman, E. (1995). The failure of reform: United States, 1865-1965. In *The Oxford History of the Prison: The Practice of Punishment in Western Society* (pp. 151-177). N. Morris and D. Rothman (Eds.). Oxford University Press, Oxford, England.

Rusche, G., & Kirchheimer, O. (1939/1968). Punishment and Social Structure. NY, NY: Russell & Russell.

Sampson, R., & Laub, J. (1993). *Crime in the making: Pathways and turning points through life.* Cambridge, MA: Harvard University Press.

Sanders, C. (1993). Understanding dogs: Caregivers' attributions of mindedness in canine-human relationships, *Journal of Contemporary Ethnography, 22,* 205-226.

Sanders, C. (2003). Actions speak louder than words: Close relationships between humans and nonhuman animals, *Symbolic Interaction, 26,* 405-426.

Sanders, C. (2006). The dog you deserve: Ambivalence in the K-9 officer/patrol dog relationship, *Journal of Contemporary Ethnography, 35,* 148-172.

Schlessinger, L. (2001). The potential sex murderer: ominous signs, risk assessment. *Journal of Threat Assessment, 1,* 47-72.

Schlosser, E. (1998, Dec.). The prison industrial complex. *Atlantic Monthly.*

Scott-Hayward, C. (2009). *The Fiscal Crisis in Corrections: Rethinking Policies and Practices.* NY, NY: Vera Institute of Justice.

Sellin, T. (1976). *Slavery and the Penal System.* NY, NY: Elsevier Scientific Publishing.

Shaffer, J. (2008). Shaving off the stigma, *The News and Observer.* Retrieved October 8, 2008 from www.newsobserver.com/news.

Shapland, J. (2003). Restorative justice and criminal justice: Just response to crime? In A. von Hirsch, J. Roberts, A. Bottoms, K. Roach, and M. Schiff (Eds.), *Restorative justice and criminal justice: Competing or reconcilable paradigms?* (pp. 195-217). Portland, OR: Hart Publishing.

Sheldon, R. (2000). *A Critical introduction to the history of criminal justice.* NY: Allyn and Bacon.

Shepherd, A. (2008). Results of the 2007 AVMA survey of US pet-owning households regarding use of veterinary services and expenditures. *Journal of the American Veterinary Medical Association, 233,* p. 727-728.

Shere, D. (2005). *Cain's Redemption: A Story of Hope and Transformation in America's Bloodiest Prison.* Chicago, IL: Northfield Publishing.

Shrum, H. (2004). No longer theory: Correctional Practices that Work. *Journal of Correctional Education, 55,* 225-235.

Shutt, A. (1982, Aug 17). Burger backs prison rehabilitation. *Christian Science Monitor,* p. 2.

Siebert, C. (2009). *The Wauchula Woods: Toward a New Understanding of Animals*. NY: Scribner.

Sitomer, C. (1984a, July 13). A rare encounter with America's chief justice. *Christian Science Monitor*, p. 1.

Sitomer, C. (1984b, June 19). High court's aim: catch more criminals; Burger's goal: make prisons productive. *Christian Science Monitor*, p. 3.

Skloot, R. (2009, Jan 4.). Creature comforts, *The New York Times Magazine*.

Smith, C. (2004, Dec. 8). Islam in jail: Europe's neglect breeds angry radicals, *The New York Times*.

Smith, L., & Silverman, M. (1994). Functional literacy education for jail inmates: An examination of the Hillsborough County Jail education program. *The Prison Journal, 74*, 414-432.

Souter, M., & Miller, M. (2007). Do animal-assisted activities effectively treat depression? A meta-analysis. *Anthrozoos, 20*, 167-180.

Sterngold, J. (2002, March 21). In Los Angeles, a traveler's best friend. *The New York Times*, A24.

Strimple, E. (2003). A History of prison inmate-animal interaction programs. *The American Behavioral Scientist, 47, 1*, 70-78.

Strom, S. (2006, October 27). Trained by inmates, new best friends for disabled veterans. *The New York Times*, A31.

Sykes, G. (1958). *The society of captives: A study of a maximum security prison*. Princeton, NJ: Princeton University Press.

Taylor, J. (1992). Post-secondary correctional education: An evaluation of effectiveness and efficiency. *Journal of Correctional Education, 43*, 132-141.

Taylor, W. (1999). *Down on Parchman Farm: The great prison in the Mississippi Delta*. Columbus, OH: Ohio State Press.

Tewksbury, R., & Vito, G. (1994). Improving the educational skills of jail inmates: Preliminary Program Findings. *Federal Probation, 58*, 55-59.

The New York Times (1916, Feb. 13). State board urges razing of Sing Sing: Prison commission would put convicts on a great model farm.

The New York Times (1911, April 16). Work to begin soon on Sing Sing's successor: New Wingdale prison will include acreage for open air employment of prisoners, will raise much of their own food and run a farm of 600 acres.

The Pew Center on States. (2008). *One in 100: Behind Bars in America 2008*. Washington, D.C.: The Pew Charitable Trusts.

The Sentencing Project. (2010, July 27). *House approves national criminal justice commission act*. Retrieved July 27, 2010 from www.sentencingproject.org/detail/news.cfm?news_id=965&id=167.

Thompson, D. (2009, April 14). Prisons press fight against smuggled cell phones, The San Diego Union-Tribune.

Tischler, E. (1998). Making amends, building futures, *Corrections Today, 60*, p. 83-84.

Toch, H. (2000). Altruistic activity as correctional treatment. *International Journal of Offender Therapy and Comparative Criminology, 44*, 270-278.

Travis, J. (2005). *But They All Come Back: Facing the Challenges of Prisoner Reentry*. Washington, D.C.: Urban Institute Press.

Travis, J. (2000). Prisons, work and re-entry. *Corrections Today, 61*(6), 102-105.

Travis, J., & Petersilia, J. (2001). Reentry reconsidered: A New look at an old question. *Crime & Delinquency, 47,* 291-313.

Trulson, C., Marquart, J., & Mullings, J. (2004). Breaking In: Gaining entry to prisons and other hard-to-access criminal justice organizations. *Journal of Criminal Justice Education, 15,* 451-478.

Turner, W. (2007). The experiences of offenders in a prison canine program. *Federal Probation, 71, 1,* 38-43.

Van Ness, D. (2003). Proposed basic principles on the use of restorative justice: Recognizing the aims and limitations of restorative justice. In A. von Hirsch, J. Roberts, A. Bottoms, K. Roach, and M. Schiff (Eds.), *Restorative Justice and Criminal Justice: Competing or reconcilable paradigms* (pp. 157-176). Portland, OR: Hart Publishing.

Veysey, B. (2008, May/June). Rethinking reentry. *The Criminologist, 33,* 1, 3-5.

Visher, C. (2006). Effective reentry programs. *Criminology and Public Policy, 5,* 299-302.

Visher, C., & Travis, J. (2003). Transitions from prison to community: Understanding individual pathways. *Annual Review of Sociology, 29,* 89-113.

Volant, A., Johnson, J., & Gullone, E. (2008). The relationship between domestic violence and animal abuse: An Australian study. *Journal of Interpersonal Violence, 23,* 1277-1295.

Wacquant, L. (2001). Deadly symbiosis: When ghetto and prison meet and mesh. *Punishment and Society, 3,* 95-133.

Walsh, P., & Mertin, P. (1994). The training of pets as therapy dogs in a women's prison: A Pilot study. *Anthrozoos, 7(2),* 124-128.

Ward , T., & Maruna, S. (2007). *Rehabilitation: Beyond the Risk-Paradigm.* Key Ideas in Criminology Series (Tim Newburn, Series Ed.). London: Routledge.

Webb, C. (2005). Parchman Farm, Mississippi State Penitentiary. In M. Bosworth (Ed.) *Encyclopedia of Prisons and Correctional facilities* (pp. 666-668). Thousand Oaks, CA: Sage.

Weiss, R. (2005). Labor. In M. Bosworth (Ed.) *Encyclopedia of Prisons and Correctional facilities* (pp. 529-535). Thousand Oaks, CA: Sage.

Weiss, R. (2001). "Repatriating" low-wage work: The political economy of prison labor reprivatization in the postindustrial United States. *Criminology, 39,* 253-291.

Whitehead, P., Ward, T., & Collie, R. (2007). Time for a change: applying the Good Lives Model of rehabilitation to a high-risk violent offender, *International Journal of Offender Therapy and Comparative Criminology, 51,* 578-598.

Wilson, E. O. (1984). Biophilia. Cambridge, M.A.: Harvard University Press.

Wilson, C., & Turner, D. (Eds.) (1998). *Companion Animals in Human Health.* Thousand Oaks, CA: Sage.

Wingfield, V. (2003). People's Institute Records, Manuscripts and Archives Division, The New York Public Library. Retrieved July 28, 2009 http://www.nypl.org/research/chss/spe/rbk/faids/peoplesinst.pdf.

Wise, M. (2003, Aug. 10). Partners, horse and man, in prison pasture. *The New York Times.* Retrieved August 9, 2009 from http://newyorktimes.com.

Woods, B. (1991, Winter). The effects of canine therapy sessions with SBH.

WARDS: Science and Animal Care, 3-4.

Wright, P. (2003). Making slave labor fly: Boeing goes to prison. In T. Herivel and P. Wright (Eds.). *Prison Nation: The Warehousing of America's Poor* (pp. 112-119). NY: Routledge. pp. 112-119.

Yomiuri (2007, Sept. 22). Inmates to raise guide dogs in private sector jail project. The Daily Yomiuri (Tokyo) p. 3.

Zimring, F., & Hawkins, G. (1993). *The Scale of Imprisonment*. Chicago, IL: University of Chicago Press.

Index

Alabama, 36, 39, 79, 143
Angola, 37, 38, 39, 40, 61, 63, 64,
    65, 66, 137, 163, 164
Animal assisted therapy (AAT), 1–
    161
Arizona, 61, 62, 78, 79, 96, 149,
    150, 165
Arkansas, 78, 79
Birdman of Alcatraz, 68
Black Codes, 36
Bureau of Land Management, 71,
    73, 83, 96, 164
Burger, Warren, 45
Bustard, Leo, 69
Cain, Burl, 64
California, 24, 27, 49, 55, 56, 68,
    70, 79, 91, 94, 96, 142, 166,
    170
Cell phones, 147, 149, 165, 173
Center for the Interaction of
    Animals and Society, 24, 165
Civil War, 35, 36, 37, 38, 164
Colorado, 49, 61, 71, 74, 79, 91,
    94, 96, 146
Comfort animals, 9
Community service programs, 82,
    84, 86, 88, 89, 99
Companion animals, 2, 15, 17, 51
Connecticut, 79, 94, 101, 149
Contraband, 147, 148, 149
Contract system, 34, 44
Convict leasing, 34, 38, 39
Correctional quackery, 151, 166,
    168
Courthouse Dogs, 16
Delaware, 78, 79, 149
Delta Society, 24, 69, 76, 165, 167
Earned redemption, 139, 164
Eastern State Penitentiary, 34, 43,
    144
Equine, 70
Farm animals, 3, 14, 33, 62, 65, 70,
    77

Florida, 36, 59, 79, 92, 96, 164,
    168
Georgia, 36, 79
Good Lives Model, 136, 174
Hawaii, 78, 79
Hines, Linda, 69, 76
Horses, 71
Human Animal Interaction, 23
Idaho, 79, 149
Illinois, 78, 79, 140
Illiteracy, 34, 53
Indiana, 35, 75, 79, 92
Inmate labor, 34, 42, 58, 59, 61,
    62, 66, 81
Institute for Human-Animal
    Connection, 158
Iowa, 78, 79, 149, 150
Kansas, 68, 78, 79, 82, 92
Kentucky, 62, 78, 79, 82, 96
Less eligibility, 43, 51, 54
Livestock Care Programs, 11
Louisiana, 36, 37, 39, 40, 63, 64,
    65, 78, 79
Maine, 78, 79, 94, 137
Maryland, 14, 79, 96, 148
Massachusetts, 35, 49, 79, 92, 94,
    108, 147, 149
Michigan, 29, 30, 35, 79, 82, 92
Minnesota, 46, 78, 79
Mississippi, 36, 37, 38, 63, 78, 79,
    173, 174
Missouri, 23, 80, 172
Montana, 80, 82, 166
Multi-modal programs, 84, 85, 86,
    88, 132
Music, 143, 164
National Criminal Justice
    Commission Act, 4, 28
National survey, 3, 67, 99, 117
New Hampshire, 78, 80
New Jersey, 49, 56, 60, 80, 93,
    101, 107, 108, 164, 169
New Mexico, 73, 74, 80, 95

New York, 5, 14, 27, 28, 30, 34,
    35, 40, 41, 45, 49, 56, 60, 67,
    80, 96, 100, 103, 104, 153,
    163, 164, 165, 166, 168, 169,
    171, 173, 174
North Carolina, 80, 92, 142, 163
North Dakota, 80, 82
Nothing works, 6, 25, 53
Ohio, 17, 41, 49, 80, 82, 92, 95,
    168, 173
Oklahoma, 66, 68, 78, 80, 82, 92,
    96, 163
Oregon, 61, 74, 80, 95, 141, 142
Parchman Farm, 37, 171, 173, 174
Pennsylvania, 24, 34, 35, 43, 56,
    59, 60, 67, 80, 165
People-Pet Partnership, 24, 69
Pet Adoption Programs, 11
Physiological, 77, 118, 123, 163
Pit bulls, 145
Plantations, 3, 33, 37
Politicians, 2, 4, 24, 27, 47
Prison farms, 3, 40
Prison industrial complex, 42, 59,
    62, 172
Punishment, 2, 3, 4, 6, 7, 8, 25, 35,
    36, 38, 42, 43, 50, 51, 52, 66,
    68, 74, 77, 97, 120, 135, 140,
    141, 152, 156, 158, 160, 166,
    168
Quinn, Pauline, 69
Reformatory Movement, 35
Republicans, 28, 44
Research Center for Human-
    Animal Interaction, 23, 172
Restitution, 3, 48, 51, 52, 58, 59,
    61, 65, 67, 73, 91, 137, 138,
    139, 141, 153, 159, 170

Restorative Justice, 136, 140, 174
Rhode Island, 78, 80
Rodeo, 51, 52, 65, 66
Service Animal Socialization
    Programs, 11
Service animals, 9, 75, 158
Shelter animals, 2, 70
Sing Sing Prison, 41
Slavery, 34, 35, 38, 40, 48, 62, 63,
    163, 170, 171
Social support, 17, 21
Solitary confinement, 43, 44, 68
South Carolina, 36, 59, 61, 80
South Dakota, 80, 149
State use, 44, 60
Tennessee, 80, 92
Texas, 36, 56, 60, 66, 78, 80, 147
Theater, 144
Theory, 21, 22, 40, 143, 151, 166,
    172
Unions, 34, 44, 104, 113, 114, 159
Utah, 78, 80, 143, 149
Virginia, 4, 28, 69, 75, 80, 94, 95,
    148, 153
Visitation Programs, 11
Volunteer, 164
War on drugs, 25, 160
War veterans, 30, 158, 159
Washington, 24, 39, 46, 48, 59, 61,
    69, 80, 94, 95, 141, 167, 168,
    169, 170, 171, 173
Wildlife Rehabilitation Programs,
    11
Wisconsin, 80, 83, 94, 137
Yoga, 142, 143, 166, 171

About the Book

Gennifer Furst provides the first comprehensive look at prison-based animal programs, an innovative approach to rehabilitation that draws on the benefits of human-animal interactions.

Analyzing a national survey of these programs and also presenting in-depth case studies, Furst pinpoints the mechanisms that transform prisoners' lives and reduce the chances of recidivism. The result is a thought-provoking exploration of a correctional programming idea that promises to benefit inmates, animals, and communities alike.

Gennifer Furst is assistant professor of sociology at William Paterson University of New Jersey.